BRICKTOP

BRICKTOP

BRICKTOP

with James Haskins

NEW YORK

Atheneum

1983

Library of Congress Cataloging in Publication Data

Bricktop, 1894–
  Bricktop.
  1. Bricktop, 1894–   .   2. Singers—
Biography.   I. Haskins, James, 1941–
II. Title.
ML420.B777A3   1983   784.5′3′00924 [B]   82–73006
ISBN 0–689–11349–8

Published simultaneously in Canada by McClelland and Stewart Ltd.
Composition by Heritage Printers, Inc., Charlotte, North Carolina
Manufactured by Fairfield Graphics, Fairfield, Pennsylvania
Designed by Kathleen Carey
First Edition

This book is dedicated to
the world in general

"My greatest claim to fame is that I discovered Bricktop before Cole Porter."

F. Scott Fitzgerald

"You know, I think Brick must have been a queen in some former life."

Elsa Maxwell

"No, an empress."   *Cole Porter*

"When Brick sings 'Embraceable You,' she takes twenty years off a man's life."

John Steinbeck

"To heck with yesterday! What are we gonna do tomorrow?"

Bricktop

ACKNOWLEDGMENTS

THERE ARE SO MANY PEOPLE who should be acknowledged for this book—all the thousands of people who went out of their way to be nice to me—that I couldn't possibly fit them all in, so I won't even try. I would like to note in particular, though, my gratitude to Ruth Ellington Boatwright, Lydia Jones and the Jones family, Earl Blackwell, Mabel Mercer, Joe Attles, Ethel Taylor, and the late Hugh Shannon. And, of course, to Cole Porter, the man who made Bricktop.

Jim Haskins wishes to thank Laurel Burns, Diane Chun, Jim Hinton, the late Jack Jordan, Bob Rhone, Barbara von Eitzen, and especially Kathy Benson.

INTRODUCTION

JAMES HASKINS

I WAS ABOUT eleven or twelve years old when I first became aware of the existence of a woman named Bricktop. No doubt I saw an article about her in *Ebony* or *Jet*, or perhaps it was in the *Pittsburgh Courier*, which purported to be the key to "understanding the progress of the race" and which was widely distributed in Southern black neighborhoods like the one in which I grew up. Or, I may have first heard the name Bricktop while listening to the grownups talk. Negroes who had made it were a common topic of discussion, and though my small town in Alabama was light-years away from the great cities of Europe, and the lives of my parents equally as alien to the life of a cosmopolitan nightclub operator, it was a peculiar fact of existence for the average American black to be on intimate terms with the stories of those few of us who had managed to burrow out from under.

The grownups talked about Josephine Baker, Ralph Bunche, Jackie

Robinson, and Bricktop as familiarly as they talked about Cousin Eliza and Aunt Cindy. Oh, yes, the grownups would nod knowingly, Bricktop had all the kings and queens and dukes and duchesses at her feet over there in Europe; and a small boy whose only image of royalty came from the stories of King Arthur, and for whom Europe was a remote, exotic place, was suitably awed.

As I grew up and read more widely, I kept coming across the name Bricktop—in stories of Paris's golden era, while researching a book about the Cotton Club, while reading *Tender Is the Night* by F. Scott Fitzgerald. She was a legend. In fact, I never thought of her as a flesh-and-blood person, and I was amazed when, in 1979, I met a man who said he was a close friend of Bricktop's. I had assumed that she was long dead.

Jack Jordan, a producer and promoter and a confidant of Josephine Baker in her later years, had known "Bricky," as her friends call her, for many years. He had been like the son she'd never had—concerned, attentive, seeing to her day-to-day needs now that she was unable to get out much. Understanding my eagerness to meet her, and approving my idea to help her publish her life story, he promised to do what he could to arrange an interview. He warned me, however, that she didn't receive many visitors, suffered from high blood pressure and arthritis, that her memory was fading, and that she could be cranky. Between my own peripatetic schedule and Bricktop's illnesses and whims, it was weeks before the meeting could be arranged, but at last one crisp October day I found myself walking down Broadway on my way to meet a flesh-and-blood, eighty-five-year-old legend.

Her apartment was just seven blocks away from mine, and she'd been there for years—but of course in New York one can live a mere seven yards away from someone and never know him or her. Her apartment door was the only one on her floor that did not have a nameplate. It was adorned only with a picture of Martin De Porres, the first black saint to be canonized in the Roman Church. I pressed the doorbell button and, amid other sounds behind the door, heard a slightly querulous voice say, "Just hand me my cane. I can walk. You don't have to help me." Bricktop opened the door herself. No matter how old or arthritic, she had not ceased to be the perfect hostess.

She was much smaller than I had imagined, frail-looking and slightly stooped over her cane. The famous red hair had long ago gone gray, but the eyes were bright and sharp, and as they stared up at me I felt as if I were being inspected. Slightly nonplussed, I quickly introduced myself, then started toward the familiar figure of Jack Jordan. His eyes moved from mine to the space behind me, causing me to turn. There was Bricktop, still standing at the open door, her cheek raised in my direction. Embarrassed, I retraced my steps and planted a kiss on her cheek. *Then* she closed the door.

The room was filled with fresh flowers. I had not brought a thing, but that was the first and last time I arrived empty-handed. I was to learn that one never visits Bricktop without first calling to see if she needs anything, that she always needs beer (she doesn't drink, but her friends do), and that although she never asks for flowers she nevertheless expects them. I was to become the visitor who always arrived with one long-stemmed red rose.

Bricktop sat down in her wing chair by the window, and I remember thinking that her bearing was regal, like royalty holding court. I took a seat as well. She offered me a beer, which I gratefully accepted, and then she began the interview with a barrage of questions for me— where was I from, who were my family, where had I gone to school, what did I do besides write, had I traveled much, where, when, with whom, what had I seen, what had I learned? At last she pronounced, "Well, it seems like you've been well bred for a Negro man," and she signaled to Jack Jordan that she was tired. My audience was over. It had been exactly one hour to the minute since I had arrived. We had not even begun to talk terms.

Months later—months of 3:30 p.m. visits on Saturdays every two weeks, of innumerable long-stemmed roses and six-packs of beer, Bricktop agreed to let me help her tell her story. Over those months I had become as fascinated by the flesh-and-blood Bricktop as I had ever been by the legend.

She was a saloon singer in Chicago during the rough-and-tumble days of Jack Johnson, Florence Mills, Bill Robinson, and Legs Diamond. In Prohibition Harlem she gave Duke Ellington his first big New York break. In café-society Paris she took a young Josephine Baker under her wing and worked with a busboy named Langston Hughes. Cole Porter had breakfast in her first Paris *boîte* one morning, heard her singing one of his songs, and started bringing his friends; soon Noel Coward, Tallulah Bankhead, all the great and glittering names of Europe between the wars had made Bricktop's their own private enclave. Later, Porter wrote "Miss Otis Regrets" with her voice in mind, and took it to her to sing.

F. Scott Fitzgerald, during his carefree Paris days, did not consider a night complete without a visit to Bricktop's; Ernest Hemingway incurred her wrath; T. S. Eliot put her in a poem; Cole Porter asked her to give dance lessons at his parties; and the Duke of Windsor spent many early mornings on the floor by the piano in her clubs, listening to the music of Bricktop's. When Hitler's soldiers advanced on Paris, the Duchess of Windsor, in concert with Elsie de Wolfe, Lady Mendl, aided her escape.

Relocating in Mexico City, Bricktop became friends with Cantinflas. Back in Paris after the war, she comforted the people who had made their way back to Bricktop's in search of an era that would never exist again. In Rome the movie celebrities flocked to her club. She watched the marriage of Frank Sinatra and Ava Gardner break up, played mother hen to the likes of Anna Magnani and Shirley MacLaine, and unwittingly presided over the first appearances together in public of Elizabeth Taylor and Richard Burton. Martin Luther King, Jr., in Europe to accept the Nobel Prize for Peace, phoned to ask if he could meet *her*. In Bricktop's story there is such an array of famous names and places that the mind short-circuits.

I already knew about the Bricktop legend, however. What fascinated me, and still does, is Bricktop's refusal to be awed by her own life or by the galaxy of people she knew. Far from being eager to enter their orb, she insisted on distancing herself. She was a communication satellite from which they often bounced off transmissions to one another, and to themselves; and that is exactly the way she wanted it. Though, in that role, she was privy to many secrets, she continues to respect those secrets, knowing that they were shared with her in trust, and refusing to believe that the terms of a spiritual trust are altered by such mundane events as passing years and death. Throughout her association with the most famous people in the world, Bricktop retained a healthy sense of her own identity, and it is *her* story, not theirs, that she has chosen to tell—though, through the telling of it, she evokes their world as few people ever have. It is the life story of an original "one-hundred-percent American Negro with a trigger-Irish temper"—a life that has always been exuberant, elegant, and truly remarkable. That is the way she lived it—and that is the way she tells it.

Gainesville, Florida
September 1982

CONTENTS

EARLY YEARS   3

ON THE ROAD   24

SALOON SINGER   38

THE WAR YEARS   53

PROHIBITION   70

PARIS   83

COLE PORTER . . . AND JOSEPHINE BAKER   100

BRICKTOP'S   113

SALOONKEEPER PAR EXCELLENCE   126

THE GOLDEN ERA   148

AND WE ALL PLAYED ON   171

THE CRISIS   190

NEW YORK   207

MEXICO CITY   223

RETURN TO PARIS   235

THE HOLY HUSTLER   250

HOLLYWOOD-ON-THE-TIBER   265

OLD WARHORSE   281

INDEX   291

ILLUSTRATIONS

AN ALBUM OF PHOTOGRAPHS FOLLOWS PAGE 206

BRICKTOP

EARLY YEARS

WHEN I think back on my early life, some of the parts fit so well with what happened later that I wonder if I'm making them fit. It's true, though, that Mama was running a restaurant when I was born, and it's true that she made a point of getting out of that restaurant when she felt the pains coming on. Mama was not about to give birth in a restaurant. What, and have her child grow up with no more ambition than to wait tables? Heaven forbid!

Well, I ended up in the restaurant business anyway, only they wouldn't be called restaurants. They were saloons, and I was one of the most famous saloonkeepers in the world. Wherever I opened up a club, whether it was in Paris, Biarritz, Mexico City, or Rome, the wealthy and famous would be there even if it meant flying halfway around the world to do so. And if you asked them why, they'd say, "Just because she's herself— just Brick."

3

Mama had given birth to four children before me—three lived—and so I'm sure she took the onset of her fifth labor in stride. Knowing Mama, she made certain everything was in order and the money in the cash drawer counted twice before she paid much attention to me. Then she let her partner, Miss Ellen, help her up the stairs to the rooms above the restaurant where our family lived, while someone else ran for the doctor. And so on the fourteenth day of August 1894, in the little town of Alderson, West-by-God-Virginia, the doctor said, "Another little split-tail," and on that day Bricktop was born.

I was the third "split-tail"—girl—and the last child born to Thomas and Hattie E. Smith. My father had dark brown skin and so did my brother Robert, who was three when I was born. My mother was seven-eighths white, with blond hair and gray-blue eyes. If she'd wanted to, she could have passed for white. My oldest sister, aged eleven at the time of my birth, inherited my mother's hair and eyes. Her real name was Etta, but everyone called her blond Etta, which became Blonzetta. My five-year-old sister, Ethel, had that golden-brown skin that looks as if there is a light underneath it. Then along I came with white, white skin like my mother's, and red-gold hair.

Since they already had two girls, I think Mama and Papa wanted me to be a boy. It helped, though, that I had that red hair. I was the talk of the town, the first red-haired baby, Negro or white, born in that area in many a year. The only other redhead in town was an Alderson. People said he had the kind of flaming red-gold hair that women just don't seem to get—naturally, anyway.

All the neighbors came to visit and make a fuss over me, and a lot of them wanted to name me. Mama and Papa had a hard time choosing. They didn't want to hurt anyone's feelings—especially not the local pharmacist's, who said he would give Mama all the soaps and powders and sponges she needed to take care of me, if she would let him give me a name.

So Mama and Papa tried to please everybody and named me Ada Beatrice Queen Victoria Louise Virginia Smith. I don't know who gave me the other names, but Beatrice was to please the pharmacist. Queen Victoria? That was probably Mama's idea. Knowing Mama, she was really thinking big when she put that one in. She used to call me "Ada, my queen."

I didn't get my freckles until I was three years old. I fell off the porch and was unconscious for ten days. The doctor puzzled and puzzled, tested and tested, but couldn't find out what was wrong. After I came out of it, my skin began to darken and the mass of freckles I still have began to appear.

The freckles worried Mama and Papa, but the doctor told them they would never be a handicap. He was right—the freckles, along with my hair, became my trademark. People used to say that if you had a lot of freckles you'd be very lucky. They also said that if you had red hair, you'd have a fiery temper. In my case, they were right on both counts.

I don't remember Papa at all. I was four years old when he died. Mama said he was a smallish man, slightly hunchbacked. He ran a barbershop which catered only to white people. In those days you catered either to whites or to blacks. There was no mixing them up.

Papa was either a Baptist or a Methodist. Whichever, he was a big shot in the church—a deacon; highly respected by all. He enjoyed giving parties at our house, but I was told that he didn't always stay long at them himself. Sometimes, while everyone else was having a good time, Papa would go upstairs to his room, read the Bible, and go to bed.

Years later I'd do the same thing: disappear to my room and go to bed while my guests were still partying. When I was missed, someone would say, "Oh, she's having her *petit relax.*" I wonder if I got that from Papa.

Papa was only in his mid-forties when he died after a series of strokes. Practically the whole town came to his funeral. He was well liked and admired. Thirty-five years later a friend in Alderson sent Mama a clipping from the town newspaper. It was a list of the town's most prominent citizens of the past, and it included Tom Smith. A line in that clipping gave me the most vivid image I have of him: "When Tom Smith had on his high silk hat and carried his gold-topped cane, he was one of the toniest men in town."

I wish I knew something about my father's background, but I don't. I don't even know much about my mother's. Children were not supposed to ask questions. They could learn plenty if they were willing to sit around and listen to the grownups talk, but I wasn't that kind of child. I couldn't sit still for more than two minutes. Blonzetta was quieter, and years later she filled me in on what she'd heard.

Mama was born in slavery, but only two years before the Emancipation

Proclamation. Her mother had white skin, blue-gray eyes, and blond hair and was mostly Scotch-Irish. She was a house slave, and so she had an easier time of it than the field slaves. Mama's maiden name was Thompson, and her father was probably her mother's master.

Whoever my grandfather was, he must have had deep roots in the land, or high social standing. Mama was constantly telling us, "Don't ever forget you're all FFV [First Families of Virginia] and people expect us to be polite."

I didn't have to go to Europe to learn manners. Mama's heritage and upbringing accomplished that.

As a young girl, Mama was sent to St. Louis to live with a grandmother. This grandmother was either white or a Negro who was passing. Mama was enrolled in a Catholic convent school, and though she never practiced that religion, it somehow fits that I would one day convert to Catholicism. Mama told us that the nuns at the school were very strict about etiquette and manners. They also instilled in Mama a lifelong passion for reading—not fiction but books about what was going on in the world and how it got that way.

I don't know how she met Papa. The details of her courtship and wedding are gone with her, but I think she and Papa must have had a happy marriage. She never said an unkind word about him in the forty years she lived after him, and she was fond of telling us children what he had said before he died: "Never worry, Hattie. Never worry about anything when I'm gone. I'll be looking after you. Never forget that."

Mama was thirty-seven years old when Papa died. A handsome woman of medium height, she wore the "widow's weeds" that were proper at the time, but she had four young children to think about and she didn't act mournful in front of us. She firmly believed in Papa's promise, and it wasn't long before she made up her mind to leave Alderson. Kindly as the people were, the town just didn't offer many possibilities for a young widow.

Chicago was her first and only choice. Chicago was the home of her Uncle Adam, who was light-complexioned like the rest of her family and who was passing as white. Uncle Adam was a railroad conductor, an unheard-of job for a Negro at that time.

Mama made it clear to Uncle Adam that she didn't want to make any trouble. She didn't expect to move in with him. She only wanted to know he was there and that she could count on his help if she needed it. Uncle Adam wrote Mama to come ahead and he'd help her get started.

News spread fast in a little town like Alderson. When the townspeople heard that Mama was planning to pack up her children and head for Chicago, they were horrified. The attitude of small-town folk toward the big city hasn't changed much in the past eighty years. They tried to talk her out of it. "You might starve to death in Chicago," they warned. But Mama had made up her mind. "Then we'll starve together," she said.

The neighbors decided to pray for us. They prayed round-the-clock as the time came for Mama to leave. Mama knelt with them and asked God to watch over us in the big city.

We went to Chicago in two stages. Mama went first, with Robert and Ethel. I was left in the care of Blonzetta until Mama could get a job and set up a new home for us. It wasn't long before she'd gotten a very good job with the Applegate family, publishers of the newspaper *Inter-Ocean*.

She probably went to work for them as a maid, but the word "maid" was never mentioned in front of Mama. Madison Avenue hadn't discovered the knack of upgrading the service occupations in 1900, but Mama had. Whenever she talked about her work, she referred to herself as "governess" or "housekeeper."

Just as soon as Mama settled in at the Applegates', she sent for Blonzetta and me. We were sent off with more fervent prayers by the people of Alderson. I've never been back.

Mama had bigger plans than just working as a "housekeeper." She always said, "If you can do it for others, you can do it for yourself," and so she looked around for a roominghouse to run. The first one she found was at 171 East Chicago Avenue. It was over an Italian barbershop (maybe Papa steered her there). She fell naturally into the routine of running a roominghouse, where she was the mistress of her own domain. She was accountable to no one, and everyone was accountable to her. She kept on working for other people for a while, until she was able to make enough just running boardinghouses. After that, she seldom worked for other people again.

The East Chicago Avenue place was the first of several that Mama had during the years I was growing up. All were more or less the same. Six or seven rooms. Running water. Inside plumbing in all but one place where we lived. Kerosene lamps. Big iron stove in the kitchen where the water was heated. Mama was a fiend for cleanliness. Seems as if she was always heating water, either for the laundry or to scrub us in the big wooden tubs in which she washed clothes.

Usually when people asked to rent the big front room, Mama turned them down. The front room and one bedroom were for her own family. She rented the other rooms out for a dollar fifty or two fifty a week, with kitchen privileges. At suppertime there'd be two or three women gathered around the stove making dinner, with some bachelor waiting in the background for a chance to heat his soup.

The roomers were responsible for their own cleaning. If they were messy and Mama "just happened by" their room when the door was open, they'd hear about it. "Don't you people know you are guests in my house? What you pay me does not give you the right to treat my home like some fleabag!" The roomer either moved to clean up or he moved out. When Hattie Smith spoke, that meant action.

Oh, how Mama could lay them out! And those roomers who were caught at what Mama called "funny business" really got the treatment. Mama prided herself on renting rooms to "nice working people." But even nice working people engaged in "funny business."

Mama was realistic, but she laid down her rules. Whenever a person applied for a room, Mama asked the same question: "Are you married?"

The answer was usually, "Yes. And no. I have a friend."

"I understand," Mama would say pleasantly, "but the first friend you bring in here must be your last. I won't have you changing partners in front of my children." She meant it. Chicago could be in the midst of a raging blizzard, but if Mama found someone breaking her "funny business" rule, both roomer and friend landed right out on the street.

There wasn't much that got past Mama's eagle eye. But one roomer really kept her wondering. He had no "friends," ate out all the time, kept to his room when at home, and kept it in good order. You wouldn't have looked twice at him except for one thing: he had smooth, smooth skin just like a girl's.

Mama wondered if he had anything else like a girl's. So one day she just happened to walk past his room when the door was ajar. There was ladies' underwear on the chair. Mama was thrown off balance, but she didn't say anything. She just tiptoed away.

The roomer must have seen Mama peeping into the room, because the next day he told her he was moving out: an urgent message had arrived and he had to leave. Though his week wasn't quite up, he didn't ask for a refund. Mama didn't have any complaints about him and might have let him stay on. He was quiet and neat, no "funny business"—but that ladies' underwear had her stumped.

Later Mama found out that her roomer really had been a woman. She'd killed someone in another state and was running away from the law. Her disguise didn't work. The police caught up with her. The newspapers carried the story. "Mercy!" cried Mama. "We might have all been murdered in our beds!"

After a while Mama told the Applegates she was leaving to devote full time to the roominghouse. They were sorry to see her go. They asked if my sister Blonzetta could come to work for them as a nursemaid. They'd taken to Blonzetta right away when they'd met her. At first Mama wasn't very keen on the idea, but the Applegates said they would take Blonzetta with them when they went to New York and Philadelphia, and my sister wanted to see those places. Mama consented at last, and it was a good experience for Blonzetta. She watched and listened, and she learned something about how people made money, and how they kept it. She would put what she learned to good use later on.

Something like that almost happened to me when I was around seven. Mama was working for a family at their estate in La Grange, a very fashionable weekend place for rich people. Next door was the estate of the Armours, the Chicago meat-packing family. They had a granddaughter named Lolita, and when Mama took me to work with her I'd go next door to play with Lolita.

She was an invalid. There was something wrong with her hip and she could hardly walk. When the Armours brought a doctor from Vienna to operate on her, the story made headlines. It was big news to bring a doctor all the way from Europe in those days.

The Armours decided I would make a good companion for Lolita and they asked Mama if they could adopt me. Mama realized I'd have all the advantages—good schools, travel, and all that. She told the Armours they could have me until I turned eighteen, but they said, "Oh, no, we want to adopt her legally. You will never see her again."

Mama wanted the best for her children, but she wasn't about to give them away.

Many years later my sister Ethel was living at 37th and Wabash Avenue. Not far away, at 37th and Michigan, was the Armour estate with its big iron fence. Sometimes when I visited Ethel I'd say, "Now if Mama had let me be adopted, I'd be over there behind that fence wearing expensive clothes, going to parties, and you'd be outside on the street looking in."

And Ethel would say, "Yeah, you'd be running around inside in your beautiful clothes, and I'd be running around outside calling, 'Nigger, nigger, nigger!' " We'd laugh until we cried.

In 1950, just after I opened my place in Rome, the American Ambassador to Italy—a man named Dunn—came in with his wife. She was an Armour. She said, "Come over here, Brick, and sit by me and tell me how we nearly became cousins."

It seems as if Mama had quite a few chances to give up her children. If it wasn't some rich white family asking her, then it was some man friend. Her first year in Chicago, Mama had a sweetheart who wanted her to send us away so he could have her alone. Mama said no, and that was the end of that.

The same thing happened when I was eight or nine. Mama had a friend and they were very much in love. He called her Laura and she called him Chicken. His real name was Charlie Jordan. He was a tall man with reddish-brown skin. I don't know what kind of work he did, but he must have earned good pay. He offered to pay our tuition at boarding school.

Mama wasn't having any part of that. He went off and married another woman, more to spite Mama than anything else, but he still came around. Five or six years later Mama was still fooling around with him. I'd hear her crying over him. I was still very young when I promised myself, "Nobody's ever going to make me cry."

Most of my early memories of Chicago begin when we moved to 3237 State Street, way over on the South Side. As usual, Mama took over the big front room and one bedroom for her family and rented out the other rooms.

It was a working-class neighborhood. Typical of most working-class neighborhoods in big cities at the turn of the century, it was divided among Jews, Irish, Italians, and Negroes. The apartment buildings were segregated, but Negro and white buildings stood side by side. When we spilled out into the street each day, we lost sight of color and nationality and behaved like neighbors.

It was a tightly knit community. Everyone knew everybody else's business, and that wasn't as bad as it sounds. We helped each other out.

Parents were strict with their own children, and they didn't hesitate to bawl out or spank their neighbors' kids. Working mothers didn't have to worry about their children when they left in the morning. There were no baby-sitters. There was always a neighbor to watch over the young ones. Mama was one of those neighborhood-watchers, and the other mothers couldn't have asked for a better one. Mama's standards were very high, and no one knew that better than her own children.

She taught manners with a capital "M." It was "Please," "Thank you," and "Excuse me." When in doubt, use all three. And never open your mouth unless you were spoken to, when Mama had company.

She demanded instant obedience. In the evening, when the neighborhood relaxed and the women gathered outside their apartments to chat and the men headed for the saloons, we children would play. But no matter how much fun we were having, bedtime never varied. Standing on the sidewalk talking to the neighbors, Mama knew without looking at a watch when it was my bedtime. She raised a finger, went right on talking, and someone, usually Blonzetta, would say, "Ada, Mama's finger is up." That raised finger meant I was to go to bed, right then and there. Away I'd run, because when Mama hit you, she hit! She'd close the doors and windows, put a pillow over your mouth, and go right at it.

Mama wasn't very affectionate. I can't remember her hugging or kissing me more than five times in my life. But if she wasn't affectionate, there were other qualities that made up for it—mainly her protectiveness. I never spent a day under her roof, as a child or a woman, when I didn't feel secure.

We didn't have a lot of creature comforts, but we had enough. If I ever went hungry as a child, it wasn't for lack of food. It was because Mama was such a terrible cook. The only thing she could make without ruining it was vegetable soup—put a kettle of water on the stove and throw some vegetables in it.

There were two things Mama never stinted on—good shoes and a good bed. She'd say, "My children are not going to run around barefoot with their feet spread out all over the world. Feet are the body's foundation. Go around without shoes, you're bound to wind up with flat feet and an even flatter head."

She'd take us to the best shoe store in Chicago and buy us three-dollar shoes. In those days, paying three dollars for shoes was like paying a hundred dollars today. Of course, in time—a very short time with children—the soles of even those expensive shoes wore out. Then they'd have to go to the shoemaker to be resoled.

When my shoes were being resoled, I'd have to wear a pair of Ethel's. Since she was five years older than I was, her shoes were far from a perfect fit. Little Ada was having none of that. Oh, I'd put them on and start out for school, but I'd never get there. Mama had made me so conscious about how my feet should look that I was sure the minute I walked into school a hundred pairs of eyes would all be looking at my feet.

When Mama found out I was playing hookey, she couldn't really whip me. She was the one who drummed into us the importance of always looking our best.

Wearing the right shoes was not the last word in the foot department. We had to wash our feet every night before jumping into bed. We also had to wash the part of us that made girls different from boys.

We could understand washing our feet, but why those other parts had to be gone over with soap and water Mama never explained. I don't know how she expected us to find out about the facts of life. She had little or nothing to say. If we went to her with a question about something the kids were whispering and giggling about at school, she'd put us off by asking if we'd done our homework. If we had, she'd find another way to make us forget what we'd come to ask her about.

We found out about the mysteries of life by bits and pieces, mostly at school.

I was probably Mama's "problem child," because I was terribly nervous. When I was two, I went through a bout of St. Vitus's Dance, an exciting-sounding disease to have. It was years before I found out what it was. The medical term is "chorea," and it is usually connected with childhood rheumatic fever. I must have had a mild case, because my coordination wasn't affected, but I was fidgety, quick of movement, and incapable of sitting still for more than a few moments at a time.

Mama, who had been taught that young ladies didn't twitch and squirm, offered me a penny if I'd learn to sit still in a chair for five minutes. A penny was big money, and I did my best and my body began to learn discipline.

Being a victim of St. Vitus's Dance had some advantages that I learned to exploit. I knew that Mama was afraid to carry her whippings too far with me, for fear that she would bring on another attack, so when she was getting ready to punish me, I'd start to jump up and down. She'd usually think better about hitting me.

I used my affliction to get out of washing dishes for a while. I hated washing dishes and still do. To get out of dishwashing, I dropped a couple of dishes "accidentally on purpose." Mama got wise in a hurry, though. She said I could trade chores with Ethel. Since Ethel was five years older, she had a lot more to do—polishing the furniture, sweeping the stairs, scrubbing down the floors. I stopped jumping up and down immediately and didn't drop any more dishes for a long time.

I was always a jumper. As a small child, I used to love to run and jump into Mama's outstretched arms. She'd swing me around and put me up on her shoulders and stride around the room, saying she was taking her little queen for a ride to Buckingham Palace.

Later I played leapfrog with the neighborhood boys. I was a tomboy. After age five or six I didn't care about dolls anymore. I wanted to play marbles and jackknife. I was a real terror, except when I was out with Mama, or if I was out on the sidewalk wearing a new dress—then I'd walk as if my feet were made of lead. The neighbors would get the message and lean out of their windows, making a fuss over me.

Not all the neighbors approved of me. Two maiden ladies decided that I was nothing but a roughhouse tomboy who had an unwholesome effect on the other boys and girls. They decided I should be sent to a correctional school, and they started a petition to have me put away.

When Mama got wind of that, she let it be known that if the sisters didn't tear up that petition immediately, she'd personally ram it down their throats. And if that didn't stop them, she'd horsewhip them to within an inch of their lives.

Mama never owned a horsewhip, but in her tempers "I'll horsewhip you!" was her favorite threat.

Well, that was the end of the petition, and the sisters didn't make any more trouble after that. Mama didn't say too much about my being a tomboy. I guess she decided that the more I jumped, ran, and played baseball and leapfrog, the quieter I'd be at home. Let her whipping arm rest a bit.

Most of the neighbors liked me because I was always willing to run errands for them. In fact, I was overjoyed to do it. I could do what I liked best—race up and down the street. The neighbors would give me a penny or so and the responsibility for their shopping. I really felt like somebody when I walked into the grocery store to order a pound of potatoes for two cents, or a half-dozen eggs for a nickel. Another way I got a few cents was by lighting the gas stoves in the homes of the Ortho-dox Jews on the Sabbath.

I ran errands for Mama, too. However, there was one errand she thought I was too young for. Whenever she wanted a can of beer, she'd send Ethel.

Mama made no bones about her liking for beer—and whiskey, too. Blonzetta's and Ethel's boyfriends discovered that a quick way to Mama's good side was to bring her a half-pint now and then. In a neighborhood with a lot of saloons, like ours, the women were always sending young-sters out to "rush the can."

You had a wide tin can with a handle on it and you took it to the back door of the nearest saloon. The bartender would fill it up for a nickel. If you were smart, you'd bring along another nickel and drop it in the can to cut the foam. That way, you'd get an extra slug of beer. Then you rushed back before the foam disappeared.

We had a neighbor named Mrs. Scott, an Irish policeman's wife. She had me rushing the can long before Mama thought I was old enough. Mama got suspicious when she found out that Mrs. Scott had me running errands for her several times a day. She finally asked, "Ada, what does Mrs. Scott send you to the store for?"

Innocent me said, "Mama, she says she gets so dry in the hot weather that I have to go to the back door of the saloon and get her b-double-e-r ginger ale."

"What?"

"B-double-e-r ginger ale."

"Not my little baby!" Mama flew out the door. She started shouting and letting Mrs. Scott have it before she got to the woman's house. The two Irish ladies faced each other. Mama's temper was at full boil.

"What kind of Irish trash would send my baby to get beer at a saloon! I'll horsewhip you blind if I ever catch you sending my baby to the saloon again!"

That was the end of my rushing the can until I was old enough to do it for Mama.

I started school after we moved to State Street. Keith School had a reputation as the toughest school in Chicago, and that was probably because it had such a mixture of students. Like the neighborhoods around it, the school had Jewish, Irish, Italian, and Negro students and a few others.

The fights I remember weren't between the different races or the different ethnic groups. They were between us and the kids who went to another school about four blocks away. Maybe Keith got its reputation because we usually won. I know I fought to win, because I didn't dare go home to Mama afterward unless I had. If I came home a loser, she'd send me right back out and tell me not to come back until I did win.

The teaching staff at Keith was as integrated as the students. Several of the teachers were Negroes, and two of them—Miss Branch and Miss Nurse—I remember to this day. They were popular with the white students, too. Even now when I go to Chicago and there is some publicity about me, invariably someone will phone or write me to say, "Remember me? We were in Miss Branch's class at Keith School."

I suppose I thought school was just an extension of the life I knew— running errands, racing through the streets, cutting up, pretty much having my own way (except when Mama was around). How I managed to get as much schooling into me as I did is a wonder.

I couldn't keep my mouth, hands, or feet still for long. I'd pass silly notes, make funny faces, ask to go to the bathroom ten times a day. I was forever getting sent home with notes from the teacher.

If Mama ever saw them, I'd really catch it, so I took the notes to friendly neighbors to be signed. I soon had everyone for blocks around acknowledging those notes. I'd say, "Will you please sign this note for me? Mama hurt her hand and can't write." I got away with that until a neighbor happened to ask Mama if her hand was better. Mama showed that it was never stronger as she gave me a slap that could be heard clear across Chicago.

Probably because I had so much energy, I was always in the school shows—little plays presented on special occasions, like holidays. I don't remember much about them. Knowing my pushy self at that age, I probably had the main part. I had a good memory for lines, and if there was any call for acrobatics, why, that was right up my alley. If ever I had a girlish dream about a career, it was probably to be an acrobatic dancer. I liked making my legs and feet move in all directions. When someone played the piano, it seemed as if my feet knew just how to move in the right rhythm.

Actually, I made my stage debut long before I started school. Shortly after I arrived in Chicago, a company was rehearsing a production of *Uncle Tom's Cabin* at the Haymarket Theatre, not far from where we lived. They needed a small child to play Eliza's son, Harry, whose biggest scene occurs when Eliza escapes across the ice, carrying little Harry with her. Someone in the company saw me and asked Mama if she'd allow me to be little Harry. Mama loved the theater and was pleased at the chance to get behind the scenes. I don't remember a thing about my stage debut, but, according to Mama, I did just fine.

Mama did not have any set ideas about what she wanted her children to be when they grew up. As long as we were well read and well mannered, she left the rest up to God. She would take note of the things we liked or were good at, but she didn't push us to develop whatever talents we showed. Mama didn't encourage me to be an entertainer except once, and that time it was for a good cause, in her opinion. She took me to dance in jail.

Mama had a strong sense of social responsibility. She and some of the other women in the neighborhood would visit the local prison and bring the inmates fresh fruit, sandwiches, and cookies. They would talk

16

to the men and tell them what was happening in the outside world. Sometimes they would write letters for those who couldn't write. They had to ask permission from the guards first, and they would have to show the letters to the guards before they could mail them.

Mama would always be proud of the work she did at the prison. With the passing years, as she looked back on it, her work got even more important. Kay Boyle, a writer friend of mine, met Mama when she was in Paris with me, and apparently Mama told Kay about her prison work. In *Being Geniuses Together*, Kay wrote:

Bricktop's mother is Irish-Negro, and she is no negligible character herself. This mother of hers was, some years back, a policewoman in Chicago . . . and was a friend of Jane Addams of Hull House. The old lady had remarkable stories to tell of her experiences, and yet remained naïve and simple, as little hardened by the world as any kindly grandmother.

Well, Mama may have known of Jane Addams, the great settlement-house woman, but a policewoman she was not. That was just Mama upgrading her position again.

How I envied Mama's visits to the jails. They were the one part of her life I didn't share. She only laughed when I asked if I could go with her. Then one day, out of the blue, she announced that the following Sunday I was going to visit the jail with her. She told me to wear my prettiest dress and to go over my songs and dances.

I don't remember much about what the jail looked like. Big rooms. Iron bars. Big keyholes and big keys that opened doors. Mama introduced me to a few of the prisoners. I don't think I was my usual outgoing self at first. These men were in jail because they had done something bad.

Then I met a man I'll never forget—a handsome colored man called Jack the Bear. He had the nicest smile. I lost all sense of fear when he spoke to me. "Say, Ada, your Mama tells me you like to sing and dance. I sure would like to see that."

I looked at Mama. She smiled and nodded her head. Off I went, singing and dancing to the songs I knew, and a few I made up as I went along. A crowd gathered around, and the more they applauded, the more I performed. Then a guard came around and said it was time to go. I didn't want to. I was getting a little crush on Jack the Bear. Mama made me say goodbye to him, and we went home.

Back home, I wanted to know if I could go to the jail with Mama again the next week. She wanted to know why. "I want to dance for Jack the Bear. He's nice." Then Mama explained to me that Jack the Bear would not be there next week. He'd been sentenced to hang the following morning. I remember running out of the house without a word, finding a place where no one could see me, and crying for what seemed like hours. I never again asked Mama to take me with her to the jail.

Crime was no stranger to State Street, or to anyone who lived on it. People got into knife fights there. The police would come and haul them off to jail, if they didn't have to go to the hospital. Sometimes innocent people were hurt, but, as a rule, if you were hard-working and law-abiding you didn't have to worry about crime. You saw it, but you were just a spectator.

Thinking back, I realize that a lot of the fights started in the saloons, but when I was a child I didn't make the connection. Even the grownups around me didn't blame the saloons. Saloons were a part of our everyday life. No one thought anything bad about his neighbor going into them. In the evening after work, a lot of the men went into them to relax and unwind, and of course us kids knew that the women patronized the saloons by way of the back door. I knew the back doors of most of the nearby saloons, but I wasn't interested in them. It was what went on behind the swinging doors up front that fascinated me.

I loved saloons. I have an idea that my fascination had to do with the fact that I couldn't go into them, and so didn't know exactly what was going on. I had a great need to know what was going on everywhere, all the time. Every time I'd go by one, I'd squat down and peer under those swinging doors and try to get a good look. What I saw never failed to pique my curiosity.

The floors were covered with sawdust, but the bar was always polished and smooth and piled high with food. Reflected in the cut-glass mirror behind the bar, the standard saloon free lunch looked like a feast to me: plates with mounds of cold cuts, salads, pickles, olives, relishes. Big loaves of bread. Chunks of butter. Specially prepared hot dishes. The smell of all this food always mingled with that of whiskey and beer, but that didn't bother me. Like the smell of sawdust, the smell of liquor was natural in a saloon.

I thought whiskey and beer smelled like medicine, and for a long time I thought the men inside the saloons must have been real sick to have to drink so much. And evidently, no matter how much they poured down their throats, it didn't cure them, because they could barely stand up when they left.

There was another pair of swinging doors inside the saloon that really made me curious: the ones that led to the back room. A lot of people set out in life with a certain goal in mind, some place in the world they aim for. I don't think I set out to want anything but to get into the back rooms of those saloons.

Women were allowed in there. They came in from the side door, the family entrance. Every so often I'd hear someone singing back there while the music came out of the player piano. Then I'd hear applause and a man's voice calling for "another round." Many years later I learned that Scott Joplin was in Chicago in 1905 and 1906. He might have been in the very back rooms I longed so much to see.

There was just no way I was going to be allowed into those mysterious and exciting places, however; I never got past the swinging doors in the front. All I could do was squat down and peek under them. The bartenders got used to seeing my red head poked under the doors. They didn't even have to leave the bar to see which kid it was. They'd just lean over the bar and yell, "Ada Smith, you go home. This is no place for a little girl." Of course, I wouldn't move from the spot until they threatened to come after me. Then I ran.

I really envied my sister Ethel when she got a chance to sing in one of those back rooms. She was not destined for a career as a saloon singer, though. She was so shy that when she opened her mouth, nothing came out. I was disgusted with her for messing up such a golden opportunity.

Not that I had any dreams of becoming a singer. Ethel was the one in the family with the good voice. I was just interested in those saloon back rooms. It wasn't until I was fourteen or fifteen that I became stagestruck, and by that time I was more interested in the Pekin Theatre than in the State Street saloons.

For a youngster who loved performing, Chicago was the right place to be in the early 1900s. Shows with big stars filled the downtown theaters. John Barrymore played Chicago as often as he did New York. Sophie Tucker, a gal Chicago claimed as its own, became a star in the Windy City in *Louisiana Lou*. The Four Cohans, Primrose and West, Bert Williams, Eva Tanguay, and Al Field's Minstrels were some of the great acts who called Chicago their home.

With any kind of success, a show that originated in Chicago could head into the Midwest with a built-in reputation. The same was true for performers.

Chicago was also headquarters for a flourishing Negro show business. It was based at the Pekin Theatre, the first theater of any consequence to be devoted to Negro drama. The Pekin opened in 1902 and was owned and operated by Bob Motts and his nephews. It was a handsome, well-decorated house that seated about six hundred. It had its own stock company, the Pekin Players, and out of it came such famous stars as Lottie Grady and Charles Gilpin, who later played the title role in Eugene O'Neill's *The Emperor Jones*. Best of all for us children, the Pekin was right around the corner from where we lived.

All our lives, going to the show at the Pekin had been a special treat for the Smith children. When I was younger, it was just as special as going to the ballpark to see the Negro teams play. (Mama loved baseball and was a walking encyclopedia of the Negro teams, which she followed religiously in the daily papers.) By the time I was fourteen or so, though, I was much more interested in the Pekin.

If I wasn't dragging my sisters or brother with me to the Saturday matinees, I'd be dragging Mama. They didn't want to go all the time. I was the one who had to see every show each time they changed the bill. I finally started going with some friends from school who also had stage-struckitis. We'd study the billboard out front and then run errands or talk our mothers into giving us the money for admission.

Sometimes I went all by myself. The doorman or the manager would sneak me inside. Afterward I'd go around to the alley and wait at the stage door for the performers to come out. Their friendliness helped convince me that I belonged in their world.

The performers got to know that whenever they saw us, there would be questions to answer—mainly, how to get a job on the stage at the

Pekin. They'd laugh and tease us about being in such a rush. We'd tell them that it wasn't a question of rushing anything, although we'd rush the can for them to the nearest saloon if they asked us. It just seemed that being on the stage was a lot more fun than going to school, not to mention how nice it would be to earn some money doing what we liked to do.

We kept on hanging around the stage door of the Pekin until the day came when we heard what we wanted to hear. Bob Motts needed some kids for the new show for the following week. They were to sing and dance with the chorus in the production numbers, and fill out the stage as silent bystanders when the scenes called for it. Above all, they had to pay attention to what was happening on stage, and not look out into the audience to see if they could spot their friends. Could we do it? Could we! Just give us a chance, Mr. Motts!

He led us to his office, where he had a piano, and we took turns singing a song and dancing a few steps. He said we had the job, but we'd have to okay it with our parents. We thanked him and rushed out of the theater, couldn't get home fast enough. We had made it. So what if it was only in the chorus? We wouldn't be in the chorus for long! How right we were.

Mama said she didn't mind my going into the show, as long as I kept up my studies at school. I told her it only meant one week of rehearsals. After that, we'd go back to school and be in the show at night. Mama was still doubtful, until I said I would get the homework from a classmate who lived near us. Mama got no peace from me until she finally consented.

I have an idea that Mama suspected, even before I did, that I was going to be an entertainer. When I used to tell her that I wanted to be an actress, she never laughed, although she confessed she couldn't understand it, since there had never been a performer in the family. Ethel's one attempt didn't qualify her. At any rate, Mama let me have my way.

The rehearsals began, and we kids took to the stage as if we'd been born to it. If the director had any complaints about us, it was that we would get too giddy, or try to jump into the routines before he told us what to do. Between rehearsals, all we could talk about was the show: what the costumes were like, which numbers we liked best.

I made few attempts to get my homework assignments, and even fewer attempts to get them done. My mind was just not about to absorb dull old facts and figures. As I sat at the parlor table trying to concentrate, the music from the show kept running through my head while my feet did little steps on the floor. Mama looked in on me from time to time. When she saw me with my book open, but my eyes closed, she told me to go to bed.

Opening night arrived. Mama, Robert, and Ethel came, and so did some friends from school. Of course when the curtain went up, we kids in the chorus did exactly what we weren't supposed to do. We stared out into the audience to see if we could recognize anybody. A backstage voice said, "The show's on the stage. Not out there."

Afterward, there were compliments from our families and friends, and also from the director. He thought one number needed more rehearsal, and we'd have to come in the next day to go over it until he was satisfied, but we didn't care. We loved being on that stage any time.

As the week progressed, so did we. We stopped staring out into the audience and started behaving like professionals. We even began to peep through a hole in the curtain before the show started, to count the empty seats and see if there was anyone out there we knew. One night we saw someone we all knew—the truant officer, sitting right up front.

She didn't wait for the final curtain to come down before she stationed herself in the wings. I was the first one she grabbed—my red hair made me stick out like a sore thumb. One by one, we were questioned and our names and addresses taken down. She gave us a lecture right there, and assured us she'd be speaking to our parents shortly.

When she came to my house, Mama started lecturing *her*. Hattie E. Smith didn't need anyone to tell her about the importance of an education. Yes, Mama said, Ada would be out of the theater and back in the classroom, but Mama wasn't going to listen to anybody's lecture.

It was very hard to go back and have to sit behind a desk. It was hard to make up the ten days' work I'd missed. However, I put all I had into it. Mama had been good enough to let me go on the stage, and I owed it to her not to fall behind in school.

We kids went back to our routine of going to all the Saturday matinees and hanging around the Pekin. Bad break, one of the performers said. But, after all, we weren't sixteen yet. There was nothing to do but bide our time until we could legally leave school to go to work.

We started going to the other big theaters in Chicago. When the Williams-and-Walker show came to town, we rushed to get seats. They were *the* big success of that time. George Walker's wife, Ada Overton Walker, was a great star, and of course in later years Bert Williams went on to star in the *Ziegfeld Follies*.

We never missed seeing Sophie Tucker. She was great then and became greater with each passing year. Whenever she was in town, we would be in the audience, and at the stage door, waiting for her to come out after the show. We'd all speak at once, trying to tell her how great we thought she was. She'd spend a few minutes with us and would always remark about my red hair. Twenty years later I would be astonished to find out that she remembered me as well as I remembered her.

My chance to get back on the stage came when we kids heard that Miller and Lyles, a comedy team who were regulars on the bill at the Pekin, were preparing to take a new show on the road and needed boys and girls for the chorus. By this time I was sixteen, old enough to leave school without worrying about the truant officer. Mama didn't want me to leave school. She'd begged all of her children to finish their schooling. I begged and pleaded, but I didn't begin to wear her down until I said, "Mama, please let me go. I'll become a star and I'll always take care of you." She didn't laugh when I said that. She took my ambition seriously.

It is one of the biggest regrets of my life that I didn't listen to Mama and finish my education. But when Mama finally gave in, there was no holding me back.

O N   T H E   R O A D

MILLER AND LYLES paid me five dollars a week. Out of that I had to pay my own room and board in the towns where we played. I didn't think much about the salary. At sixteen, who cared about money? I'd never had more than a nickel that belonged to me at any one time. I was a stage-struck kid, and the only thing that mattered to me was that I had a job.

Flournoy Miller and Aubrey Lyles had started out in college theatricals at Fisk University in Tennessee. After that, they'd teamed up to take a show on the road. It was a blackface act full of Southern small-town humor, dance sequences, and a fight scene that was imitated by a lot of other vaudeville acts.

The show I went out with was a good one and well received. We played a few dates in theaters several hours' rides away from Chicago, but vaudeville, especially Negro vaudeville, was risky in those days. You took your bookings as they came, and when there were no more bookings, you folded.

24

It wasn't too long before I learned that fact of show business. Suddenly, there was no more money to keep the show going. We were stranded one hundred miles from Chicago. It was every man for himself then, and we kids were among the luckiest, because we had concerned parents to write home to. Mama had money in the mail for me as soon as she got my SOS letter. In those days the mails were pretty fast.

On the train back to Chicago I had plenty of time to think. Even before joining Miller and Lyles, I knew that unless you were a dramatic actress you had to perform in vaudeville—and from what I'd seen, living on State Street around so many performers and musicians, vaudeville was not the greatest life in the world. It was a world of dingy theaters, sudden cancellations, and, as had just happened to me, getting stranded.

It didn't make sense that a chorus kid in vaudeville had to play five and six shows a day for five dollars a week, be constantly on the move, pay for her own room and board, while girls entertaining in Chicago's saloons were earning as much as twelve and fifteen dollars a week, with tips.

It was useless for me to dream about entertaining in a saloon, however. The law said that singers had to be eighteen, and the police on the beat were strict about enforcing it. Besides, I'd never been inside a saloon, and you don't learn to entertain in one just by peeking under swinging doors. I knew I'd have to serve more time in vaudeville if I wanted to remain on the stage.

Mama didn't say much about my getting stranded, especially after I announced that I had no intention of giving up the stage. She just said it would be a good idea if in the future I asked about the number of advance bookings before I agreed to go on the road with an act.

I started hanging around the theaters again, and it wasn't long before I landed a job with McCabe's Georgia Troubadours in a tour around Illinois and the neighboring states.

The McCabe show was like a minstrel show, with an all-Negro cast. Bill McCabe was an end man, a comedian. There was another end man and then Billy Young in between. There were two or three other people, and then the chorus girls. We did a lot of stock minstrel numbers, like "Rufus Rastus Johnson Brown," and we sang things like:

> Coon, coon, coon, I wish my color would fade,
> Coon, coon, coon, to be a different shade.

Coon, coon, coon, morning, night and noon,
I'd rather be a white man, 'stead of a coon, coon, coon.

Try to sing that now and you'll get *crucified*. People got mad at Florence Mills because she sang "I'm a Little Blackbird." But it didn't bother me to sing that kind of song. That's what you did in a minstrel show. It's what the audiences wanted, and if you wanted to be on the stage, you gave the audiences what they came for.

I learned about soul food when I was with McCabe, only they didn't call it soul food then. Soul was something you didn't talk about except in church. Soul food was Southern food. Mama never made it, and I don't know whether she knew about it or not. There weren't all that many Negroes in Chicago when I was growing up, so it wasn't until I went to places like Louisville and Cincinnati that I met up with Southerners and ate things like spare ribs and biscuits, sweet potatoes and cornbread, chitlins and fried chicken. I loved it, couldn't get enough of it. When I came back after all those years in Paris, what I wanted most was that good Southern food.

I managed to get in several months with the Georgia Troubadours before I left and went back to Chicago. Being in the chorus of a traveling vaudeville show just didn't pay—at least not in my opinion. Other girls in the chorus didn't mind sharing a room to save money, but I minded. Maybe it was because I'd always had to share a room with Ethel and Robert. I wanted a room of my own. After paying for a single room and meals every day, however, there wasn't much left over from a chorus girl's salary. It seemed to me that there had to be something better—and the best place to find it was in Chicago.

As I look back now, I wonder how I could have had the gall to think I could do so much better. I had some assets, sure. Besides youth, I had flaming red hair, a happy freckled face, and a pair of beautiful legs and feet. I could sing well enough to get by and there weren't many people who didn't agree that Ada Smith was a terrific natural dancer. The big handicap—and it stayed with me for a long time—was being so thin. I couldn't make anyone believe I was sixteen and in show business. Then, as now, managers were looking for "better-rounded" girls than I was.

I was determined to make it, however, and I had the advantage of my experience with two traveling shows. The world of Negro vaudeville was a small one, and as I hung around the stage doors of the theaters, I could say hello to a lot of people as if we were long-lost friends and almost get by with it.

One day Oma Crosby did more than just return my "Hello." The girl in her trio was leaving and she needed a replacement. Would I be interested? It meant going on the road, farther away from Chicago than I had ever been before. Sure! I said, but first we'd have to ask Mama.

Oma was in her late twenties. She had light brown skin, beautiful hair, a lovely body, and long, trim legs. She did a song-and-dance act and always had two kids, a boy and a girl, as part of it. In fact, she built her act around the two kids. She had a fine reputation—the Oma Crosby Trio was what reviewers called a "nice, clean act," which gives you some idea of the caliber of some of the other acts on the vaudeville circuits. Not only did Oma have a good personal reputation, she was also respected as a reliable performer. That was important in those days on the circuits, as it still is in show business generally.

Oma worked white vaudeville and bookings were rarely steady. She beat the layoffs by working the TOBA Negro circuit, which booked acts throughout the Midwest and along the East Coast. She'd take a booking anywhere at a moment's notice. Often we took the night train or steamer to Canada to play a few dates. So many managers knew and liked Oma that she was able to pop a letter in the mail saying she was available and grab an engagement.

Oma went in person to ask Mama if I could join her act. She gave Mama every assurance that we wouldn't be stranded anywhere. Mama already knew of Oma's fine reputation and didn't hesitate too long before she said I could go.

The other part of the trio was a handsome boy named Russell, about eighteen, who had a very fine baritone voice. The act was one of those busy things. Oma did her turn, then Russell and I hoofed and sang duets. We changed costumes for every number. I remember wearing a gingham apron for one. In another, Russell dressed as an Indian and I played his squaw. For the finale, the three of us would do a number together. The act was not exactly the height of sophistication, but very little in vaudeville was. Family audiences in the "ten-twent-thirt" theaters we played enjoyed us, and reviewers always repeated the legend about our being a "nice, clean act."

"Ten-twent-thirt" used to refer to the prices of admission charged at those small theaters—ten cents, twenty cents, thirty cents. After a while almost any small theater was called that.

Clean act or not, the hours were just as killing. We arrived early in the morning, played four or five shows, and caught catnaps in between. Sometimes we were lucky enough to have a two-week engagement, but mostly we played on a one-week or split-week basis.

I was paid seven dollars a week, plus seventy-five cents a day for a room and two meals (in those days coffee was three cents a cup and you could get a whole dinner for fifteen cents). If the room and meals came to a dollar, you had to pay the difference. We stayed in Negro boarding-houses where the food was good and there was plenty of it. If I'd been willing to share a room, I would have been able to get by fine, but my tab was always coming to a dollar because with Oma I continued the indulgence I began when I first started traveling: I had to have my own room. Whatever was left over from my pay at the end of the week— usually two to three dollars—I'd send home to Mama.

With Oma Crosby I began to grow up. I turned seventeen when I was with her, and I couldn't be out touring, and hanging around backstage at the various theaters and not begin to learn about what makes the world go 'round. Part of that growing up, and the part that fascinated me most, was finally getting into the back rooms of those saloons. Getting inside still wasn't easy. At times I felt as if I were nine years old and still peeking under the swinging doors, because at age seventeen I still looked fourteen. Even to get in, I had to lower my short skirt over my waist, so it would look like an ankle-length skirt, and keep my coat on. And I suppose if I hadn't been with Oma I wouldn't have gotten in even then.

There were always plenty of saloons near the theaters where we worked—colorful, interesting places. Only a couple of visits behind those swinging doors convinced me that a saloon was where I belonged. This was where the action was.

An old-time saloon was more than a cocktail lounge. Besides beer and liquor, there was that free lunch of legend. The saloon era was the great era of American hospitality.

Saloon bartenders were fat, warm, friendly men who favored striped shirts and bright garters on their sleeves. A quick glance separated the entertainers from the prostitutes. The entertainers wore long skirts and blouses. The prostitutes dressed to the teeth, and wore their skirts several inches above the ankle.

Ladies were not permitted at the bar. They were allowed in the back room only. Some were ladies with husbands; some were with other ladies' husbands, offering companionship for the night. Saloon customers cut right through American life—on any given night you could find the steady family man, the politician, the gambler, the pimp.

The last two types were not new to me. You couldn't grow up on State Street in Chicago and not learn to recognize them. The professional gambler and the pimp always sported diamond rings with matching stickpins—the genuine articles. These sporting men, as we called them, wore tight-fitting, slick-looking suits to go with their diamonds. Sometimes they had to make do with just the suits. In that era diamonds weren't just a girl's best friend, they were a man's, too. A sporting man's diamond spent as much time in a pawnshop as on him. Performers, trying to look spiffy, too, usually wore imitations.

There was always a non-stop show going on in the back room. Sometimes there was paid entertainment. Sometimes it was a waiter or waitress who also knew how to sing and dance, and there was usually a piano player in the crowd. Other times they might have performers who were appearing at a local theater and who needed very little encouragement to get up and do a turn. When they finished, their show friends threw pennies at them as a joke. There would be lots of laughter and applause, and then someone would call out for another round of drinks.

One night, after we'd played a show at one of the Negro theaters in Cincinnati, we went down to the rathskeller in the basement of the hotel where we were staying. The saloon itself was on the first floor, and the back room, or rathskeller, was downstairs. It was my first experience in a rathskeller. Ed Gaither's place was one of the early few. He owned the entire building, including the hotel, and was the first Negro in the United States to own a Rolls Royce.

It was crowded that particular night, but we managed to get a table. Soon we were talking and enjoying ourselves, along with everybody else. I wasn't drinking any hard liquor. I'd had a few tastes of beer with Mama back in Chicago, but that was all. I stuck to drinking lemonade.

As the others at the table ordered round after round of whiskeys, lemonades kept appearing in front of me. A young man next to me was about to order for a second time when Oma, on the other side, whispered, "Now, Ada, you buy a round."

"Me? Buy a round? I don't even drink."

Oma's face broke into one of her warm smiles. "Ada, if you're with people in a bar and everybody buys a round, when it's your turn you buy a round. That's the way it is."

I dug into my purse and pulled out a crumpled dollar bill. It was plenty to take care of a round. Drinks usually cost two for a quarter. That was the first round of drinks I ever bought in my life. How many I bought in the next sixty years I don't think even a computer could figure out.

From that time on, Oma didn't have to remind me about my social obligation when we were out drinking with friends. I still drank lemonade, occasionally a beer. One taste of whiskey had convinced me I should stick to drinking what went down my throat easiest and gave me no headaches the next day. No one made fun of me or any of the other teenage performers. We were not addicted to dope or booze. Of course, there was always one joker in the crowd who'd try to force some whiskey down me, just to be smart, but there was usually a protective adult around who'd say, "No you don't."

At first we worked out of Chicago, but eventually the Oma Crosby Trio headed east on the TOBA circuit, which was probably the largest Negro vaudeville circuit. The initials stoood for Theatre Owners Booking Agency, but we all called it Tough On Black Acts (or Asses, if you used that kind of language—I didn't). TOBA paid very little except to headliners. Bill Robinson, Bessie Smith, Ma Rainey, Wilbur Sweatman, and Ethel Waters, who was known as Sweet Mama Stringbean, all worked the TOBA circuit before they went on to bigger things.

We went to Philadelphia first and worked out of there for several months, playing some of Pennsylvania's pretty country towns, the factory cities, Philadelphia itself, and the famous "Pot Circuit" of vaudeville: Pottstown, Pottsville, and Chambersville.

We stayed at a boardinghouse operated by a woman named Lizzie Mitchell. While we were there, I got to be friendly with a "street woman."

30

Her real name was Annie Williams, but she was known up and down the East Coast as "Tack" Annie, a name she had got from a man she called Tack. Tack was brown-skinned, of medium height, and in her mid-twenties at the time. Not a raving beauty, but attractive enough to get the men she smiled at on the street to follow her up a dark alley. Tack's technique, like that of her cohorts, Chippy Mama and Big Mouth Florence, who worked different streets, was to spot a foreign-looking man on the street and give him the eye. Newly arrived immigrants didn't trust American banks and usually carried their bankrolls around with them in their hip pockets. Tack would lure one into an alley, run her hands over him to get him excited, then at the crucial moment she'd skillfully lift his wallet—and make herself scarce. Tack made it hard for her victims to identify her by wearing an assortment of blond, red, and brunette wigs.

Tack took to me and treated me like a sister. When she moved out of the boardinghouse to her own place, I went along and rented a room. There I met a young fellow whose woman was in jail. We got to talking and laughing, and next thing we knew, we started fooling around. I guess we both thought we could get away with it, what with his woman locked up behind bars, but this woman had some friends keeping an eye on things for her, and it wasn't long before she got wind of what was going on between me and her young man. She sent me a message that was short and to the point: "As soon as I'm out, you're going to be on the wrong end of a knife!"

I didn't take the threat too seriously, but Tack Annie did. She knew her own people. Shortly after the woman was released from jail, Tack took me to a saloon I'd never been to before. As soon as we walked in, I could feel the tension in the place. Every eye was on me. I suddenly realized that it must have something to do with the woman with the knife.

She was there, all right. Tack Annie headed right for her table, with me trailing behind. Introductions weren't necessary. Tack leaned over and looked the woman right in the eye. "Well, here she is. This is Ada. And never lay a hand on her or you'll have to answer to me!"

The woman looked me up and down and then looked at Tack. There was a moment of silence. Then she threw her head back and laughed. "Why, this is nothing but a little show girl. She couldn't do anybody any

31

harm." The tension in the place disappeared, and people began to laugh along with the woman. Tack turned and walked out of the saloon. I was right with her. It had been a close call. Without Tack to protect me, if that woman had ever got a hold of me, little Ada Smith might not have lived to be Bricktop.

Tack was the first woman I ever saw wearing a harem skirt—a long skirt that was slit up the front. When she walked, she gave the men a good view of her legs. She created a sensation with that skirt when she visited New York one summer day. Excitable men, jealous women, and shocked old maids crowded around her. Also the police, who told Tack she'd better get off the streets and save the harem costume for her boudoir.

I'd written to Mama about what a good friend Tack had been to me, and when Tack moved to Chicago, I had her meet my family. Mama was never actually told Tack's profession, but she probably suspected it. Mama thought Tack was a fine woman.

Through the years I lost track of Tack, but in 1942, when I was in Saratoga, Tack showed up, looking well for her age and "experience." She said she was in semi-retirement but not too old to miss the racing season. She had heard I was there and boasted to friends about how she had known me as a youngster. She'd made bets with her friends that she knew Bricktop, and I guess they didn't believe her. Whether Tack collected on the bets, I don't know. We had a wonderful reunion after all those years. Tack died a few years later, back home in Boston.

Mention a city to a performer and he'll know everything about it— within the range of his "show." The name of the place where he worked, how the manager treated him, the names of the local hotels, newspapers, and restaurants, and the best saloon to simmer down in after the last show. Aside from these things, one city is pretty much like another. Except for Chicago, all the cities I performed in were blurs. I saw very little of them. I was in the theater all day, and midnight isn't exactly the time to go sightseeing.

So when Oma announced that we were leaving Philadelphia for New York, I didn't feel any special excitement. I certainly wasn't one of those entertainers who dreamed about the Palace, which was like the pot of gold at the end of the rainbow for most entertainers. I'd already decided I wasn't going to spend my life in vaudeville. Anyway, the Oma Crosby Trio wasn't booked at the Palace. We were to play the Gibson Theatre.

To me, New York was just another town, and I realize now that I was beginning to show a trait that grew through the years—an inability to get excited about things when they happen. I'm an "after-effects" person. Things can happen to me that are tremendously important, but I don't react at the time. I react later, and then, watch out!

I don't think Oma sensed my indifference. With all those manners Mama had drilled into me, I certainly didn't intend to put a damper on Oma's vision of performing in New York as the great triumph of the Trio. New York was just going to be more boardinghouses and being cooped up in a theater all day.

We stayed at a boardinghouse on Columbus Circle, 59th Street and Broadway, which was operated by a woman named Elvira Brown. It was comfortable and clean, and since we arrived late at night and I was tired, I went straight to my room after we checked in. I did my washing ritual and climbed into bed and was asleep as soon as my head hit the pillow.

I thought I was dreaming when I sensed light flickering in the room. I opened my eyes slowly, and what I saw almost made my heart stop. A woman dressed in a dark gown was standing in the middle of the room. In one hand she carried a small shovel full of red-hot coals. She passed her other hand over the coals and mumbled some words I couldn't understand. Then she started coming toward my bed.

I screamed. The woman stopped in her tracks. For a moment she didn't seem to know where she was. I screamed again, and she turned and walked out of the room, taking her shovel full of coals with her. I don't know where everybody else in the house was, but it seems no one heard me scream. The next morning I learned that our landlady was a spiritualist. She'd been chasing away evil spirits, and I'd broken her spell. She was quite upset. Well, I thought, better to break the spell than to die of fright. What's more, I wondered where she got off thinking I carried evil spirits around with me. Could it have been because of my red hair? She made herself scarce for the remainder of the time I stayed there.

The vaudeville houses we played in and around New York weren't the least bit different from those in Chicago, Cincinnati, or Philadelphia.

33

The routine never varied—long hours, food on the run, tiny dressing rooms, running for trains, subways, and trolley cars. The saloons were something else, however, especially Barron's.

It was at Seventh Avenue and 134th Street, and it was one of the best in New York. Barron Wilkins, the man who ran it, was not just big physically, but politically, too. Everything about his bar and back room was bigger and better than anything else in the neighborhood. He drew a crowd we called "sporty." I went there one night with a couple of friends named Gertie and Anita. We pulled our skirts down around our hips and kept our coats on so we'd look older. We were so proud of ourselves for getting in, even though we were under age, that we started giggling, but when we realized Barron himself was looking at us, we simmered down and behaved with decorum.

Evidently, I'd caught his eye. He was such a big, fat man that it wasn't easy for him to move around, but he managed to get over to our table. He said to Gertie and Anita, "Who's that cute kid?"

"Why, she's Ada Smith from Chicago. She works with Oma Crosby."

Barron knew how to put a fierce look on his face, and I thought for sure I'd be called on my age or something and get kicked out. Instead, he turned on a warm, beautiful smile.

"Well, Ada Smith, how do you do?"

I stuttered something about doing very well indeed, and thank you.

He smiled some more. "You know what?" he said, and pointed to my mop of red hair. "I think I'll call you Bricktop."

And that's how I got my name. At the time, there was only one well-known Bricktop in the country. She was a white woman with red-gold hair who was a prostitute in Chicago; her pimp was a man named Needham Wright and he was one of the biggest pimps who ever lived.

Everybody started calling me Bricktop after that, but not Mama. Probably because of that prostitute.

Eventually there were no more dates to be found around New York. We had played them all. The Oma Crosby Trio packed up and returned to Chicago. I left the Trio there. I'd served my apprenticeship, and Oma understood. She had been a wonderful friend to me, and I like to think that I never caused her to regret bringing me into the act.

I was happy to be home. Although I had written often and Mama had written to me, it was nice to be able to see everyone in person. Mama's cooking hadn't improved any in the months I was away. She did get around to baking a chicken that didn't turn out too badly, and then there was that old Hattie E. Smith standby—vegetable soup—cooking on the stove all the time. It seemed as if I'd barely gotten a chance to unpack my things and get caught up on family news, though, when I was off on the road again.

I joined the Ten Georgia Campers, a fine singing and dancing act. I was delighted about this, because we were booked on the Pantages circuit. Getting with Pantages was really big-time. It made me feel that I was on my way to being somebody as we worked our way out to the West Coast and back.

Then I was home again, unpacking, sitting down to vegetable soup with my brother and sisters. By this time I had my own room at home. It was proper for a girl who was seventeen going on eighteen. Mama was to remind me of this fact in a way I would never forget.

The first time I ever felt a strange but pleasant feeling about a boy, I was ten years old. He was a very handsome Italian boy, about thirteen. He used to come to our street with an older man, an organ grinder, and a monkey. The boy would hold out his hat for pennies. Often the monkey picked up more than he did.

I'd stand there watching and listening. Every time I looked at the boy, I would get a funny feeling and start acting silly. I wonder what became of him.

I felt the same way about a few other boys before I started going out on the road, but nothing ever happened. Nothing much happened when I was on the road, either.

Dating boys while I was out on the road was not the biggest thing on my mind. I didn't stay up nights thinking about it. I stayed away from boys in show business. They were never around long enough. If I met someone I liked who wasn't in show business and there was a mutual attraction, I let nature take its course.

There was a voice inside me that kept saying "No, no, no," even though I knew I was going to say "Yes." Each time I put off doing it, I didn't feel as if I'd won any big victory. I'd wake up in the morning and feel pleased with myself, but I'd know full well that I might get right at it that afternoon. And as long as I was going to do it, I followed Mama's advice—to be the best.

Mama might have had a suspicion about what I was doing on the road besides performing in vaudeville houses, but she didn't have a chance to find out first-hand until I came back to Chicago.

His name was Chappie. We met at the skating rink on 29th Street between State and Wabash avenues. I loved to rollerskate and had started skating at the rink when I was still in school. My brother Robert and my sister Ethel were champion skaters. Blonzetta wasn't interested—we found out later that she was too busy buying up real estate.

Robert was a very quiet, very proper boy who was always running home to Mama and telling on me. Ethel must have kept him occupied that Saturday afternoon at the skating rink when Chappie came over to me and asked me to skate with him.

I already knew Chappie. We'd skated together before, even had some tricky dance steps down pat, but that was when we were younger. By now all the boys and girls in our age group were paired off and going steady, and it seemed the natural thing for Chappie and me to do the same. We started going everywhere together, even bought two Melton-style overcoats exactly alike. As a matter of fact, we even looked alike and were often taken for brother and sister.

Pretty soon we were necking and petting—and looking for a place really to get to fooling around. He was a year older than I was and more anxious to get at it than me, and he finally wore me down and I agreed to go with him to a place. But where?

I couldn't take him home and he couldn't take me home. So we decided to rent a room at Gertie Jordan's. She had a roominghouse for theatrical people over a theater at 31st and State streets. Up we went. No questions asked. Of course, it was foolish of me to think I could go up there with Chappie and not be noticed. I only lived around the corner, and since I was the only real redhead for blocks and blocks, there was no mistaking Ada Smith.

As soon as Mama heard about it, she made for Gertie Jordan's with fire in her eyes. "I'll horsewhip you on the corner of 31st and State if you dare rent a room to my baby again!"

I didn't know what to expect when Mama got me home. If there was ever a time when I thought she'd produce a real horsewhip, this was it. But Mama fooled me. There were no tantrums or rough language. She said very quietly, "We have a house here with eleven rooms. If you're going to have a man, bring him home. You take a man up to Gertie's or some other place, everyone's going to talk about you. You bring him home, and no one will talk about you."

This was a time when I fully appreciated the contradictions in Mama's character. She wasn't able to display affection, but when it came to protecting her children, she was a tigress. And her wisdom! She spared me an embarrassment that I might never have forgotten.

After that, whenever I wanted to sleep with a boy, I'd sneak him home. I still felt funny about doing it there and didn't flaunt it—never brought a boy to the breakfast table. Ethel did the same thing. Mama knew about those once-in-a-while sneak-ins, but she didn't say anything.

Blonzetta never did that sort of thing. When any young man came to call on her, Mama was right there in the living room with them, and if Mama couldn't be there, then Robert was, or me, or Ethel.

Chappie and I saw each other a few times after the episode at Gertie Jordan's, but it wasn't the same. I was away on the road quite a bit. I think Chappie was aiming to be a small-time pimp—not with me, of course, even though those Melton overcoats we wore were the kind pimps had: the latest, sportingest style. I heard later that Chappie had moved to Detroit or Cleveland and become a *big-time* pimp. With his good looks, I didn't wonder. I also learned that he had started smoking hop. It finally got him, and Chappie was probably gone from this world at a very young age.

After the Gertie Jordan episode, I went on the road again, this time with the Kinky-Doo Trio. Kinky, whose real name was Madeleine, was a great little dancer about five years older than me who had come out of the Pekin Theatre. Together with another girl, Lola Wicks, we danced and sang and did skits in vaudeville houses, mostly on the TOBA circuit. I remember one line of dialogue that would put the audience in stitches. Kinky would say to me, "Are there any more at home like you?" And fresh me would answer, "No. Papa died and Mama lost the pattern." That line was considered quite risqué in those days.

SALOON SINGER

By 1911 THE NEWSPAPERS were estimating that bustling, brassy Chicago had ten thousand saloons. They employed lots of entertainers, and I knew a lot of them and didn't need glasses to see that they had a much easier life than vaudevillians. They made good money, lived in real homes, dressed well, and enjoyed friendships that lasted. In vaudeville we were forever losing friends just when we were really getting to know them. I was nearly eighteen now, and I was more determined than ever to get off the road and into those saloon back rooms.

I didn't have to wait long to get my first break as a saloon performer after I left the Kinky-Doo Trio. One of our neighbors was Rose Brown, a great tap dancer who worked in vaudeville and also entertained at Roy Jones's saloon. She knew about my comings and goings on the road from Mama, so one night when she took sick she hollered across the alley to Mama to ask if I could take her place.

Mama didn't hesitate to give her permission. She was always big on helping neighbors. She knew that I'd be going into those back rooms sooner or later, and that if I knew how to handle myself on the vaudeville circuit I'd sure know how to behave in a cabaret. While she pinned me into the nearest thing I had to a dress suitable for a saloon back room, she tried not to laugh at me for being so excited.

Roy Jones's was a big-time place. That back room at 21st and Wabash was rated as one of the best in Chicago, if not in the whole United States. Everybody in Chicago knew Roy Jones, a dapper little man who was married to Vic Shaw, one of the three biggest brothelkeepers in the city (the other two leading "housekeepers" were Black Mag and the Everleigh sisters). He didn't draw a high-class clientele just because of his social connections, though. The entertainers who worked in his back room were first-rate. Once you appeared at Roy Jones's, you were certain to go on to work in other saloons with high-class reputations.

My nerves were jumping around inside me as I made my way to the saloon. I wasn't nervous about performing. I shook inside at the thought of being in the company of great performers like Sidney Kirkpatrick, a large, light-skinned Negro with a beautiful voice, and the James Sisters, Ethel and Rina.

I wasn't even nervous about what Roy Jones would say when he took a look at me. I was skinny—nothing like Rose Brown with her soft, round body. I was below the legal age for saloon entertaining and looked younger still. I'd learned from experience, though, that you had to show your real talent just to get a job, and I must have had real talent to convince him to hire me even though I didn't look like the type of girl he usually engaged.

Against his better judgment, Roy Jones hired me, and I began a career as a saloon singer that lasted sixty years and gave me a life I could never even have imagined at the time.

I gave the piano player a list of the songs I knew. He told me which entertainer I would follow. There would be no formal introductions. There never were in those back rooms. The piano player played some of your introductory music and you were on. While you were singing and dancing, the customers threw money, and you picked it up and put it into the kitty. You kept doing number after number as long as the money kept being thrown. Since all the tips were split between the entertainers and the musicians, no one cared how long you stayed on the floor. Of course, that was to change in later years, when you split your tips with no one but the piano player and other musicians. Then the other artists wanted you to get off the floor so they could get on—especially if there was a big spender in the house.

When you finished your turn, you took your seat with the other entertainers and waited until the piano player played your music again. You never knew ahead of time which of your numbers he would choose. It depended on what the mood of the room was like at the moment. He would sense the mood and pick the appropriate song. He knew when it was time to jazz up a dying room, or when to play a sentimental ballad. Whenever you heard your music, you got up and performed. That's the way it was all evening. It seemed like you met yourself coming and going.

Between performances, the entertainers sat at a table together. City ordinances did not allow the artists to sit with the customers. If someone wanted to buy us a drink, he sent it over to our table, but there was practically none of that. Anyway, we performers would much rather have had the tips.

I don't remember much about that first night at Roy Jones's. I was so excited it was pretty much all a blur. I only know that I sang and danced as hard and as well as I could. I went home that night feeling happier than I ever had before. I'd suspected all along that the saloon back room was the place for me, and now I was sure of it. When Rose Brown recovered from her cold and came back and Roy Jones kept me on, I thought my career was all set.

It was a fantastic time for the saloon business in Chicago. The city was on a big crusade against vice and had shut down all the whorehouses, but that just made business better in the saloons, and didn't stop prostitution. The girls simply moved into the saloons, picked up their tricks there, and worked out of roominghouses, and the pimps and madames moved into the saloons to keep an eye on what was going on.

I fit right in with the pimps and prostitutes. Almost from the beginning I was a pimps' pet. Don't ask me why—they just liked me. Of the dozens I knew, not one ever invited me to join his stable. It was just the opposite—they went out of their way to protect me. When I moved on to other saloons, it was pimps who recommended me. Saloonkeepers were always on the lookout for new girl entertainers and depended on pimps to tip them off.

In my last years in the saloon business I had only a nodding acquaintance with pimps. They seemed a different breed from those I had met when I was starting out—too busy making money to waste their time on friendship.

At Roy Jones's you could make a lot of money if you were smart, and I got smart pretty fast with a little help from Roy. The entertainers were given a choice: they could be paid a straight twenty-one dollars a week or take twelve dollars and split the tips the customers threw on the floor. When I first started, the other entertainers suggested that I work for the straight twenty-one dollars; because I was new I thought it was a good idea. I'd never been paid that much in my life, and I was having so much fun I would have worked for nothing.

After a few nights, however, Roy called me over. "Little girl," he said, "why did you take the twenty-one dollars a week instead of the twelve and tips? My customers like you. I think you'll get a better shake the other way." After I made the change, I quickly started taking home much more money.

Come to think of it, the change was better for Roy Jones, too. Reduced his overhead by nine dollars a week.

If we were going to make money, we needed a constant supply of new songs, so we went regularly to the music publishers. They'd give us lead sheets and teach us the new tunes. The song pluggers from the various publishing houses would also come into the saloons to do new songs. You never really knew about a song, though, until you learned it, sang it, and saw how the tips flew.

One person you absolutely had to get along with was the piano player. Although we were forced to split our tips with him, he was anything but a partner. Mostly, the girls wanted to kill him. We'd bring in our lists and think we were set for the night with numbers we knew and could really get over. If there was one thing sure in the hurly-burly world of saloons, it was that the piano player would get you out on the floor by playing something familiar, then throw away the list and play his own sets, letting you stumble through them as best you could. I guess that was his way of letting you know that entertainers were a dime a dozen and good piano players weren't. There was no use getting mad.

We sang and danced from seven p.m. to one a.m., delighted when the tips came in a shower, grateful if they hit the floor in a slow trickle. After the place closed, everyone who shared in the tips waited while they were counted and split evenly. Sometimes I'd go straight home. Other times I'd go to some after-hours place with friends. I'll never forget the first night I got drunk.

It was one of those Chicago summer nights—so hot that you felt as if someone somewhere had left the door open to a huge oven. Walter Jones, a well-known sporting man from Detroit, suggested we go drink some cold champagne. I said champagne would really hit the spot.

We not only wound up hitting the spot with champagne—we made sure we hit it with a beer chaser. I don't know what Walter wanted with me. When something inside me said I should go home and go to bed, he saw that I got home all right. I got myself into the front bedroom, which was my room, threw off my clothes, and put my whirling head on the pillow.

I couldn't have been in bed long when I started dreaming that the bed was moving in every direction. I woke up, but the bed was still moving. I headed for the bathroom. To get there, I had to go through the dining room. I never made it. All that champagne and beer fighting in my stomach spilled out onto the dining-room floor.

I didn't know it, but Mama had been sitting there all the time. Without a word, she took me to the bathroom, cleaned me up, and put me back to bed. The next day, when people asked what was wrong with me, Mama said, "Oh, Ada must have eaten some fish."

That was a common saying then. If anyone was drunk, he'd "eaten some fish." When I first heard the expression, I avoided fish because I was afraid it was going to make me sick. I'm glad I got over that notion, because I do like fish once in a while. But not the combination of champagne and beer.

The other night from that period that I'll never forget is the night I met Jack Johnson. I didn't know at the time that I was already friends with quite a few people who would become famous—like Shelton Brooks, who wrote "Some of These Days" and "Darktown Strutters' Ball." Jack

Johnson was my first real celebrity, though, and he wasn't just mine, but all of Chicago's and every Negro's in the United States.

Jack came from Galveston, but after hitting the big leagues as a boxer, he made Chicago his home. I can understand why—it was big and sprawling, full of vitality and excitement, just like Jack. Chicago really went wild the night Jack won the title from Jim Jeffries. One group of people that included his sisters got so carried away that they toppled a streetcar off its tracks. It was a crazy thing to do, but that's how people celebrated then, and the police usually looked the other way.

Jack played the role of champion to the hilt. Everything about him had to be the best—elegant clothes, fancy cars, beautiful women—and now he was going to open a cabaret that would outshine every other place in Chicago. The front pages of the newspapers were full of Jack's elaborate plans—the exquisite furnishings, plush rugs, masterpiece paintings, and hundred-dollar cuspidors.

Jack stopped traffic wherever he went, and he was never too busy to give a warm smile or a ready handshake. People loved him, and when he stopped in at Roy Jones's place that night, surrounded as always by friends, fans, and hangers-on, you could feel the electricity in the air. The entertainers put a little extra into their performances, and whatever I sang must have pleased him. The "no entertainers at the tables" rule was suspended for me when Roy Jones said, "Ada, the Champ wants you to join his party."

Excited as I was, I was certainly not tongue-tied. I was a talker then, just as I am now. Mr. Johnson, as I called him then and every time we met afterward, was a charmer. There were reasons why his smile was so famous. It reflected the real champion, the warm, generous, impulsive, wonderful, lovable man. That smile gave him a handsomeness his looks didn't really deserve.

Jack started telling me about his plans for his new club. I listened intently, even though I'd already read about it all in the papers. My ears really perked up when he said, "When the club is ready, little girl, I'd like you to work for me." I didn't waste any time telling him that I'd enjoy it, and he told me that all I had to do was drop by after the place opened, ask for the manager, and say that Jack said I was to work there.

Well, when I walked home after work that evening, I walked on a cloud. I told anyone I met on the street that I was going to work for the Champ. I must have had a hard time falling asleep that night. It isn't every day that the man of the hour singles you out.

The Cabaret de Champion, which was quickly shortened to Café Champ, opened at Armour and Dearborn in October 1911. It was everything that Jack said it would be. He'd already traveled a lot, seen the great cafés of Europe, and been impressed with their richness and elegance. He wanted to re-create that atmosphere, and he succeeded.

It was a handsome place with thick rugs, a low, highly polished bar, good, sturdy furniture, and a number of paintings that Jack had picked up in the course of his travels and that he considered masterpieces. They weren't, but did it matter? Jack Johnson had given Chicago something different—an elegantly furnished, racially integrated saloon. It was an overnight hit, and while its prices eliminated many Negroes and whites, those who could afford it enjoyed an atmosphere free of discrimination. Jack's friends were many and important, and they filled the place night after night.

I didn't waste any time following up on Jack's invitation. I went right over to see Earl Walker, the Champ's entertainment manager. I told him Mr. Johnson had sent me. He looked me up and down and burst out laughing. "Oh, go away, little girl. You're too young. Besides, you don't have the kind of experience it takes to work in this place."

I started to tell him about my working at Roy Jones's with all those great entertainers, but he wouldn't listen. There was nothing for me to do but go back home. When people asked me when I was going to start entertaining at the Café Champ, I told them I wasn't ready to go down and see about it just yet.

The idea of my singing for the Champ did seem a little too good to be true, but I refused to believe that he'd just been pulling my leg. He didn't seem like that kind of man. The whole thing didn't seem fair, but even pushy me wasn't pushy enough to go looking for the Champ to find out if he'd meant what he said.

I kept on working at Roy Jones's and put Jack Johnson's place out of my head for a while. Then one day as I was walking along State Street, I caught sight of a big red racing car—the kind of car that could have belonged to nobody but the Champ. His secretary, a white Englishman by the name of Levy, was with him. The Champ saw me, made a quick U-turn in the middle of the block, pulled up beside me, and said, "I thought I told you to come and work for me."

I told him what had happened. He thought it was very funny. "Now listen," he said, "after you get through working at the end of the week, I want you to come to my place with your music. Go right up to the orchestra and hand it to them. And if anybody says anything, you just tell them that *I* said you were working there!"

I did exactly as he said. Walked into the place, handed my music to the orchestra leader, and went over two or three songs. The manager came running over to give me an argument, but I stood my ground—and with that I began an engagement that I will always remember as the most wonderful of my life.

The Café Champ consisted of three floors. The long, beautiful bar was on the first floor. Adjoining it was a long, narrow room with rows of tables along the walls and down the middle—one of the fanciest back rooms I've ever seen. On the second floor was a private dining room with a piano, and on the third floor was Jack's apartment.

There were eight pieces in the orchestra, which was quite a lot for a back-room orchestra then. Six or seven singers would sit on the end of the platform next to the musicians and take turns performing. You began your song from the platform, then started down and went from table to table. At each table—there were about forty—you stopped and sang half a chorus of your song. You carried a little skillet—the "kitty"— and the customers would drop money into it. It was nice to hear the tinkling sound of coins, but even nicer when the money was a bill and made no sound at all. Any time you got to the table where the Champ was sitting, you knew you were going to get a lot of that silent green money in your skillet. Big bills, too. People naturally showed off for the Champ.

Each entertainer had a song to sing especially for Jack. Mine was one that the Whitman Sisters sang on the TOBA circuit. It went, "When you do the teddy, and you do the bear, but when you do Jack Johnson, kid, you're there!" Jack had taught me a fighting stance, and I'd get my fists up at the proper time in the song.

He was a wonderful man. I never saw him once being ordinary or vulgar. When he hit the door of the place at night, the millionaires from Lake Shore Drive and everybody else would all be screaming, "Jack, come over here!" He would just stand there with his big, wonderful self and say he'd be right over. Sooner or later he'd hit all the tables, having a drink at each. He never drank anything but champagne. He cleverly covered up for his lack of education by letting other people do the talking. There was always a twinkle in his eye, as though he was saying, "This is all a funny game, isn't it?" He wasn't a bowing man.

The Café Champ was a happy place to work in. Jack took a lively interest in the entertainment, and we girls were mighty pleased when he winked at us. If I brought more scowls than winks to Jack's face, it was because I was always late. I was a chronic late one as a young woman, and I didn't change until recently. Now I've learned to pace myself a little better for the good and practical reason that I can't make the last-minute dash. It's a concession to advanced years, and I don't particularly like it. The mad dash was fun—part of living.

Jack didn't agree. This champion of the world, driver of fast cars, escorter of beautiful women, symbol of the wild, irresponsible sporting man, was well mannered and conservative in business. Unluckily for me, he lived by his version of the idea that punctuality is the courtesy of kings.

It was a rule at the club that whenever entertainers were late they had to report personally to Jack in his apartment. In my case, that was just about every night. I'd climb up those stairs to hear a stock lecture about how I wasn't being fair to the others, wasn't being professional, and so on. I tried to be on time, but I still managed to arrive late.

One of those times he really gave me a calling down. I thought he was being too harsh, and I got angry. I said, "Just wait, Mr. Johnson. Someday I'll be bigger than you are and you'll be sorry that you bawled me out this way." I wish I could remember his reaction to my brave boast, but I was so full of myself that I didn't notice. Many years later he would remind me of the incident.

There were all kinds of whispers about Jack's private life. He was married to a white girl named Etta Duryea, and of course that was bound to cause comment. She was a handsome brunette, but I doubt that I spoke three words to her in my life. She kept to herself in the third-floor apartment.

46

It was said that Jack had soured on Negro girls and didn't think they could be trusted. He even wrote that in his autobiography, but now and then we'd hear something that suggested that wasn't quite the case.

There were rumors that Jack was fooling around with Adah Banks, one of the singers. She was a good-looking, brown-skinned girl with a lovely soprano voice. The rumors must have been true, because she was a haughty, big-timey girl who had no use for the rest of us. I think she went out of her way not to speak to us, but we didn't lose any sleep over it. The rest of us were considerate and encouraging to one another, but Adah Banks paraded around like she was too good for us.

On September 11, 1913, Etta Duryea Johnson killed herself. I was singing in the private dining room on the second floor at the time. Every entertainer did about forty-five minutes a night up there. I was singing Shelton Brooks's "All Night Long" when a shot rang out. Everything came to a standstill in the private dining room. No one heard it on the first floor, and the orchestra kept playing.

None of us knew where the shot had come from, and whoever investigated took care of things quietly. Jack wasn't in the café at the time. He was at the railway station saying goodbye to some friends. When he finally did arrive, the police were there and the place was in great confusion. An ambulance came, and only then did we learn that Mrs. Johnson had shot and killed herself.

Jack closed the café for the night, and we stayed closed until after the funeral. During that time we all speculated about why Mrs. Johnson had killed herself. Some of the entertainers said it was because of Adah Banks. Adah probably shared that view, and when the club reopened she was even more impossible to be around. The wheel of fate is funny, though. Sometimes you win, and sometimes you lose, and the times you are too sure of winning are the times you had better watch out. A white girl was about to come into the picture and start spinning that wheel in a different direction for Adah Banks.

About two weeks after the funeral Jack came into the club with Lucille Cameron on his arm. She was a white girl from Minneapolis. Jack had known her before Mrs. Johnson died. Before the tragedy Lucille had possessed just one outfit, as far as we could tell—a checked suit that she wore all the time—but that night, when she and Jack walked in after seeing Thomas Shea in *The Bells*, Lucille was wearing a black

47

broadcloth suit, a big hat covered with white egrets, and diamonds all over her hands. Whether these things had belonged to Mrs. Johnson, I don't know, but we knew Lucille had never worn a diamond before. Naturally, our eyes went from Lucille to Adah Banks. We giggled among ourselves, because Adah had been so nasty and mean to us because she was Jack's girl.

Thomas Shea and some other people were with Jack and Lucille. It was a big, laughing party. We all went over to do our songs. I did my song with the prizefighter stance. Jack's favorite song for Adah to sing was "My Hero," and when her turn came she started to sing it. She went along fine until she got to one of the high notes, then her voice cracked and she broke into tears. She ran through the café, with me behind her. Trailing me were two or three of the other girls telling me to leave her alone—she deserved to cry, the way she had treated everybody.

A few nights later Adah and Lucille met in the ladies' room. Adah said, "We'll see who's going to be the next Mrs. Johnson!" The white girl didn't open her mouth. She *knew* who the next Mrs. Johnson was going to be, and that is what she became.

About a month later Adah and Jack had a row and she shot him in the leg. The injury wasn't serious and Jack didn't press charges.

After Etta Duryea Johnson's death, the scandalmongers got a good chance to let out their bigotry and hatred for Jack. A lot of us may have loved him, but a lot of other people would have given anything to see him brought down. It all started when he beat a white fighter to become champion of the world. Then he added insult to injury by flaunting his success with his flashy cars and high living—and especially by his going around with white women. White preachers devoted whole hellfire-and-brimstone sermons to him, and some black preachers would have done the same if they hadn't been afraid of the reaction of the Negro community. Having closed the brothels, the blue-noses looked for another target, and Jack was an obvious scapegoat.

Jack just made matters worse by going around with Lucille. He was arrested on a trumped-up charge of transporting Lucille across state lines for immoral purposes.

Those who stood by Jack in spite of the scandal came back to the café. We worked harder than ever out of our own sincere admiration for him, but the place wasn't the same. It seemed to be under a cloud that wouldn't go away. After Adah shot Jack, the police used that as an excuse to suspend the café's liquor license. Business dropped way off. Eventually the café closed.

The clients had ten thousand other cafés to go to, but we missed the Café Champ. I missed Jack. From time to time over the next twenty-odd years I read about him and his travels through Europe making personal appearances at music halls, circuses, wherever he could use his name and fame to hustle a living. I wondered if I would ever see him again.

By the time Jack Johnson's café folded, I was well-known enough to have my pick of several saloons in Chicago. I was shaping up as an entertainer. I knew my way around a floor and could hold a table's attention. That was the trick of saloon singing—you weren't trying to get the whole audience, just one table after another as you went along.

Saloon behavior was becoming a little more sophisticated. There were still customers who threw the tips on the floor. I didn't like it, but I wasn't too proud to pick them up. A new breed of customer was coming along. He'd single out an entertainer, invite her to his table, and slip her some folding money. I did pretty well under that system, and I decided it was time to test my wings outside Chicago. I went to St. Paul, Minnesota, to entertain at George and Gus's saloon.

While I was there, Mama wrote me that my brother, Robert, had died of consumption, which was what we called tuberculosis in those days. He'd been sickly for a long time. I remember being warned, "Don't pick up that glass. Robert drank out of it." He was only twenty-two when he died.

My first impulse was to want to be with Mama and my sisters, but Mama wrote that I shouldn't come home. There was no need for me to travel to Chicago and get all upset and nervous at the funeral. She said she'd be all right, and I knew she would be. Mama practiced the philosophy that it's how you treat the person in life that counts, not how much you weep and wail after he's gone. So I said my silent goodbye to Robert and went on working.

When my engagement in St. Paul was over, I went back to Chicago for several months. In the fall of 1913 I went to Minneapolis to entertain at the Twin Cities Stag Club. Although the club was stag, I was allowed to live upstairs. The owners, Daddy and Florence Stuart, didn't like the idea of my having to go home alone late at night. It's hard to believe, but I was just nineteen years old.

My youth was a plus. It made people feel protective toward me, especially the pimps. It was pimps who recommended me to other saloon-keepers, trying to help me boost my career. A pimp recommended me to Billy Crutchfield and Jack Broomfield, owners of a famous saloon in Omaha, Nebraska. That's where I went next.

Billy Crutchfield was a big-shot politician, important downtown as well as in the Negro community. His place was part saloon, part gambling house. The gambling, mostly poker, craps, and blackjack, went on downstairs. Upstairs there was a small room with a few tables and a piano. We started entertaining in the afternoon and stopped at ten p.m. The room wasn't licensed for entertainment beyond that hour. Three singing waiters entertained with me. We danced and sang for the customers who wanted to take their minds off gambling for a while.

I went over very big, especially with Billy Crutchfield. One day he gave me a five-carat diamond ring. It seems he had ideas beyond my singing and dancing for him. I had the same ideas, but not about him. I got dreamy-eyed over one of the singing waiters. I started going out with him while wearing Billy's ring on my finger. Billy was having none of that. He took back the ring and fired me. I got out of Omaha and went back to Chicago.

Even if I'd liked Billy, I wouldn't have fooled around with him. He was married and he was my boss. His being married might not have stopped me if I'd liked him, but I had no intention of going out with the boss. I don't know why I felt so strongly about that, but it was a feeling that would stay with me. By the time I became boss of my own place, there was nothing in the world that would make me fool around with the personnel—or the customers.

The singing waiter followed me to Chicago. I didn't try to stop him. We took a room up at Gertie Jordan's—the *same* Gertie Jordan's where I'd gotten into trouble before. Mama was away, taking care of the graves in Alderson.

Within a few days the waiter was looking less and less attractive to me. Having a waiter for a sweetheart in Omaha was one thing, but in big-time Chicago? Not for up-and-coming saloon singer Ada Smith! I told him it was all over between us. I thought he would just accept the fact and leave, but he wasn't as cold-blooded as I was. He told me later he'd turned the gas on, but then had thought better of it and turned the gas off. I guess I wasn't worth leaving this earth for.

I'd been home about a month when a letter arrived from Omaha. The sporting men at Billy Crutchfield's had taken up a petition to get Billy to hire me back. Billy wrote a nice note saying there were no hard feelings, so I got myself on the train to Omaha.

Billy was a gentleman throughout my second stay in Omaha. We had many a laugh together. When I left, he told me he would always be happy to recommend me. He added, "So long, Ada. Don't take any wooden nickels—or diamond rings."

I can't leave Omaha, here, without talking about Tommy Lyman. Whenever I think of him, I remember that old show-business joke about the entertainer who spends hundreds of dollars to buy new material and orchestrations, goes out on the floor and sings his heart out, and, when he's just about to drop from exhaustion, hears someone call out, "Sing 'Melancholy Baby.' " Though I've laughed at that joke, it always occurs to me that this person in the audience might have been privileged to hear that song as it should be sung—by Tommy Lyman. No one could ever imitate him, although many tried.

That wistful, thin, almost shy little man had a way of singing that song that could grab hold of you and twist your heart. Moments later he'd do another type of song and have you laughing your head off.

He was working at a top cabaret in downtown Omaha. It was a Jim Crow club, and I might never have gotten the chance to hear him at all if he hadn't been so generous with his talent. Every day he'd drift into Crutchfield's.

I remember that the first time I saw him I couldn't believe he was *the* Tommy Lyman, the saloon singers' singer, but when I saw him work in that quiet way of his I understood what it was all about. All the chatter and clinking of glasses, not to mention almost everyone's breathing, came to a standstill when Tommy sang. He'd stand at the bar, his eyes heavy-lidded, his long, tapering fingers resting on the edge, and he'd sing sooo quietly. And yet you could understand every word and exactly what each one meant.

There was no song he sang better than "Melancholy Baby," and we

wouldn't let him quit until he'd done it. The way he sang it was un-
forgettable. Maybe it was because he was such a melancholy man himself. He was an opium smoker, even way back then in Omaha. I used to
find it hard to believe how that wisp of a body could take the effects of
the drug and still keep going. But Tommy did. I knew that he was someone I wanted to hear again and again, and over the years I tried to see
him perform as often as I could.

THE WAR YEARS

By 1914 I WAS BACK in Chicago again. World War I was raging in Europe, but in the United States people just read about it, shook their heads, and kept on going to the saloons. Most people thought: What the foreigners are doing has nothing to do with us, so let's go get a few drinks, hear a little music, and have a good time.

I was playing at the Panama on 35th and State Street. It ranked with the Elite No. 1 and the Elite No. 2 among the city's top cabarets and catered to integrated audiences. I didn't have any trouble getting hired there. My experience at Roy Jones's and the Café Champ convinced the owner, Isadore Levine, that I was good enough for the Panama. He never told me in so many words, of course. Izzy was a manager, and so he'd tell you to your face that you were lousy and then go out front to the bar and bet his saloon that he had the best entertainers in Chicago.

I know he had one of them—Mattie Hight. She was the greatest female I have ever seen on a floor. Al Jolson never missed her if he was playing the same town. Mattie was from Atlantic City, and so was Cora Green, who wasn't in Mattie's league then, though she was certainly on the way up. Both Mattie and Cora were staying at Gertie Jordan's theatrical boardinghouse.

In a few months another girl moved in there. She was working on the TOBA circuit and was tired of the four and five shows a day. She asked if I could help her get a cabaret job. Since she seemed an eager, pleasant sort of girl, I took her to Izzy.

Izzy wasn't impressed. "She's too skinny," he said. I had to admit that the girl was skinny—she was of medium height and her skin texture was beautiful—but the same thing had been said about me often enough that I was all the more determined to help her. I pointed out that she had a gorgeous voice, but Izzy wasn't big on sopranos.

"Listen, Izzy," I said, "me and Cora can work up some numbers with her." I finally wore him down. "Okay," he said at last, "go ahead if you want to. But you're responsible." That's how I got Florence Mills out of vaudeville and into the cabaret business.

It wasn't easy to keep her there, however. Izzy never took to Florence. He called me aside one night and told me to fire her. I warned him that it was a mistake, but his mind was made up. I didn't like the responsibility of firing the kid, but it was part of what was slowly happening to me. I had started to run things, and Izzy was right in there making me do the dirty work. I learned a good lesson: there's a price tag on everything, including running the show.

Florence took her firing good-naturedly. She had been performing long enough to realize she didn't have a cabaret style. That night, before the crowd came in, she was in the back room rehearsing "Little Gray Home in the West." Out front, Izzy heard her and sent for me. "Who's that singing?" he wanted to know.

"The girl you told me to fire," my fresh self said.

Izzy thought a moment. "Listen, why don't you take her and show her how to move about. Can she dance?"

Florence sure could dance. She was one of the greatest dancers we had, and I said so to Izzy. I went back and told her that the boss had agreed to keep her on if she would learn how to move on the floor. She was willing. I did a turn around the empty tables.

"Oh, is that it?" she said.

Well, this girl not only learned how to move around the floor, she got to the point where she was so good she ran everyone else off. I don't think it would be remiss for me to take a little pat on the back for giving a few pointers to the girl who would go on to become one of the greatest Negro stars.

Florence, Cora, and I started doing some numbers and billed our-selves as the Panama Trio. We were singing harmony and dancing to-gether long before the Boswell Sisters became big stars. When the three of us were out on the floor, we really kept the audience applauding and wanting more. One night Bill Robinson complimented us, and then we knew we were really something special.

Bill Robinson would go on to be world-famous as Bojangles. At the time, he was part of a top vaudeville duo on the Keith circuit—Cooper and Robinson. He told us we were great and that he was going to send someone in to hear us. A few nights went by, but there was no sign of anyone saying that Bill had sent him.

One night a man and a woman came in just before closing time. The place was almost deserted. Florence, Cora, and I were anxious to get out of the place, so we went out on the floor, walked through two or three songs, and then got off. I was standing by the door when the couple left. I remarked that their faces looked familiar. He looked like the head of the Keith circuit and she looked like Eva Tanguay, "The Girl Who Made Vaudeville Famous," the highest-paid single performer in vaude-ville. I was to find out the next day that the lookalikes had been the real thing.

Bojangles could be a very explosive fellow, and when he came to see us the next day, he really took aim at us and fired! There was no fight-ing back, because everything he said was true. We'd been unprofes-sional. How did we expect to get anywhere? That was the last time in my life that I didn't go out on the floor and do my best. After that, I demanded it of myself and certainly of those who worked for me. I'd say, "I don't care if there is just one person out in the room or at the bar, you go out and do your best. You never know."

55

While I was at the Panama, I met Joe Frisco. He didn't work there; he hung out at Big Jim Colisimo's and at Freiburg's. Izzy Levine wouldn't even have considered hiring him. He was a sandy-haired, undersized, nondescript man. He wore such big, thick glasses that you could barely see his face, and to top it all off, he stuttered terribly. He had a dry wit, though, could dance a little, could juggle a cigar with a derby hat, and had made up his mind to get into show business.

Every so often he'd wander into the Panama and want to do Shelton Brooks's "Walkin' the Dog." When Izzy wasn't around, I'd let him take the floor for a few minutes. Since the chorus took two people, I'd wind up getting out there with him. Florence and Cora would never dance with him because they said he had bad breath. "Walkin' the Dog" wasn't one of those up-close numbers, so I didn't mind doing it with him. He showed all the traits of a born hoofer; he just needed polishing.

I knew he was trying to hustle himself some cash, so I let him keep the money the customers threw on the floor while we danced. Sometimes I'd let him go on by himself and do his act, a crazy sort of thing where he'd shuffle around the floor with his hat pulled down over his eyes, smoking a big black cigar.

One night he stammered, "Aaaaadddda, wwwwhyyyy dddon't yyyou cccome to Nnnew Yyyork wwwith mmme?"

I laughed. "New York with you? To do what?"

"IIII hhhave hhhad an offffer."

I couldn't imagine what kind of offer he could have. I thought he was out of his mind and that I would be, too, if I went with him. Me in New York with a white boy? A white boy who had no money? So he went off to New York himself.

Some time later I happened to pick up a sheet of new music. I stared at the cover in complete disbelief. There was no mistaking that impish face, that hat he wore, that big cigar. Underneath his picture was written: "JOE FRISCO, *Ziegfeld Follies.*"

Soon all of Chicago had seen that sheet music, and I was in for a lot of ribbing. Did I know that Joe Frisco and his dancing partner, Loretta McDermott, were one of the hit attractions of the *Follies*? Yes, I'd heard that. Yes, I knew that it could have been me up there with Joe. Everyone really rubbed it in. What could I say? I couldn't say I hadn't been asked.

Joe's star brightened Broadway for many years, but as fast as he made money, he lost it all on the horses. During the Depression, Broadway stars were asked to take a cut in their salaries, but independent Joe said no. He said he needed his thousand-dollar-a-week paycheck to pay off the bookies. He'd quit rather than take a cut. True to his word, he never played a vaudeville theater again. He drifted to Hollywood and made a few pictures, then wound up as a regular at a San Fernando Valley club run by Charley Foy of the Seven Little Foys. A lot of performers envied his independence. When he died, he was still in hock to the bookies, but, except for that, he'd lived his own happy life.

Around the same time that Joe was coming into the Panama, I met Benny Davis and Benny Fields. Benny Davis would go on to be a hit songwriter. Benny Fields later became what many people called the first crooner. I always saw him as a blues singer.

White people have their own style of singing and dancing. Negroes have another. I cannot put my finger on what the difference is, but I know that there are very few white people who can really sing the blues. Benny Fields was one of them. He had a big and lazy kind of voice that was wonderful for blues.

The two Bennys were teamed up with another chap whose name I can't remember, and were working at Al Turney's, 35th and Calumet. After the cabarets closed at one a.m., Florence, Cora, and I would meet the three fellows and go to one of the buffet flats that had become part of the Chicago scene.

Buffet flats were after-hours spots that were usually in someone's apartment—the type of place where gin was poured out of milk pitchers. The customers paid ridiculous prices for watered-down liquor, and there was a joke that they even watered the ginger ale. It didn't matter. Nobody drank very much. I could sit all night with a tiny shot of gin and a glass full of orange juice. I hadn't been drinking long. I thought I was raising hell. Drinking wasn't the big thing it is today. The three-martini lunch wasn't even imagined. I could count on the fingers of one hand the entertainers I worked with in the saloons who were out-and-out drunks.

We really paid for a place to get together where we could sit around and harmonize. We'd have one drink, do some close harmony, then move on to another buffet flat . . . till six or seven in the morning.

Benny Fields and I sort of paired off. I really liked him, and I know he liked me, but there was no hanky-panky. Everyone around us thought there was something going on, but there wasn't. I loved listening to Benny sing, and I liked being with him. He was big and handsome, as gentle as a lamb with his old sleepy eyes. He was something rare then— a fellow with perfect manners, especially when it came to women.

One early morning—it must have been about seven or eight o'clock— Benny said he wanted to take me to Al Turney's for a drink. I said sure. In those days Negroes didn't go to white saloons—except for Jack Johnson—but I wasn't thinking anything about it. I just went along with Benny.

When we got to Al Turney's, the porter was mopping the floor. Benny asked him to get behind the bar and serve us a drink. The porter was so embarrassed he didn't know where to put himself. "Mr. Fields, you know that's not allowed. The little lady there—isn't she colored?"

Benny glanced at me with those wonderful eyes of his. "You bet she's colored. Now serve us a drink."

To this day I can't remember whether or not the porter did pour us some drinks. I do recall that the whole idea of being served or not served was a joke as far as I was concerned. I knew where you were supposed to go, and what you were supposed to do. It was one of the few times in my life that my being a Negro created an incident.

Of course Benny moved on and so did I, and we never saw each other after those days. Benny went on to play in vaudeville with Blossom Seeley, a San Francisco girl who had made it to stardom as a rhythm singer. They called it ragtime, and Blossom could really swing. She knew how to put over a number by working the full stage. She worked with two pianos, always made a dynamic entrance, and even sprayed the curtain with perfume before it went up.

A few years later I was in San Francisco appearing at Lester Mapp's and I read in the papers that Benny and Blossom had come to the city on a Keith-circuit engagement. Benny Davis was on the bill with them. Show business was a much smaller world then, and he must have known that I was in town and where I was playing. I felt sure he would be down to say hello.

As the nights went by, however, there was no sign of Benny. That wasn't like him. Then one evening Benny Davis and another fellow who was in the show with him came in. I was glad to see Benny and his friend, but I wanted to know, "Where's Benny Fields?"

The way Benny Davis looked at me I thought something terrible had happened. But then he said, "Well, Brick, Benny's pretty thick with Blossom."

There wasn't much I wanted to say. I went to the show, but didn't go backstage. There was no point.

After the two Bennys left, things went on pretty much as usual for me and the Panama Trio. At the club there was never a dull moment, and I guess part of the reason was that it was integrated. There were a lot of chances for men and women of the two races to get together.

In those days they had a thing at the Panama, as well as at the other cabarets on the South Side, called "grenades." These were notes that usually read something like "Call me at such-and-such a number." White women with a fascination for Negro men would pass these "grenades" to a waiter or entertainer, who in turn would deliver the note to the intended party. These women used to come over to the South Side because the Negro men couldn't go downtown or over to the North Side. If a Negro man became involved with a white woman, he'd better have a lot of money or else someone else would take her away from him.

Twinkle David and several of the others working at the Panama would deliver the grenades, but I wouldn't. I don't know why. I had an instinctive aversion to doing it, even though there was no prejudice or jealousy involved. Maybe I just had a good nose for trouble.

One night a white girl who'd come in with a white fellow got up and went to the ladies' room. One of the female entertainers who passed grenades followed her in. The entertainer came out with a grenade and took it to a Negro man. He sent a note back to the white girl. Naturally, all of this was done as discreetly and secretly as possible, but the note fell out of the white girl's bag and her boyfriend picked it up and read it. All hell broke loose. The girl got the tongue-lashing of her life, and Izzy promptly fired the entertainer who had passed the note.

I suppose that's how grenades got their name. They exploded every which way if they got into the hands of the wrong people.

Another night Cora and Florence and I found what the preachers called "the heartbreaking side of love's harvest." It was a hot night and we had gone out to get some air between sets. Cora thought she heard a noise in a nearby garbage can. We walked over to investigate and found a newborn baby in a shoebox.

While Cora held the infant, crazy me ran around screaming that we'd found a baby. Somebody do something quick! The police arrived and took the baby away to the hospital.

All that evening Cora and Florence and I schemed and planned about how we were going to get that baby and keep it ourselves. After all, if no one claimed it, we should get it. We'd get some nice baby clothes, a crib to put it in, and so forth. After all that talk, however, we finally had to admit that we didn't know the first thing about taking care of a baby. We decided to leave it in the hands of those who did—but it gave each of us a warm and tender feeling to think about taking care of a little breath of new life that someone had discarded along with the rest of the day's trash.

Those days were great days for entertainers in Chicago. The city seemed to draw the best performers from all over the country, and up from its own neighborhoods. Alberta Hunter was born in Chicago and became a star without ever leaving. She is a blues singer who started off working at Hugh Hoskins's saloon at 32nd and State streets, then became the reigning queen at a place called the Dreamland. After the Panama closed, that became the big cabaret on the South Side. After many years she retired to New York City and took up nursing, then went back to singing and is still going strong.

The great trumpet player King Oliver, master of New Orleans jazz, came to Chicago and worked next to the Panama at an upstairs place called the Deluxe. A few months later he brought his great protégé, Louis Armstrong, up from New Orleans.

The Panama and the Panama Trio were flourishing. I don't know how long Florence and Cora and I might have played there if there hadn't been a shooting out at the bar. Someone got killed, the Panama was closed down, and for the second time I was out of a job because of gunfire.

Because we had an act, the next step was vaudeville—at least that's how Cora and Florence saw it. I wasn't too happy with the idea, but I went along. Our first booking came easily and quickly. We were spotted at the Grand Theatre on 31st and State streets, right where Mama and us kids used to live. The old house had been torn down in order to build the theater. It was mostly sentiment that caused me to perform on the very spot where I'd once lived.

Mama came to see us. She'd sit in the front row and tell me to pull my skirt down in front or in back, or she'd turn to the person sitting next to her and say, "That's my baby up there in that trio. My Ada. You know Ada Smith. Why, everyone knows my Ada."

We were having a nice success at the Grand, and of course it was fun to have Mama come to see me perform in someplace other than a saloon. The stage just wasn't for me, however. I had come to grips with something I'd suspected but hadn't really understood until I played behind the footlights again. I was just plain uncomfortable. I'd found my style in saloons, and I just wasn't happy playing to a sea of darkness, unable to see the reactions of people beyond the first three rows. I left the Trio. Florence and Cora replaced me with a girl named Carolyn Williams. That was the last time I ever performed in a theater.

It wasn't easy saying goodbye to Florence and Cora. We'd been through a lot together. I joked that I would be catching up with them sooner or later. Any trio that harmonized as well as we did could never get too far apart. While I was saying that, however, I had plans to get very far away from Chicago and the old Panama Trio. Guy Hart, a pimp I knew in Chicago, had often told me that I ought to give the West Coast a whirl. With the Panama Trio shot out from under me, I decided the time was right.

It was 1917 by now, and America had entered the war. I was exchanging a lot of tearful goodbyes with young friends as they went off to serve their country. Now I exchanged a tearful goodbye with Mama and set off for California.

I guess I decided that since I was going to a new place, I ought to have a new name. I wanted to be so theatrical and so mature—I was almost twenty-three years old, after all. Everybody else in the entertainment business seemed to be changing their names, so I decided I'd be Adah Smith. "Adahhh" sounded so much more theatrical than Ada. I had my picture taken for postcards once I got to Los Angeles. I had on a long, lacy white dress, and I sat in a chair and rested my chin on my hand. I sent one to Mama. I signed it, "To My Mama, From Her Baby, Adah." Mama wrote right back, "Your name is A-D-A, Ada," and that was that. When my Mama spoke, everybody jumped, and that was the end of "Adah Smith," at least when I wrote to her.

I arrived in Los Angeles in May of 1917, and in no time at all Guy Hart had set me up with George Henderson, who ran the Watts Country Club on the outskirts of Los Angeles. Entertainers could always depend on the pimps to get things done faster and cheaper than the theatrical agents who were beginning to move into the business. The Watts Country Club was quite a surprise, however.

It was in the country, all right—wilderness was more like it. Watts was a woodsy, weedy place, and the club itself was little more than a barn. It consisted of one large room with a bandstand on one side, the bar on the opposite side, and tables set out around the dance floor. There was drama to the place, though, because these were dramatic times. People were tense and nervous. There was a desperate feeling that you had to enjoy everything now, that tomorrow would be too late. You'd see a fellow in a civilian suit one night, and the next night he'd be there in uniform saying goodbye. It touched me to see young men turned into soldiers overnight. Still, performing at the Watts Country Club would have been just another job if it hadn't been for one thing: it was there that I fell in love with Walter Delaney.

Walter was a pimp. His woman was one of those street women who lifted wallets from men when they ran their hands over them. She'd bring the money home to Walter, and I could see why. He was handsome, dapper, all the things a pimp usually is. He was a regular at the Watts Country Club, but I never really talked to him until one night when he stayed behind after the place closed.

There were five of us—three men and two women. The men were Neil Martin, another pimp; Walter; and George Henderson, the owner. Neil and Walter were so close that people thought they were brothers. The women were me and Carolyn Williams, the gal who had replaced me in the Panama Trio. She'd quit the act when it had played Los Angeles and was working at a place downtown.

George and Carolyn were making it. This didn't sit too well with Bertha Henderson, George's wife and one of the best street women in the business. That night Bertha took it into her head to do something about George and Carolyn. We were sitting there, laughing, talking, enjoying a drink, when all of a sudden the door burst open and there was Bertha waving a knife. She made straight for Carolyn. She got in a few swipes, but they weren't serious because Carolyn knew how to duck fast. Before Bertha could cause any real damage, Carolyn made it out the door and hid in the woods.

As usual, I didn't react right away. George calmed Bertha down and talked her into going home. He asked me to come along. I was living at their place anyway, but I had an idea he wanted me as a buffer. Their place was the last place I wanted to be right then. Walter and Neil stepped in then. They said maybe George and Bertha ought to be alone for a while. They'd take me to a buffet flat.

It was after we'd got to the flat that I started getting nervous and scared about going back to George and Bertha's. Walter suggested I stay at his place.

Two weeks later I was still living with him. We were never apart except when I was working or when he went out to satisfy his habit. Walter was an opium smoker. Finding it out didn't surprise or shock me. Pimps usually were opium smokers, and so were a lot of sporting men and entertainers.

I never tried opium myself, but in Chicago I learned to cook it to help out a friend. He was a sporting man who said he had eyes only for me. I was to learn differently when he begged me to help out his woman. She was a street woman and she'd been badly cut by a trick who'd thought she was the same woman who had robbed him a few weeks before. The woman's arms had been severely slashed while she'd protected her face. She and my so-called friend were opium smokers. She couldn't cook her stuff. I was the only person in Chicago who could be trusted to cook it for her.

I said that I'd do it, but that once I'd done it I'd never have anything to do with him again. He didn't believe me.

I burned my fingers and I don't know how many dollars' worth of opium before I learned to cook it right. After a couple of weeks I could manage that little old yen stick pretty well. By that time the woman's arms had healed enough so she could cook her own stuff. I got out of there and never saw that pimp again.

No telling what Mama would have done if she had found out I was cooking opium. Mama was scared to death of any kind of drug after seeing a friend of hers back in Alderson become addicted to morphine through illness. Mama may have been negligent about telling her children some of the facts of life, but she had drummed into us the dangers of becoming addicted to drugs. As a result, I was over forty years old before I took my first aspirin. If we got sore throats as children, Mama would blow sulfur powder down our throats, or she'd rely on that old standby—gargling with our own pee.

Except for people like Mama, only the police worried about opium smokers, and even they didn't pay much attention until some new vice campaign began. The smokers didn't bother anyone, as far as I know. They didn't have to steal or kill to satisfy their habit, because there was plenty of "stuff" around. When they felt the need, they holed up in a hotel room, fixed a wet blanket to the door to camouflage the smell, enjoyed their kicks and got it over with.

This was how things went with Walter. He never smoked in my presence. From time to time he'd say he was going to kick the habit, and once he really tried. I saw him sweat cold turkey, but he couldn't go through with it. He'd been on opium too long.

I suppose I decided I was in love with Walter when Bertha Henderson found out where I was staying and asked me to come back. I said no, that things were fine the way they were. Bertha was put off, and I decided that that was the end of my association with the Hendersons.

I left the Watts Country Club to go and work at Murray's on Central Avenue. Murray's was near the railroad station, and every night when I went to work I could see the trains being loaded with young boys going off to war. One of the entertainers at Murray's was a chap I'd met in Chicago, but I really got to know Jelly Roll Morton at Murray's. He was still trying to figure out what to do with his life. He couldn't decide whether to be a pimp or a piano player. I told him to be both.

Walter's woman eventually found out what was going on. She came to Walter's place and didn't waste words. "Who do you want? Me or this little entertainer?" Walter told her quietly that he'd take me. It caused quite a stir in the sporting world. Pimps didn't usually take up with entertainers. We didn't make enough money. A pimp's woman brought big money to him.

Walter and I moved into a little bungalow, and I started learning how to keep house. I hadn't had a broom in my hand since I used to help Mama with the housework when I was a kid, and as for cooking, well, I had seen Mama make her vegetable soup so often that I could have made it blindfolded. There were few complaints from Walter. He loved me, and we were happy just being together in our little house. For once, I wasn't restless. I didn't want to be anywhere else.

We lived pretty well. Walter gambled, and at times there was quite a bit of money to spend. Otherwise, we lived on what I brought home. It was a comedown in life-style for Walter, and no woman was going to give him money while he was living with me. He said he didn't care about that. He wanted to get away from pimping. He got a job working on the troop trains, but that didn't last. Then he tried a few other things, but it was hard to keep a job when you were an opium addict.

He tried to quit, but he couldn't. Had I been older, more experienced in what to do for him, I would have fought tooth and nail to get him away from that pipe. I tried. I encouraged him to do anything that might help him, but nothing seemed to work. It was a problem we both lived with.

I got word one day that a fast gal around town was boasting that she was going to get Walter for herself. I laughed it off. When I didn't see Walter for a few days, however, I began to wonder if that girl had started making good on her boast. Some of the entertainers at Murray's made it their business to have me overhear a conversation they were having: "That gal is trying to get Walter. She gave him a whole lot of money."

I began to get nervous. I had to find out what was going on from Walter himself, so I went up to the hotel where Walter and a friend of his used to smoke opium and knocked at the door of his room. When he found out it was me, he told me to go away. I wouldn't. He opened the door and came out into the hall. "I want you to go home," he said. "Just go home."

I went home. Later he came to the house, his pockets full of hundred-dollar bills. He also had a gold chain with a twenty-dollar gold piece dangling on it. He told me about the girl, laughing as he did so. I wasn't to think anything about it. It was me he loved, only me.

Well, if that was so, then I decided it was up to me to prove it to everyone else. The following night I put on the chain with the twenty-dollar gold piece and went out to show it off. The girl found out about that and decided to pin Walter down. Again, faced with an either-or choice, Walter chose me. I didn't like the idea of his being with another woman, but it made me feel kind of good to wind up always as number one.

Then the Los Angeles police started a big vice clean-up. Just like in Chicago, the first step in the campaign was to round up all the whores, pimps, and addicts. They're the easy marks. Walter had been busted a couple of times before, and he knew he'd be in for another bust soon. He decided to head for San Diego. All the sporting people on Central Avenue decided to leave town and air out the street.

Walter hadn't been gone more than a couple of days when I got so lonesome I couldn't take it. Walter was the only thing that mattered—not the police, not the questioning, not the problems of being an addict's woman. I headed for San Diego, too, but Walter talked me out of my brave decision. He wanted me to have nothing to do with his troubles, and packed me back to Los Angeles. When the atmosphere of self-righteousness simmered down a bit, Walter headed for San Francisco, where I eventually joined him.

Earl Dancer, a bright young Negro promoter, helped me to get to San Francisco. He later discovered Ethel Waters on the TOBA circuit, put her into white vaudeville and then on Broadway. He not only got me a job at Lester Mapp's, he also got me a higher salary than any of the other entertainers at Lester's.

The going rate at Lester's was one dollar a night plus a percentage of the drinks. Earl told Lester that a hotshot like me, who'd entertained at Jack Johnson's at the Champ's own invitation, wouldn't take less than twenty-five dollars a week. At the time, that was quite a sum of money. It wasn't as much as a good prostitute made, but I still felt pretty proud to be able to rejoin Walter making that kind of salary.

San Francisco seemed like one great town when I got there. It was wonderful being with Walter again. Lester Mapp couldn't have been nicer. All the attention I was getting led me to believe that I was something special. I felt like the hotshot Earl Dancer said I was when I walked out on the floor of Lester Mapp's for the first time and everything stopped. The owner, the waiters, the other entertainers, the barmen, the customers—everyone gave their undivided attention to a new entertainer who was getting twenty-five dollars a week.

I went on the floor and did what I always did—went from table to table, singing, bowing, smiling, dancing. When I left the floor, I got a good hand, but I recognized it for what it was—what's called "polite applause." That's how it went for several days until finally Lester called Earl upstairs and asked, "When's that girl going to cut loose? When's she really going to *do* something?"

Earl was a champion sweet-talker. He told Lester that I'd never worked in a place like that before and it would take a while for me to get used to it.

He was right about that. My first nights at Lester's were confusing, to say the least. Lester Mapp's was a speakeasy. It didn't have a liquor license. You'd be on the floor singing, a buzzer would sound, and you'd quickly sit down at the table nearest you. The piano top would be closed, the drinks whisked away. When the police came downstairs to look around, all they'd see was some slightly happy people drinking ginger ale or Coca-Cola and talking about the weather. When the police left, things went back to normal. The booze would appear on the tables and the piano player would get busy at the keyboard. Lester Mapp's place was well protected.

Earl explained to Lester that I couldn't concentrate on my singing and dancing with all this going on. Thanks to him, I managed to squeeze in one more week at twenty-five dollars. By the third week Lester had cut my salary to eighteen, and pretty soon I was working on the same deal as the others—a dollar a night and picking up my own tips. It was quite a comedown, I admit, but, frankly, I was relieved. I was able to relax and have fun.

There were times when we'd perform out on the floor. Other times we'd sit right at the table with the customers and sing. I'd be singing

"Hello, Central, Give Me No Man's Land" at one, someone else would be singing "Darktown Strutters' Ball" at a table nearby, and across the room someone else would be singing the "Hesitation Blues." I started having fun at Lester Mapp's.

I was happiest when I was with Walter, however. We lived over in Oakland above a saloon. There were pool tables downstairs, and one upstairs on our floor that was used for private games. I already knew how to play pool, but I practiced up, and pretty soon I was a regular pool shark.

I also had the pool shark's ability to bluff. The owner of the place would tell a customer that the little girl upstairs was just a beginner, but that she'd love to play a few games to pass the time. Up the man would come. We'd play for fifty cents a game—no slouch of an amount in those days. I'd let him win a few games, then I'd start knocking the balls into those side pockets. The man wasn't going to let any girl beat him, so he'd keep playing, raising the stakes. When I'd won about twenty dollars, I'd suddenly remember an important engagement and take off. After a while, word got around about how I conned men that way. Walter and I had some good laughs about it. Shark or not, I always won legitimately.

Walter wasn't working at anything. Once or twice he ran across an old dumb broad who thought she was going to get him by parting with her dollars. They never lasted long. I didn't care.

I did care, though, that Walter was still smoking opium. He would talk for hours about how he was going to kick the habit. His words were just words that never went anywhere, much as we both wanted to believe them.

One morning I came home from work to find that Walter wasn't waiting for me as usual. There was a note on the bureau. Walter seldom, if ever, wrote notes, and I hesitated before opening it. I read it and had to sit down. I felt weak. He'd gone to Seattle and wasn't coming back. Not because he didn't love me anymore—quite the opposite. He loved me too much to drag me down with him. He just couldn't get away from the opium. He wanted the best for me, and the best, according to him, was not Walter Delaney.

I was torn up inside, but my pride wouldn't let me follow him. He wrote to me. I answered. There were letters back and forth. Several times we thought we might get together again, but we couldn't, not as long as Walter was an addict.

Many years later I heard that he talked about how much he still loved me. As for me, if I ever loved anyone in my life, it was Walter. How can you help but love a man who tries to lift himself up because he loves you? He was bitter with himself because he failed to do what he wanted to do. But he did try. What else can you ask of a man but that he try?

PROHIBITION

PEACE WAS DECLARED and the Armistice signed while I was still in San Francisco. License or no license, the liquor really flowed at Lester Mapp's on November 11, 1918. Most of the entertainers, including myself, were not big drinkers, but a special occasion called for an extra drink or two, or three or four or more, until you lost count. After Prohibition came on, every night became a special occasion for some people.

It was the craziest law. You can't stop people from doing what they want to do. If you try, you just make them want to do it more. It was Prohibition that gave the gangsters a chance to become big-time. Prohibition made a lot of people *start* drinking, and it didn't make anybody stop.

I was still working at Lester Mapp's when Prohibition started in 1919. It didn't make any difference at Lester's, because he'd never had a liquor license in the first place. The buzzer still buzzed when the police came around. The difference between Lester's and the other places was that now *they* had to get buzzers, too, and they had to learn what we already knew—how to cover things up quick.

Around 1920 Lillian Rose, a fellow entertainer, and I went up to Vancouver with some musicians to work for Billy Bowman. I'd known him in Chicago, and he wanted me to open up his new place. Lily and I lived at a boardinghouse first; then, seeing that we liked working at Billy's and that Vancouver could be fun, we found an apartment to share.

There was no Prohibition in British Columbia, but the liquor laws were so complicated that Vancouver was what we called a dry town. Outside of the private clubs and speakeasies, the only place you could buy a drink was at someone's house. It was like those after-hours places in Chicago, only in Vancouver you could buy a drink night or day at someone's "open house."

When friends started coming to our apartment to see us, they'd say they wanted a drink and we'd give them one. They said we were crazy fools to give liquor away, so Lily and I started selling a shot of whiskey for fifteen cents, or two for a quarter.

Anyone who was going to have liquor in the house, to drink or to sell, had to buy it from a Chinese laundryman. They were the only ones selling it. Whenever it was my turn to go for a bottle, I made someone go with me. Because of the stupidity of race prejudice, I was deathly afraid of going near a "Chinaman."

As a kid on State Street, I was taught to be afraid of the few Chinese around. They were harmless little people who ran laundries and carried their babies slung across their backs, but we heard stories that they had big hatchets hidden under the ironing table. There were also stories of children being kidnapped by them and sold to scientists for experiments. It was silly kid's stuff, but as an adult woman I was still terrified every time I went to pick up the liquor. Eventually I got friendly with the two Chinese brothers who sold the stuff, and I learned a good lesson.

Lily and I didn't have any big liquor business at home. We were seldom there. After work we'd go to some private club where there was gambling. Lily was quite a gambler. She loved to shoot craps. I didn't play as much as she did—spent more time watching than playing. A person about to roll the dice would ask me if I felt lucky. If I said I felt "hot," he'd have me roll for him. I never did become much of a gambler. Years later, as I headed for the tables at Monte Carlo or Biarritz, I'd say, "If I'm not back in five minutes, you'll know I'm winning."

Back in the early saloon days, my favorite card game was one on the order of gin rummy called Coon Can. If anyone asked what Coon Can was, you'd say, "Some coons can and some coons can't." People would object to that now. Back then we'd all laugh—Negro and white. If anyone squawked about the game back then, it was because he was losing too much green folding money.

Bowman's biggest customers—and I do mean big—were the Swedish lumberjacks who came into Vancouver on their time off. Tall, strapping fellows, they could make a bottle of whiskey disappear in no time. Pretty soon they'd be drunk and ready to fight. I wanted no part of these fights and would make myself scarce when one broke out—except on New Year's Eve of 1920 in the fight to end all fights.

No one knows what that fight was all about. Everybody was beating up on everybody else. Bowman's was a large place, and "everybody" means about three hundred people. I remember all the fists flying and glass breaking, but that's all I remember. It was one of those "special occasions" when I lost count of how many drinks I'd had.

The next thing I knew, I was in a bed in a white room. My right leg was in a splint, and my head felt as if it were about to come off. I was in a hospital, and my leg was broken.

A gal I knew called Dago was standing by the side of my bed. I couldn't believe it when she told me I'd kept trying to get into the brawl the night before. "You kept running into the middle of all those punches and someone kept pushing you back out, but that didn't stop you. You got right back in the middle of it again, and got pushed out again. But this time you fell down a flight of stairs."

She told me that I'd given quite a time to the doctor who'd tried to set my leg. He'd just come from a party and was feeling no pain himself. We must have been quite a pair. I'd rolled and turned so violently that I broke three splints. He'd sworn and staggered. He hadn't been too drunk to do his job, though. My leg healed in the normal length of time and never gave me a bit of trouble. I never told Mama what had really happened. Just in case she happened to hear something through the show-business grapevine, I wrote and said I'd sprained my ankle.

It must have been toward the end of 1922 that I decided I'd been away from Mama too long, so I went back to Chicago, to quite a different family from the one I'd known as a child.

Mama was still running a roominghouse, but it was a smaller one. She was getting more for the rooms and didn't have to take on all the burdens of a big place. She was still the same vigorous Hattie E. Smith, though life had dealt her some hard blows. Besides losing a husband early, she'd lost her two middle children.

Ethel had died in 1920. Her death had been more tragic, because it wasn't a long time coming, like Robert's. Still, Ethel's death wasn't completely unexpected. She had a reputation for being a tough gal. She got into a fight with someone once, and when a policeman tried to break it up, she cut him in the hand. He arrested her because of the fighting. When she came to trial, the judge gave her a suspended sentence, but then the policeman stood up. "What about me, Judge?" he said, holding up his bandaged hand. The judge gave her five to ten days for that, then suspended that sentence, too.

This is the story behind Ethel's death. Ethel was married and living in Chicago Heights when she heard that her husband, Gus, was fooling around with another woman. One night she decided to go to the woman's house and catch Gus in the act. She rang the bell and knocked on the door. No one answered. She started to leave, then something caused her to change her mind. She went around to the back of the house and up the back stairs. She knocked on the door of the woman's room. The woman opened it, firing, and killed Ethel.

I did go home for Ethel's funeral. This time Mama didn't tell me to stay away. None of us were prepared for Ethel's death. After the funeral Mama took Ethel's body back to Alderson, too.

At least the two other Smith children were doing all right. I had reason to be mostly proud of how I'd gotten ahead as an entertainer. Blonzetta was way ahead in the dollars department, however. I had some exciting experiences to tell about, some pretty clothes, and lots of shoes. Blonzetta owned mortgages on a string of Chicago properties.

Long before Blonzetta had left home to marry Peter Belfant, she had started buying second mortgages. Before she was twenty, she owned a major interest in a building. Her cleverness at business continued throughout her life as she gradually doubled and tripled her interests. When asked how she'd managed to be so successful, Blonzetta would say, "Simple. I worked for rich people. I listened to them and got to know how they did business. I saved money and invested it the way they did. It's like Mama says—if you can do it for others, you can do it for yourself."

After a short, happy reunion with Mama and Blonzetta, I was itching to get out on the cabaret floor again. Prohibition was in full force by this time, and the pace of the sporting life had stepped up. Atlantic City was at its height as a chic resort town. The owner of the Paradise, a mixed cabaret there, decided to bring a show in from the West, and a group of us who were in Chicago at the time set off for the East Coast. Bertha Ricks, Justine McKenney, three or four others, and I invaded Atlantic City, but we never stood a chance.

We were a flop, but a proud one. When we danced, we picked up our skirts, showed an attractive bit of knee and thigh, and let the skirts fall, according to the rhythm. The Eastern entertainers belonged to another school. They rolled their dresses around their waists and did the grind, and a few of them didn't mind going to the tables and picking up quarters and half-dollars with a certain portion of their anatomy.

We complained that we hadn't been engaged for that sort of work. The Eastern girls shot back that we were afraid to lift our dresses because we didn't have nice underwear. All this may sound naïve today, but this was the era of the can-can, and smart entertainers had fastened on the technique of working with the skirt and adapted it to American dance styles. An entertainer spent as much on her underwear as she did on her dresses. Not being as chintzy or as underpaid as the Eastern girls, we probably spent more.

I gave them more back-talk than the others, so of course when it came time to fire us, I was the first. A fellow named Ramsey offered me a job at the New Whirl, which he managed. He said he wanted one entertainer who didn't depend on bumps and grinds. I worked there a few weeks, but I'd had enough of Atlantic City and decided to get out.

Before I'd left Chicago, a girlfriend who knew I was headed East had written Barron Wilkins in New York. She'd told him I might be around New York and would he be interested in hiring me? She reminded him that I was the redhead that he'd nicknamed Bricktop years before. Barron wrote back that of course he remembered me and that he'd heard that I'd blossomed into quite an entertainer. I'd be welcome any time.

So I got in touch with Barron, was hired on the spot, and walked into a grandstand seat at the carnival called New York in those Prohibition days.

It was 1922 and Harlem was really jumpin'. Harlem was the "in" place to go for music and booze, and it seemed like every other building on or near Seventh Avenue from 130th Street to 140th was a club or a speakeasy. There was Broadway Jones's Supper Club, the Bamville Club, the Clam House, the Alamo Café, the Cotton Club, dozens of others. Some were hangouts for musicians and other entertainers, small neighborhood places that stayed open after the big clubs closed. Some were high-class nightclubs that catered to an integrated clientele. In others the only dark faces you saw belonged to the waiters or entertainers.

Barron's was called Barron's Exclusive Club, and it *was* exclusive. Only light-skinned Negroes could get in, unless you happened to be someone special like Jack Johnson or the great Negro comic Bert Williams. Men had to wear jackets and ties, and women had to wear long dresses. It was *the* Harlem spot. Frank Fay, the actor—he played the original Elwood P. Dowd in *Harvey*—hung out there, and so did Al Jolson, and a chorus girl named Lucille LeSueur who would later be known as Joan Crawford. Every night the limousines pulled up to the corner of Seventh Avenue and 134th Street, and the rich whites would get out, all dolled up in their furs and jewels. Going to work at Barron's was the new high point of my career.

I was making eighteen dollars a week as a guarantee against tips, but the way the tips came at Barron's, you didn't need any guarantee. Barron catered to big spenders, and I mean big. People would come in, plunk down a hundred-dollar bill, and ask for change in half-dollars. At the end of a song they'd throw all of it onto the floor and go back to change another bill so they'd be ready to do the same thing when the next song was over. Even split among the singers and the band, these tips could really add up in a night, but, believe it or not, I hardly saved a thing. Aside from the rent on my furnished room, my biggest expense was clothes.

Entertainers had moved out of the blouse-and-skirt stage and now went in for dresses. Colorful, flashy costumes were expected, and you had to have a big variety. This put a big crimp in an entertainer's budget.

Every night salesmen would come to the back of the club to show us so-called "hot goods." We were supposed to believe that the dresses had been stolen from warehouses in New York's downtown garment center. Probably some of them had been, but I think the Seventh Avenue boys liked to say "hot goods" just to excite our interest and make us feel we were buying tomorrow's Fifth Avenue models today. They were pretty and a bargain at the ten or fifteen dollars we paid. One night, though, a customer right up front stared so hard that I was convinced I had on a real "hot dress." I got so nervous I went home and changed.

The customers at Barron's were the "Who's Who" of New York's Roaring Twenties, when gangsters rubbed elbows with high society, and people in show business came uptown after the Broadway theaters closed.

I always enjoyed singing for a nice, quiet Irishman who came in regularly. Sometimes he'd come in with his brother Eddie and sometimes he'd come in with a fly girl named Alice. She loved to dance and was sharper than a tack. He was a very likable fella—a good sport. He'd buy a drink a minute. When he wasn't with Alice, he'd say, "Bricky, come on, let's you and me . . ." And I'd say, "Oh, no, that ain't the play." I wasn't going to start messing around with customers. He was Jack "Legs" Diamond.

I knew he was a gangster, but I didn't pay much attention to that gangster stuff. That was the game in those days. They weren't killing anybody but themselves—they weren't killing you and me. It wasn't like it is today—they kill up anybody now. Anyway, it wasn't until later on that he got that reputation as the killer of killers. He walked into the Hotsy Totsy Club in Manhattan with a bunch of thugs and gunned down five of his enemies. When he went out to shoot you, he seldom missed.

I'll never forget when he came to Paris. One night Mabel Ball, who was one of the "show-business set," came running into the club crying, "Bricky, I've just left Chez Florence because that Jack Diamond is over there."

We used to call her Mimsy, and I said, "Mimsy, Jack Diamond don't want nothin' you got."

She wasn't convinced, but she sat down. And she had no more than sat down before Legs and Alice, who was now his wife, walked in. Alice walked right over to Mabel and said, "You old bitch, why are you screaming and carrying on? We don't want none of that junk."

Mabel looked like she was going to have a heart attack. Jack was saying, "Come on, Alice, come on, Alice." Finally, Alice left Mabel alone, but I think it was a long time before Mabel got over that experience.

The Barrymore brothers often came to Barron's. John Barrymore was one handsome devil. Whenever I danced he'd sit there and watch my legs and feet. He came to Bricktop's in Paris one night, and I went over to his table and said, "Do you remember me?" He turned to his wife, raised that famous eyebrow with a "Watch this" look, and said to me, "Can you dance?" I broke into one of the routines I'd done at Barron's. Barrymore roared with laughter.

Another of my favorites was Charles MacArthur. He married Helen Hayes and became one of America's greatest playwrights. They're still performing *The Front Page*, which he wrote with Ben Hecht. Charlie swore that he was going to star me in his first Broadway show, *Lulu Belle*, but by the time David Belasco got around to producing it, I was in Paris. The role of the half-caste made a great star out of Lenore Ulric. I'm sure things turned out for the better.

Barron Wilkins and I got along fine, and pretty soon he started depending on me the way Izzy Levine and other club owners had. He asked my advice on music, the scheduling of performers, and lots of other things. When the manager tried to make a pass at me, like he did with all the girls, Barron himself stepped in and told him to stop.

Barron didn't mind when I took a day off now and then, or even left for a while to work out of town. I did that quite often. I really liked Washington, D.C., and every chance I got I went there. One of the reasons was a combo called Elmer Snowden's Washingtonians.

There were five of them: Elmer Snowden, Sonny Greer, Arthur Whetsol, Otto Hardwick, and a tall, incredibly handsome piano player named Duke Ellington. I met them when I was singing at the Oriental Gardens at Ninth and R streets, N.W. Later on I partied with them and made sure I caught them wherever they were playing. I'd already been lucky enough to meet some great musicians, but I knew a good outfit when I heard one. The Washingtonians were something.

⌈On one of my trips to Washington, I heard that the kids—they were only about five years younger than me, but I thought of them as kids, maybe because I was many years older in experience—weren't playing anywhere. They were unemployed and anxious to go to New York. I saw my chance to help them. The outfit we had at Barron's wasn't good, which didn't surprise me. I'd discovered that most nightclub owners had tin ears. I'd complained to Barron every so often, and he'd said that if I ever found another outfit to let him know. So when the Washingtonians became available, I went to bat for them with "Daddy." He hired them immediately, and they joined the other three singers and me at Barron's.

I really felt good about being able to help the Washingtonians, but I also wanted to make sure they could get along in New York. I don't remember exactly what I said to them, but Duke would. Half a century later he wrote in his autobiography, *Music Is My Mistress*:

> I shall never forget Bricktop's speech. "You know that you kids are making your living on tips," she said. (The salary was fifty dollars a week, but tips at around a thousand a night, split nine ways, averaged over a C-note a day for each person.) "Always remember it," she continued, "and always be generous when tipping, because the man who depends mostly upon tips for a living is one of us. And our people are always generous when we tip."

After several months at Barron's the Washingtonians went downtown to the Kentucky Club at Broadway and 49th Street. The club had an all-Negro show and the band was there for several years. Then, in 1927, they went to the Cotton Club, and the rest is history.

Florence Mills came back into my life while I was at Barron's. She was with an act on the Keith circuit called the Tennessee Ten, headed by Kid Thompson. Kid had a thing for Florence and was about to break up his marriage because of her. The whole situation was too sticky for Florence, and she needed an out. She asked if I could find her a spot at Barron's, and I didn't have any trouble. "Daddy" was delighted, and, as it turned out, the timing couldn't have been better for Florence.

Downtown the all-Negro *Shuffle Along* had been playing to sell-out audiences on Broadway for a couple of years, but now its star, Gertrude Saunders, had decided to quit and go into burlesque, which paid more money. The producers of the show were two Negro entertainer duos, Noble Sissle and Eubie Blake, and Flournoy Miller and Aubrey Lyles. Miller and Lyles were the team I'd started out with, and in the small world of show business at that time I'd kept in touch with them. I'd also met Sissle and Blake.

Harriet Sissle had a drinking problem, but I liked her. She liked me, too. When she told me that Gertrude was leaving and they needed a replacement, I didn't hesitate to say, "Why not Florence?" Harriet came to Barron's to see for herself, and then she got Noble to come with her.

Gertrude Saunders was going to be a hard act to follow. Noble Sissle was so sure Florence was not the right type that he didn't even tell his three partners why he came to Barron's that night. Poor drunken Harriet wouldn't leave him alone, however, and he went mostly to humor her. In spite of himself, he liked what he saw. He asked Florence downtown for an audition.

She auditioned, and auditioned, and auditioned. I don't know how many times they had her try out. I think Actors' Equity has a rule now that makes producers pay actors if they audition more than a couple of times. If that rule had existed then, Florence would have made a fortune. I wanted to tell all of them, "Stop fooling around and hire her." I was beginning to feel guilty about what I'd started—what if they didn't choose her after all this?—but I kept quiet and kept my fingers crossed. Anyway, Harriet Sissle was saying whatever I could have said, and she had more influence.

Finally, they gave Florence the job, and the night she took the floor from Gertrude Saunders, she had seventeen encores. *Seventeen encores!* She never looked back. After that, Florence Mills was a *star*. She conquered Broadway. Later she conquered Europe. And when she came back in 1927, Harlem, not to mention the rest of New York, was hers.

There's no telling where she could have gone, what she could have done. To this day, I can't figure out the logic—that someone like Florence had to die at the peak of her career because of something as stupid as appendicitis.

A regular customer at Barron's was a big man with curly red-blond hair named Connie Immerman. He and his brother George had a delicatessen business, and all the show people went there. One of their delivery boys was Fats Waller. The business Connie really wanted to be in, however, was the nightclub business, and maybe that's why he came to Barron's so much. We became friends, and he started telling me about his dreams. When his dreams were still just dreams, he was already talking about a name for his place. One night I volunteered, "How about Connie's Inn? That's your name, isn't it?" He agreed that it had just the right sound, and it had a Harlem touch.

The name was the least of his worries. Even after Connie found a place, he had a lot of trouble opening up his club.

There was a lot of competition in the Harlem club business. There were tremendous profits to be made in those Prohibition days when the money and the booze flowed. There was plenty for everyone, but it's human nature to be greedy and want more. When the Shuffle Inn at 131st Street and Seventh Avenue closed after a couple of years, the other club owners were not too interested in seeing it resurrected as Connie's Inn. Connie and his brother George were stubborn, though. In June 1923, Connie's Inn opened with a new entrance on Seventh Avenue facing the famous Tree of Hope, a lucky tree that people just about killed by taking pieces of bark from it—the stump is still there.

Connie's Inn had been open about a month when Connie sent word that he wanted me to work for him. He was putting all his dreams into practice and had Wilbur Sweatman's Rhythm Kings and Leonard Harper to stage the shows. Now he needed a soubrette, and I fitted the bill.

I was ready to move on. As I explained to Barron, "Look, Daddy, Florence Mills is a star. Cora Green is a hit in *Running Wild*. I'm the only one left who's still working the tables. It's my turn now."

Barron asked me how much Connie had offered. I told him. Barron said, "If you can get that much more, it's okay with me." I don't remember the exact figure, but it told Barron that Connie thought a lot of me.

I made quite a debut at Connie's Inn. I came out in a flower number with all the girls as flowers. I danced in at the end as a red rose. I held the petals over my head so you couldn't see my face. I wore little short pants.

I was a headliner at Connie's Inn, and I loved it, but I was still kind of restless. Every little while I felt the need to take off and work somewhere else. I still loved Washington, D.C., even though the Washingtonians weren't there anymore. Whenever I got a chance, I'd go down there. Connie didn't mind, any more than Barron had. There were plenty of girls around to take over my numbers.

I went to Washington, D.C., quite a few times in order to meet up with Mama. Although we wrote regularly, we seemed to be seeing less and less of each other as the years passed. I almost never got back to Chicago. At the same time, her visits to the family plot in Alderson were becoming more frequent as she grew older. They were charmingly impulsive visits. Mama didn't wait for special days like birthdays or anniversaries or Memorial Day. She'd wake up in the middle of the night, decide she was going to Alderson, and head for the train station. If she thought to send a wire to me, I'd try to arrange to go to Washington, D.C., and we'd meet.

I got word that Mama was going to Alderson around Eastertime of 1924, and I booked myself at a very nice club operated by Louis Thomas so Mama and I would have plenty of time to visit. I hadn't been there more than a couple of days when who should show up at the club but Sammy Richardson, a top Negro entertainer in Paris. Show people are never surprised at meeting their own even in the middle of a desert, but the news Sammy brought surprised and excited even the normally unexcitable me. *I* was wanted in Paris.

At the time, there weren't more than eight or ten Negro entertainers in all of Paris: Opal Cooper, a singer; Palmer Jones and Sammy Richardson, piano players; a cornet player we used to call Gut Bucket; and a few others. There was exactly one female Negro entertainer. She was Palmer Jones's wife and her name was Florence.

She was a sharp-dressing little girl, very haughty, and she'd been so popular at a place called Le Grand Duc that she was leaving to headline at a new place down the street.

Florence's leaving gave Gene Bullard, the Negro who was managing Le Grand Duc, the unwelcome problem of having to replace her. Florence's husband, Palmer Jones, had a suggestion. "Why don't you send to New York? There's a little girl over there called Bricktop. She don't have no great big voice or anything like that, but she has got the damnedest personality, and she can dance. She'll be a big success over here."

Bullard said, "But won't she be competition for your wife?"

"My wife needs some competition," said Palmer. "Her head's gotten so big that nobody can get along with her."

So they cabled Sammy Richardson, who was in New York at the time, and asked him to find me and make me an offer. Sammy tracked me down in Washington and followed me there. He stated the salary and told me I'd get an advance to pay for my ticket.

It all sounded good to me. I said to Mama, "What about it?" And she said, "Go ahead, I'll be over." She'd go anywhere, biggity as she was. There was nothing left to do but accept.

I raced back to New York and told Barron and Connie. They were both delighted. So were all of my friends. I packed and made preparations without any idea of what was in store for me. It was a spur-of-the-moment thing, a new adventure just for the sake of adventure. I wasn't running away from anything. In fact, I was happy with my life in New York, but it turned out that the timing of the move was perfect, for the glittering, happy world of the Harlem nightclubs was soon to end. When I said goodbye to Barron Wilkins, it was the last time I was to see him. Soon he would fall victim to the stepped-up competition among the bootleggers who were trying to control the Harlem trade. As I heard it, he got a shipment of bad booze and refused to pay for it. Early one morning in 1926, Yellow Charleston, a well-known junkie, stabbed and killed Barron in front of the Exclusive Club. The club closed after that, the third club I'd played in that was closed by violence. Only this time I was an ocean away.

PARIS

I DIDN'T SAIL for Paris right away. I had to get a passport first, and in those days it took at least two months for a passport. People didn't travel very much then—there weren't any cheap, package tours. If you said you were going to Europe, everybody knew you had money—unless you were one of those eccentric writers.

It wasn't unheard of for an entertainer to go to Europe, but not many did, and hardly any blacks did. I was quite a celebrity to my New York friends. In fact, they were more excited than I was.

I wasn't excited. I wasn't nervous. I barely knew where Paris was and didn't know a word of French, but I'd traveled to a lot of cities in the United States, and it didn't seem to me that Paris would be much different.

When the big day finally arrived, Mama came to see me off. She made it easy to say goodbye, at least outwardly. There were no warnings, no last-minute instructions about how to behave, just a warm embrace and a prayer that I was taking the right step. Mama had done her duty and brought me up to take care of myself. The future was up to me. Neither of us knew how long I would be away.

I sailed out of New York harbor on the *America*, one of those grand sister ships of the time when the only way to get to Europe was by ship. Traveling by ship is the highest form of elegance, and if I'd ever learned how to sail, I would have had a yacht long ago. There was such glamour! The champagne corks popped, the ship's orchestra played, and a girl could dance until dawn.

Unfortunately, all the glamour was lost on this little gal, whose only previous acquaintance with a boat had been on the Great Lakes steamers that plodded between Chicago and Michigan City. The *America* and I had nothing in common.

I was so miserably seasick that I would have swapped Paris for Michigan City in a minute. All I remember about the crossing was that I was the only Negro and the only passenger who didn't seem to have a good time. I shared a cabin with another woman, and I hated having anyone else around when I was feeling so bad. In between attacks of nausea, I vowed never again to share a cabin, and I kept my word.

The trip took eleven miserable days. On the morning of the eleventh day I was staring into the fog when the gray blur suddenly seemed to break up and I saw land. Le Havre emerged, and it had trees, buildings, and roads. I was so happy to see land again that I knew conquering Paris had to be easier than getting there.

Gene Bullard, manager of Le Grand Duc, was waiting for me when the *America* docked. A tall, handsome American Negro, he'd come to France in 1914 because he couldn't get aviation training in the U.S. After serving in the French Foreign Legion, he'd gone on to become a pilot with the Lafayette Escadrille in World War I and had received fifteen medals, including the French Legion of Honor. After the war he'd stayed on in France, for it had been a lot more friendly than his native land. He was so self-assured, and I needed to be with somebody who knew what he was doing. In the excitement of docking, I managed to lose my purse and the whole twenty-five to thirty dollars that was in it.

He told me not to worry. He'd take care of me. It was May 11, 1924, and I was twenty-nine years old.

We took the boat train from Le Havre to Paris. Gene had brought a bottle of champagne and we celebrated. Between sips, I tried looking out the window, but then thought better of it. My seasickness was not completely over. Gene told me when we were approaching Paris, and I swallowed hard and peered out at the red-roofed, close-set buildings. I wasn't impressed. Maybe I would have been if it had been one of those beautiful Paris spring days, but it was gray and blustery, and by the end of the two-hour trip, after eleven days at sea and too much champagne, I was kind of gray and blustery myself.

A rickety, open-air Paris taxi took us to Montmartre, atop a hill above the rest of the city. It was a tumbledown little place, with red and yellow one-story buildings lining its narrow, twisting streets, and as many cafés and dance halls and bordellos as on State Street in Chicago. We stopped at the hotel where the owners of Le Grand Duc had booked me a room, just long enough for me to check in and freshen up, then we headed for the club.

Le Grand Duc was at 52 Rue Pigalle, on the angle where the Rue Pigalle met the Rue Fontaine. A triangular sign jutted out above the single-door entrance. It didn't look very impressive, but I had played enough saloons and cabarets to know better than to judge a place from the outside. We walked into a tiny room that contained about twelve tables and a small bar that would feel crowded with six pairs of elbows leaning on it. I smiled my prettiest. "My, this is a nice little bar. Now where's the cabaret?"

There was a long silence. Then Gene said, "But *this* is the cabaret. This is Le Grand Duc."

I burst into tears. That was one of the few times in my life that I reacted to anything immediately, and maybe it was because of the long trip and everything. I sat down at one of the tables. "But it can't be. Do you mean to say this is the whole place? Have I come to Paris to entertain in a bar about the size of a booth at Connie's Inn? I had a twelve-piece band backing me up in New York."

I might have gone on and said something I would have regretted later if a handsome young Negro busboy hadn't come out of the kitchen just then. He smiled and said, "You need something to eat." He took me by the arm and led me back to the kitchen and gave me some food. He said I would like Paris and the Grand Duc. I don't remember what he called himself.

Years later Carl Van Vechten was in my place and he said, "Bricky, have you any of Langston Hughes's books?" I said no, but I'd like to have some. And Carl said, "You know who Hughes is, don't you Bricky?" And I said, "No, only by reading about him." He said, "Langston Hughes was that colored boy that was working here when you came." I said, "What?"

I didn't know, the waiters didn't know, nobody knew who he was. The first trip I made back to the States was years and years later, and I called him up as soon as I got in town. "You dirty dog!" I said. I'd written him, though—I'd found out where he was living in the meantime.

The Jamersons, who owned the club, were nice to me, too. He was a small-time gangster from an important French family. His family connections were so good that he didn't need to be a big-time gangster.

I calmed down, and Gene took me back to the hotel. It was Tuesday, and I decided that I'd start work on Thursday. That sounded good, because I'd be opening at the beginning of the Paris weekend.

The next two nights Gene took me out to see Paris, and I learned something about the nightlife. After the sun went down, Paris did become the City of Light, and Montmartre changed from a sleepy little village to a jumpin' hot town.

The Moulin Rouge was tops among the big places. Casanova was a popular little spot. Maxim's had faded during World War I and hadn't been able to recapture its great name. As a matter of fact, Maxim's stayed in the doldrums until after World War II, which shows how fickle the restaurant business can be. There were dozens of other clubs in Montmartre. Most of them featured jazz. Even the smallest clubs were classy. The hostesses were beautifully dressed—no bummy girls hanging around. The patrons dressed to the hilt and wore their chic clothes with the ease of people accustomed to finery. Most of them were French.

The few white Americans I saw were very rich—you had to be rich to travel to Paris in those days—and it took only the two nights to see just about every Negro American in Paris. Opal Cooper, Sammy and

Harvey White, Charlie "Dixie" Lewis, Bobby Jones, and maybe ten other Negro musicians were the only Negro men in Paris when I got there. They all wore tuxedos and looked so handsome. Some of them had wives, but they weren't in the business. After Florence, I was the second Negro female entertainer to arrive.

Of course, there were a lot of Negroes from Guadeloupe and other French colonies, but they were French. There was no American Negro colony then, like there is now, with all those blues singers.

I got very drunk the first night, on more champagne, which seemed to be the only thing the French drank. The next morning I met the French language head-on. I wanted ice, and I couldn't seem to make anyone understand me. Finally, a couple of American entertainers who saw me in the lobby helped me out. I blame the hangover for the trouble, because afterward I never had any trouble communicating. I picked up words and phrases and began speaking my own brand of French. It paid off years later by inspiring a whole set of funny and popular songs in my repertoire.

After two nights of hitting the Montmartre clubs, I felt better about the smallness of Le Grand Duc. Plenty of other clubs were just as small. The patrons packed into them and nobody seemed to mind. Anyway, I didn't have to depend on tips. My contract called for me to be paid seventy-five dollars a week, and I would repay the hundred advanced to me for my ship passage.

My opening night at Le Grand Duc is best forgotten. Oh, the trimmings were there all right. My name up in lights. One side of the triangular sign said, ADA SMITH ENTERTAINS! The other side said, BRICK-TOP. Gene and the Jamersons sent me flowers. The waiters and the kitchen help wished me well. I arrived early to rehearse with the piano player and began the long wait until after midnight when the Montmartre clubs came to life.

Well, there may have been plenty of life in the other clubs, but there was exactly none at Le Grand Duc. *Nobody* came in for hours. In the small hours of the morning, after everything else had closed down, the Negro musicians wandered in. They were boys I'd met the two nights before, and they came to help me look good and feel good. Some of them had another motive. American Negro women were scarce in Paris, and most of the boys hadn't been to bed with someone of their own complexion since leaving the States. I was twenty-nine, but still looked nineteen, and that had something to do with all the champagne they drank and the attention I got. They weren't just welcoming me, they were trying to make me.

On Friday night I doubled over in pain. My side felt as if it were going to burst. Gene bustled me into a taxi and headed for the nearest pharmacy. Pharmacists were almost like doctors there. After he heard my symptoms, the pharmacist said, "This young lady had better see a doctor right away."

Another taxi. More minutes of agony. In the doctor's office I learned that I had acute appendicitis. He told Gene, "If this woman isn't operated on immediately, she'll be dead in twenty-four hours." Gene translated for me and I nodded to say, "Go ahead."

When Gene told the doctor to go ahead, the man said it wouldn't be possible until Monday. Gene lost his temper. He raised the roof, hollering that as a flyer he'd done so much for France and now he wanted something done for his countrywoman. He ended up in tears. I wish I could have enjoyed the performance more. The doctor gave in and scheduled the operation for Sunday. We were now well into Saturday morning.

An appendectomy usually lasts fifteen mintes, but mine took forty-five. My appendix had grown to my intestine, and when they cut it out, there was a bone about the size of my thumb in there. They said it was a pig foot! Anyhow, it came right out.

Later I asked Gene what he'd said to make the doctor change his mind. All he'd done was tell the doctor he'd kill him if he didn't do the operation real quick.

Gene wanted to know what I'd thought about in the hours between entering the hospital and the operation. I showed him two letters I'd written, one to my mother, telling her about the operation, and one to Gene, asking him to ship my body home if anything happened. Gene shook his head. "What a cold-blooded girl!"

I went back to work at Le Grand Duc, and it turned out to be a fine place in which to recuperate. The club stayed as quiet as on my opening night. They didn't do any advertising in those days—no ads in the paper, no leaflets or anything—it was all by word of mouth. The play in that part of Montmartre was still going to Florence Jones, who had been at Le Grand Duc before me. She'd moved down the street to a place called Mitchell's, run by Louis Mitchell, a singer and drummer who had come to Europe with Vernon and Irene Castle. In Paris he had worked as a musician until he'd gotten hold of the place he was running.

Florence's husband, Palmer, had been the one to suggest me to the Jamersons because, he'd said, she needed the competition, but I'm not sure who was really bothering who in the Jones family.

Florence was a little woman with lovely brown skin, not pretty, but striking in her beautiful clothes. She was a wonderful dresser, and I once asked her why she paid so much attention to clothes. She answered simply, "Because my husband fools around quite a bit and when he comes home I have to look pretty and chic."

Florence and Louis Mitchell were involved in a long-running argument about why the place had not been named for her. She could have saved her breath, because I was doing a good job of steering customers her way. Night after night I was alone at Le Grand Duc when people would come in and ask, "Where's Florence?" I'd say, "She's down the street," and they'd duck out, saying, "We'll drop in sometime to hear you." Only a handful ever did.

I wasn't jealous of Florence. She'd been in Paris before me. She had attracted a loyal following. However, I wondered why the Jamersons kept paying me. There was nothing in my contract about how long I was supposed to stay. Of course, the overhead on the place was very low. Just a few customers running up a fair-sized bill once a week could keep it open.

I kept on working. My piano players changed a lot, because there were so few good ones in Paris that those who could play for me could earn more elsewhere. I never gave anything less than my best. If only one man stood at the bar, I entertained as if the place was full. I kept telling myself that I was learning, and that when people did start to come to hear me I'd be ready.

I was learning other things in Paris. How to dress, for instance. There was nothing to be ashamed of in the wardrobe I'd brought from America, but I could see a difference between my appearance and Florence's. An old friend, pianist Kid Cole, took me in hand and said bluntly, "Brick, you've got to get some clothes." I protested that I had clothes. "No, no," he said, "not those things you're wearing. You're in Paris now. I'll send my girlfriend over and she'll take you shopping." When I stepped into those Paris gowns, I understood what Kid was talking about. They bring assurance to a woman, and on the floor I found new poise and confidence.

Le Grand Duc closed for the month of August, as did everything else. Nobody would be caught dead in Paris in August. We didn't have tourists then, like they do now. I spent the month traveling in Spain with a group of musicians, where I fell in love with the bullfights. In the years that followed, I went back to Spain as often as I could.

Fall found me back at Le Grand Duc, and since it appeared that I would be staying in Paris for a while, I moved out of the hotel and got an apartment at 36 Rue Pigalle, right down the street from the club. It was the first of many apartments I would have in Paris.

They were all furnished. Furnished apartments and furnished homes were the big thing in Europe in those days. You could have any kind of place that you wanted—deluxe, with antiques and all that, or just a flat where you could sleep and cook food and keep your things. I'd always wanted to have a home of my own. When I was a little girl, Mama said, I was always playing house. So I got myself a nice furnished apartment—not one of those with antiques or anything, but a place I could really call my own.

Business at Le Grand Duc hadn't changed much since the spring of 1924. I was still having trouble with pianists. They came and they went until the spring of 1925, when I tried out a new combination, the Jackson Brothers. They were Negro boys—one a drummer, the other something of a piano player. They took club work more seriously than the others, and soon the boy at the piano knew what he was doing. I prayed he wouldn't fly away, and he didn't. The Jacksons stayed with me for about a year.

That spring of 1925, was warmer than the usual Paris spring, and I'll always be grateful for that. One night I was waiting for customers as usual when a man came in and sat down at the bar. He looked tired. The Jacksons and I went to work as if twenty people had come in to be entertained. After the first set a waiter told me the man at the bar wanted to meet me.

I crossed the room and introduced myself. He was smiling, and the smile never left his face as he talked. The first thing he said was, "Are you colored?" I said yes. He said, "I didn't know there was another colored girl in Paris. We only know Florence Jones down the street, and that's usually where we go. Tonight it was awfully warm and crowded, so I came outside to get some air. Then I saw Le Grand Duc and came in. It hasn't changed much."

I started to say that the only difference was that there were no customers, but thought better of it. He wanted to know how long I'd been in Paris. "About a year," I said. Then he said, "Do you know my wife, Fannie Ward?"

I said I didn't even know *him*.

Still smiling, he said, "I'm Jack Dean and my wife is Fannie Ward. I'm going to bring her to see you tomorrow." Then he ordered another drink, finished it, and, still smiling, left.

If I hadn't met Fannie Ward, I certainly knew who she was. Fannie Ward had been a stage and screen star and now was rich and owned a collection of fabulous jewels which she loved to wear in public. At the time, Fannie and Elsa Maxwell were in a neck-and-neck race to see who could outdo the other as the most popular hostess in Paris.

The next night I went to work hoping that Jack Dean would come with Fannie Ward as he'd said he would, but I was trying to be prepared not to be disappointed if he didn't. I made myself sit with my back to the door between sets.

I was sitting with Tony Mitchell, Louis's wife, during one break. It wasn't surprising to find the wife of a rival club owner at Le Grand Duc. It was typical of Montmartre. Although there were jealousies sometimes, we dropped in on each other's clubs and helped the other fellow out when he ran low on champagne. Tony saw Fannie Ward come in with a bunch of people, and she grabbed my wrist. "Bricky, if you can make this woman like you, you're made. She can really fill up this place."

I went out on the floor and got to work, and I was good. I hadn't been finished long when a waiter told me I'd been invited to join Fannie Ward's party. Jack, that grin still on his face, introduced me to Fannie and their guests.

Fannie was a tiny thing, blond, blond, blond. She was covered with jewels—her arms from wrist to elbow were heavy with diamonds. She was quite a contrast to Jack, who was a bit on the plump side, with a double chin. Still, they looked alike in an odd sort of way. Just like Jack, Fannie had a strange, fixed smile.

Fannie spoke right up. "You're a wonderful performer. I didn't know there was another colored girl in town until Jack told me." I smiled a thank-you. Then Fannie's tone changed. She challenged me, "Can you stand success?"

Much as I wanted it, I wasn't going to get drawn into any game. "Nothing excites me," I said.

Fannie didn't know quite what to make of that. "Florence Jones got excited," she said.

I answered, "Her name is Florence. My name is Bricktop."

I got a feeling that it didn't matter what I said. Fannie had her mind made up. "Florence needs a lesson. She's too spoiled. I'm going to pack this place for you."

I told her I'd be grateful, and we chatted a bit. Then the party left. I went back to Tony Mitchell, wanted to know about those perpetual grins on Jack's and Fannie's faces.

Plastic surgery, Tony explained. It wasn't really new, but people were talking about it now more openly than before. Fannie had wanted to have it, but Jack wouldn't permit it until it had been tried out on him first. In spite of the eternal grin that had appeared on Jack's face, Fannie had considered the operation successful and had had it done on herself. She'd come out with her own grin. Those grins set you back a bit, but after a while you got used to them.

Fannie never won her battle with Elsa Maxwell to be the top hostess. Fannie's set were people on the fringe and theatrical personalities. However, her influence was considerable, and she did what she promised: she packed Le Grand Duc.

The next night Fannie and Jack and about a dozen of their friends arrived in a fleet of taxis. They were all dressed in their elegant best, and the room looked wonderful with them in it. I sang set after set, with the Jackson Brothers accompanying me, and we just bathed in the rounds of applause. The receipts, when they were tallied in the morning, looked pretty good, too. Fannie and Jack came back night after night with their friends, and some of their friends got into the habit of coming by even without Jack and Fannie. ADA SMITH disappeared from her side of the sign over Le Grand Duc, and BRICKTOP took over.

Fred and Adele Astaire used to come in. So did Clifton Webb and Mary Hay. They'd get out on the floor and dance the routines they'd be doing on Broadway the following year, in *Sunny* or *Treasure Girl.* I think Jimmy Walker, the mayor of New York, came in around that time, too, and there were probably a lot of other people whose names should have impressed me, but I was too busy entertaining, trying to make sure they'd come back.

Fannie Ward and her friends, and the buzz they started to make around town, combined to make a big change in the fortunes of Le Grand Duc. There was a good-sized crowd every night now. George Jamerson raised my salary to a hundred dollars a week and gave me a percentage on each bottle of champagne sold.

I was beginning to consider Paris my home. Light housekeeping in my apartment brought me in touch with the simple French people— shopkeepers, flower sellers, pharmacists. I liked them, and they liked me. They laughed at my French, but they did so in a warm, friendly way. I started realizing that even the simple people had elegance and chic. A shopgirl could put on any sort of gown, draw a belt tight or loosen it, and look stunning.

Then I started to be recognized on the street. Café entertainers seldom made the newspapers at that time, but items about me started to creep into the French and English-language newspapers. One young man, who was studying *haute couture* in Paris and writing for *Vogue* at the same time, wrote, "Bricktop is a pale, unspoiled beauty who sings and dances like a star. She's young and new to Paris." He would later become the famous designer Mainbocher.

I worked hard at my still-modest success. I stood at the door and shook hands with the customers as they entered. That was the custom in those days. It was also the custom to shake hands with the patrons as they left, and usually, when the patron's hand left yours, you'd find a nice tip in your palm.

Some of the customers started inviting me to join them at their tables between sets. I thought the friendly thing to do was to accept, but gradually I realized that I was getting lots of champagne but fewer tips. Louis Mitchell heard me complaining one day and advised me, "When you sit too long drinking with people, you get too intimate. Then they're embarrassed about giving you a tip. It's all right to sit down and have a drink, but excuse yourself as soon as possible and say you have to get back to the door. And even at the door, be careful. Never raise your hand to shake a customer's, let him raise his hand first."

I never forgot Mitchell's advice. Tips were *it*—the butter on the bread, the rent on the room, the new dress. After World War II, things changed. It was expected that you would sit with the clients. I couldn't object if the entertainers did, since I was doing it, but I told them to keep their visits brief. I didn't want a customer arguing with me about a bill with, say, eight drinks and then find that half of them had been ordered by the entertainers. It looked too much like a hustle.

Toward the end of the 1925 season Fannie Ward and Jack Dean and their friends gradually drifted away. They spent only the spring in Paris. In the summertime they went to Biarritz, Deauville, Venice. Business dropped off drastically at Le Grand Duc, and when we reopened in the fall of 1925, it didn't get much better. A few of Fannie's friends reappeared, but it wasn't the theatrical crowd that kept me going during that period. In fact, there were nights when we'd play to a single customer, like in the old days. What made the difference was that the Montparnasse crowd of writers and artists discovered Le Grand Duc, led by F. Scott Fitzgerald.

Paris in the twenties was the artistic capital of the world. I was in Harlem in the 1920s. I saw the excitement of the Renaissance there, but Paris was even more exciting. The whole city was like a great big ongoing celebration. World War I had been all too real to the French. Now that it was over, they wanted to forget all that heartache. They wanted to party and dance. The city was like a magnet to goodtime-loving people from all over the world.

A lot of these people were rich Americans. They knew how to get the most value out of their dollar, which is why they were rich in the first place. In Paris after the war the dollar was the best kind of money to have. My hundred-dollar-a-week salary at Le Grand Duc translated into something like two-thousand francs. Just a few years earlier it would have been only about five-hundred francs. And I was just a poor working girl. Imagine what the French inflation did for an American millionaire.

The nice thing about a lot of these American millionaires was that they didn't just bring over their money. They also brought over their interest in helping young writers and artists. Fannie Ward helped a lot of young people. So did Robert McAlmon and, later, Peggy Guggenheim.

There were a lot of young, talented people around to be helped. Paris was filled with so many young people who didn't have a dime. They all clung together at the Dôme or the Sélect, the two big places in Montparnasse—on the sidewalk in the summer, indoors in the winter. We entertainers joined them when we were through work. A lot of people who had money were there, too. I can't tell you how many people there were who wanted to write or paint or perform, and who had the money but not the talent—and then on the other side were all those people who had the talent but no money. The beautiful thing was that the rich ones took care of the poor ones. Scott Fitzgerald later wrote that in those days in Paris it didn't matter if you were broke, because there was so much money all around you.

Of course, by that time Scott was already successful and had plenty of money. The way he threw it around, he was naturally the star of the Paris art scene. Money burned in his pocket. When he'd go out for an evening, he'd stuff his pockets with bills. It's lucky he lived in a time when mugging wasn't the nighttime sport it is today. He would usually stay out partying until all that money was spent.

Scott and his wife, Zelda, were a beautiful, fun-loving couple. They came into Le Grand Duc one night in the fall of 1925 with Dwight Wiman and his wife, Steve. The Wimans were regulars at Le Grand Duc, friends of Fannie Ward. After that first night, so were Scott and Zelda.

Scott was almost thirty, but he acted like a big, overgrown kid. Their baby, Scottie, had been born, and I couldn't believe Zelda was a mother. She was a wisp of a girl, feather-slight, with lovely hair and very white skin. She was very outgoing, but next to Scott she seemed almost retiring. He was so mischievous, he'd take over the whole place.

It was impossible not to like him. He was a little boy in a man's body.

He hadn't grown up and he didn't intend to, and I liked that. He brought out the mothering instinct in me.

When Scott got drunk, he was never mean or malicious. He just got more playful. He'd deliberately do things to get people excited or annoyed, but not bad, bad things. I wouldn't allow that in the club, and he respected me too much to do anything in Le Grand Duc. However, there were plenty of times when I helped him out of situations he got into outside the club.

I'll never forget the night—actually the early morning—when the doorman came in and said, "Madame, Mr. Fitzgerald is outside with two gendarmes."

Outside, I found Scott dripping wet, and two angry and confused policemen. One asked, "Do you know this man?" I said I did. "Well, you can have him."

I took him off their hands. He'd been at the Lido, he said. The Lido, on the Champs-Elysées, was an arcade-type building with a fountain in the middle. In those days it was famous for its tea dances. Scott and Zelda had been there and he'd decided to jump into the fountain. "Zelda," he said, "being a dutiful wife, jumped in, too."

When the police had arrived, Zelda had managed to get away, but they'd taken Scott and were going to lock him up, when he said, "You can't lock me up. I'm a friend of Madame Bricktop."

I was surprised that I carried so much weight with the police, but I did know a few gendarmes personally, and they all knew who I was. The ones who arrested Scott didn't believe him, but they agreed to drive him over to Le Grand Duc.

After they left him, Scott wanted to get inside. I said, "Honey, you can't come in like this."

"Just for one drink?"

"No, you'll make a puddle."

Scott wasn't going to leave without a drink, so I sent the doorman to fetch a bottle of champagne, and there we stood outside on the sidewalk, drinking champagne. I managed to convince him that he would catch a cold if he didn't go home and change. I called a taxi and put him in it. He wanted me to go with him. I said no. Pouting like a baby, he rode off.

In a few minutes the doorman came to me again. Scott was back, this time in the custody of a furious taxi driver. Anyone who has ever visited Paris knows there's no fury like that born in the breast of a Parisian cabbie. Scott had kicked out every window in the cab.

That was one time I was grateful that Scott carried all that money around with him. I made him dig into his pockets and helped him count out enough francs to buy the whole taxi. Luckily, the fellow simmered down. Then Scott turned to me and said, "See, Brick, I'm not responsible. I was just trying to teach you a lesson. You've got to take me home."

I don't know how many times I did take him home. Night after night I said to him, "Scott, you've had enough to drink. Go home." The answer was always the same: "Brick, I'll go home if you take me home."

Scott and Zelda lived in a house out in Neuilly and there I was in Montmartre. Yet I'd get in a taxi and take him home. The ride took every bit of fifteen minutes, but as soon as we got there, Scott would say, "Brick, let's go back and have another bottle."

Sometimes I made the trip three and four times a week, often back and forth in the same night. The other regular patrons noticed. They wanted me to take *them* home, too. I said no to that one. One spoiled youngster on my hands was enough.

The reason I got saddled with taking him home so often was that Zelda didn't stay out as late as he did. They'd come into the club together, but pretty soon she'd go home, just walk out and get into a taxi. Of course, in those days you were as safe on the streets as you would be in your mother's arms. Scott was never going to go when you wanted him to go. She'd just say, "Well, I'm going," and he'd turn around to look and Zelda would be gone.

She had Scottie at home, of course, but that wasn't the reason she went home early. In Paris in those days, every time you turned around, there was a maid there to do this and a maid to do that. And then the maid had *her* maid.

Zelda was just quieter. But she wasn't dull. She tried to keep up with him, but I always believed that Scott knew that Zelda was a little bit off. Later on, people said that Scott neglected Zelda. If he did, I never saw it, and I knew them quite well. Theirs was one of the few homes I ever visited. It was a nice, comfortable house, well constructed. No antiques or anything like that. Scott was always a gentleman with Zelda.

A lot of negative myths have grown up about Scott. I remember the time, about three or four years ago, when I was working here in New York. I wasn't going to go to the club that night—I don't remember why, arthritis attack or something—but my pianist and partner, Hugh Shannon, called me up and said, "Brick, you gotta come to work tonight. Scottie Fitzgerald is coming." And I said, "Oh, yeah."

When I walked through the door of the club, she looked at me and I looked at her and we both burst into tears, and she said, "Bricky, tell these people that my Daddy couldn't have been drunk, drunk, drunk *all* the time, or else he could never have written the wonderful things that he wrote."

And I said, "No, no, no, he was just like everybody else. A lot of times Scott was trying to make people think he was drunk to get away with his foolishness."

Poor Scott. He came back to Paris in 1928 after his first trip to Hollywood to visit his old stomping grounds. He came back to my place. He wrote about it in "Babylon Revisited," calling Bricktop's the place where he had spent "so much time and so much money."

I was there the night he came in. I recognized him immediately, and, oh, I ran and grabbed him and told him, "Mr. Fitzgerald, come on in." He was hanging back because he was broke in those days, and I said, "No, *you come in here*, yes indeedy." I'm not demonstrative, but I hugged him so tight. But I called him Mr. Fitzgerald. I couldn't have put it too familiarly, because he was down and out and that would only have put him down deeper. That was the only time I ever saw him again.

I loved Scott Fitzgerald. He was so wonderful. He often said, "My greatest claim to fame is that I discovered Bricktop before Cole Porter."

After Scott Fitzgerald started calling Le Grand Duc his "home away from home," others from the Montparnasse crowd began coming in. Hemingway was one of them. He came in quite often. A lot of people were raving about him, but I never took to him. I wasn't the only one. He just wanted to bring people down, and he had a way of doing it, and he was liable to punch you at the same time. He didn't do it in Le Grand Duc—I had a way of saying, "You can't start a fight in here, I'm a girl" —but I didn't like the way he baited people, especially Scott.

Louis Bromfield was one of my favorites. Picasso used to come in, too. He was in the first contingent of the Montparnasse crowd. I didn't know he was going to become one of the greatest artists in the world. He was just another customer to me. What did I know then? It's hard for people to understand, but most of these people weren't great then. Even if they were, I didn't get excited. I always looked at people as just people. Man Ray and his girlfriend, Kiki, were regulars. His paintings in those days were advanced art, or whatever they called it, but he was a lovely person. He was scuffling and struggling in those days, too.

After the Cole Porter crowd started coming in, the Montparnasse crowd just faded away. Montparnasse and St. Germain didn't mix.

COLE PORTER...
AND
JOSEPHINE BAKER

ONE MORNING in the late fall or early winter of 1925 a slight, immaculately dressed man came in, sat down at one of the tables, and ordered a plate of corned-beef hash with a poached egg on top and a bottle of wine. By morning I mean between three a.m. and six a.m.—we stayed open after the other clubs closed and got quite a few customers during those hours. We only served three things at that time of day— corned-beef hash with a poached egg, creamed chicken on toast, or a club sandwich—but we served them courtesy of the house.

I got up to sing and could sense that the man was watching and listening with more than ordinary interest. He applauded when I finished the set. I bowed and took up my usual position at the door. He finished eating and got up to leave. Just then Buddy Gilmore came through the door. Buddy was a drummer who'd come to Paris with Vernon and Irene

Castle and stayed to form his own group. He grabbed the stranger and started hugging him.

"Who was that?" I asked Buddy later.

"That was Cole Porter," he said.

"Oh, my God!" I said. "I've just been singing one of his songs!"

The normally unexcitable me was suddenly shaken. It's one thing to take someone like Fannie Ward in stride. It's quite another to find out you've just performed in front of a giant-sized talent like Cole Porter— and performed one of his own songs! Everyone in Paris knew that Cole was funny about people singing his songs. If a singer didn't do it just right, Cole wouldn't embarrass him or her, but he'd leave quickly—and that would be the most embarrassing situation imaginable for the singer. I was worrying about what I'd done to "I'm in Love Again," the Porter song I'd been singing, when it occurred to me that he *hadn't* left. In fact, he'd applauded. I was to find out that he was interested in me for other reasons.

Cole came back the very next night. I was excited. It meant he liked me. I was also nervous, because now I knew who he was. I didn't chance singing another one of his songs.

Pretty soon he sent for me. I thought he was going to ask me to sing something, but he'd heard me sing. What he wanted to know was, could I dance? I couldn't believe it when he asked, "Can you dance the Charleston?"

The Charleston hadn't been introduced to Europe yet. Songs and dances didn't travel as fast then as they do today. They also lived a lot longer. I'd learned the Charleston in New York, and I said, "Sure can." I launched into a quick rendition.

When I finished, Cole thanked me and told me I had "talking feet and legs." I laughed. He laughed, too, and said he would see me again.

A couple of nights later he came back, this time with Elsa Maxwell and four or five other people. Again he sent for me and asked me to dance the Charleston. Elsa loved it. She clapped and shrieked. That's the way she was. If anything pleased her, her enthusiasm was boundless. She was just as intense about her dislikes. Luckily, I was on the right side of Elsa's enthusiasm. Me and the Charleston were something new for her to play with. I was in.

101

Once I had Elsa's stamp of approval, Cole got around to telling me why he was so interested. "I'm going to give Charleston cocktail parties at my house two or three times a week, and you're going to teach everyone how to dance the Charleston."

I didn't have to think twice. I accepted right away. I didn't know how much I was going to be paid or who I was going to teach. It didn't matter. If Cole Porter had asked me, I would have taught all of Paris to do the Charleston for nothing.

At the agreed-upon time on the agreed-upon date, I arrived at Cole's house at 13 Rue Monsieur. The house itself was already a legend. It didn't look like much from the outside—in fact, it looked as if it might come tumbling down any minute—but inside it was spectacular. Cole's wife, Linda, was the decorator. There were zebra skins on the floors and on some of the walls. The chairs were painted red and upholstered in white kid. There was even a room with platinum wallpaper.

The house contained all the *objets d'art* that the Porters had collected. The chandeliers were magnificent. The whole place was like a palace, and it took my breath away. Later on I learned that there was one small room, close to the front door, that didn't look at all as if it belonged in a palace. It looked more like a monk's cell. That was where Cole did most of his composing.

I was prepared to find that the Porters were living in a palace. I wasn't prepared to find royalty there. However, there was the Aga Khan, eager to learn the Charleston, along with Elsa, of course, and about fifty other VIP's. I was about to become the dance teacher to the most elegant members of the international set.

I have to give the Charleston the credit it deserves for launching me on my career as a saloonkeeper. It was a great dance. You could do it by yourself. You were never embarrassed about having to keep up with a partner. All you had to do was to keep time, and if you couldn't, who knew the difference? It wasn't so different from the dances that were popular before the disco craze. And it was a fast dance. It appealed to people who led fast lives. It caught on and I caught on, Cole Porter standing right there behind me and never leaving me until I became Bricktop, the one and only.

* * *

That afternoon of Cole's first Charleston party, I must have been a success, because people started coming to Le Grand Duc to see more Charleston. A lot of people were too shy to dance with the group at Cole's. I started teaching them at the club, but some were too shy even for that. They asked me to give private lessons. They sent their cars for me. I charged ten dollars a lesson. Sometimes I gave three or four lessons a day.

The shyest would-be Charleston dancer was the Aga Khan, and who wouldn't be, at over three hundred pounds? He was a delightful man with a very dry wit. Every time one of his horses won the English Derby, he'd tell the English, "I know you hate to see this nigger win the Derby, but I have the best horses." And he did, right up until Nijinsky. He didn't drink because of his religion, but he entertained lavishly his friends who did. He also hit all the night spots. He'd come into Le Grand Duc and bow very low and kiss my hand. "How does it feel to have royalty kiss this little freckled hand of yours?" he'd ask. I had a stock answer: "I don't feel anything. Royalty? They're only people." That always tickled him.

He never managed to ask me personally for Charleston lessons. The Marquise de Polignac was the one who told me that the Aga wanted to learn the Charleston. Would I teach him? I was really flattered then. Teaching a three-hundred-pound man would have been a challenge. I was really sorry when he backed out of the lessons. He sent his driver with a very nice note calling the appointment off.

One of my first private pupils was Dolly O'Brien, a tall, handsome society woman who always wore white and lots of diamonds. She was once linked with Clark Gable. Too bad that relationship was only rumors. Her husband, Jay, was such a cracker that he said he resented seeing a Negro man in a smoking jacket.

One of my more intriguing Charleston pupils was a famous ballerina at the Paris Opera. There she was, a prima ballerina, and she wanted to learn how to do the Charleston!

Through the Charleston lessons I began to meet the top hosts and hostesses of Paris. This was a time when there were big, big parties. The best party-givers I knew were Cole; Elsa Maxwell; Dolly O'Brien and her cracker husband; Arturo Lopez, the Chilean multimillionaire;

103

the Rothschilds; Lady Mendl; Daisy Fellowes; Mrs. George Dixon; and Consuelo Vanderbilt, who had married the Duke of Marlborough. There were many others, of course, but these were the people I knew personally.

There were so many parties in those days in Paris—everything from garden affairs to lavish costume balls to formal dinners. The very exclusive dinners were for ten to fifty guests. At a buffet affair there might be as many as five-hundred guests. In between, there were the big sit-down dinners for as many as a hundred and fifty people. The largest spring garden parties and winter balls had three hundred to five hundred people. I have no idea how expensive these parties were. Probably the hosts and hostesses didn't even know. Money was no object. I don't think those affairs could ever be reproduced today except by a government or one of those giant corporations.

When I was asked to do a party, we didn't usually discuss terms. Our fees were understood. I was paid fifty dollars for a party, and could expect another fifty or so as a tip. The piano player got twenty-five, and when I brought a combo along, the fee could be as high as three hundred dollars. I never stooped to negotiate with a host or hostess. No high-class woman ever lays down a price.

One of the first parties I did was given by Elsa Maxwell at the Ritz. I brought along the Three Eddys, a team of dancers who did a comedy act. Like many entertainers of the time, Negro and white, they blackened their faces with burnt cork, wore white gloves and big eyeglasses. It was a great party, and the Three Eddys thought they'd gone over well.

That night, however, Elsa came over to the club to say, "Brick, don't use the Three Eddys again."

My first thought was that they'd misbehaved. "Well, not exactly," said Elsa. "But when they saw all the men kissing women's hands, they must have decided that was the thing to do. About half a dozen women had their hands smeared with burnt cork. And, Brick, if you don't know how hard that is to clean off, I do. I used to wear cork in vaudeville."

I did many other parties for Elsa, and we kept in touch for years. I never got too close to Elsa, though. With her, the best thing to do was to be cordial. You could stay that way for a long time. I suppose that's why we remained casual friends and I never found myself on the wrong end of her sharp, cutting words. I could have gotten into a feud with her if I'd called her on her claim that she was responsible for my success. I could have reminded her that she took me up simply because Cole was interested. I decided it wasn't worth the trouble, however. She could be a formidable enemy.

In another time Elsa could never have made it the way she did. She was unique in a unique era. She came from nowhere and ended up on top because she managed to push herself forward without seeming brassy. That took real skill. She was a wonderful party-giver, a born hostess, a great organizer. She knew how to run things and how to give service. She also had a great imagination, and you needed that if you were going to be a top party-giver.

Hostesses stayed up all night dreaming up new party ideas. The Porters gave great affairs. For one party at the Ritz he wrote a Charleston song. The words were strung across the room so everybody could sing along with me: "A dark-eyed lady, not so shady, started winking her eye and saying Charleston . . ." Then we went into the dance.

You didn't go out just one or two nights a week in those days. You went out every night. If it wasn't to a party, it was to the opera or the theater or the Folies-Bergère, and afterward you went to one of the Montmartre clubs. Parties began at eleven, or even at midnight. I sometimes left the club to do a party, came back, and more often than not found the whole party moving into the club in the early hours of the morning. If I'd had the stamina, I could have been at a party every night.

I did a lot of parties for Lady Mendl around that time. She was the former Elsie de Wolfe and she still used her maiden name for her decorating business. An American, she had married Sir Charles Mendl, who was with the British embassy, in March 1926. A short woman with gray-white hair, she was charming and vivacious. You always knew when she was in a room. The Mendls lived in a beautiful villa in Versailles with big, formal gardens, and there they entertained all the notables of both the American and British colonies, not to mention just about every other notable in Paris.

The first time I did a party for Lady Mendl, she sent a Rolls Royce for me. The whole of Montmartre went out of its mind—"There's a Rolls Royce standing down in front of Madame Bricktop's!" I felt like a million. Very seldom after that did Lady Mendl give a party when I wasn't present as a guest or an entertainer.

At Lady Mendl's parties, and at the others, too, entertainers were treated like guests. That may sound strange to even mention today, because today's society (or what's left of it) lionizes entertainers. Back then, however, when I was going through the front doors of the most elegant homes in Paris, entertainers working private affairs in America went in the back door and ate in a separate room from the guests.

I remember a story about the tenor John McCormack. He was invited to a party given by some Long Island socialite, and after he accepted, she said, "You know, Mr. McCormack, you're the first theatrical person we've ever invited. You'll sing, of course." He told her he'd be glad to. He'd even go through the back entrance and eat in the kitchen. And then he'd bill her for his usual concert fee.

That never happened in Paris. Even though we were being paid, we ate and drank at the buffet and mingled with the other guests. It was taken for granted that we knew how to behave ourselves. After I started giving dancing lessons and entertaining at parties, I began receiving personal invitations. I turned most of them down.

That may sound strange. Here I was, two years in Paris, thousands of miles away from home, and not caring too much about making a lot of friends. Being alone never bothered me. It still doesn't.

I had plenty of opportunities for friendships—with men and women. I had some romantic involvements, and I could have had romantic involvements with women, but I never liked women. Consequently, I was never big on the orgies that some people had. You were either in on them or you weren't. I didn't play. Even meeting a bunch of other women for lunch wasn't my disposition.

I didn't even have too many friendships that weren't romantic. People would ask me to join them for lunch down at the Ritz, or to come to some party or other, but it was a rule with me then, and it still is: never get too familiar with clients. Besides, who wanted to get up and get dressed for lunch at the Ritz when you'd been working until five a.m. and had a party to do that night?

With Lady Mendl, things were a little different. She was like a god-mother to me. I often lunched at the villa, and there were times when I went to her for advice. She never failed to be wonderfully helpful.

There were a few others: Arturo Lopez, Billy Dee Leeds, producer Ray Goetz. I considered Cole and Linda Porter real friends.

However, I never tried to use my popularity as an entertainer to get me into "society." There's a story that I wanted to go to the Paris Opera Ball one year, felt left out of it, and Cole took me to it. That is the most untrue story. I was supposed to have got there and said, "Oh, I don't belong here." I have never thought that in my life. I'm not really social. I like people, but I like them in Bricktop's. I like them in an intimate setting. I never went in for big balls, and I never would have asked any-body to take me to one—I don't care how big it was.

I didn't need people. I didn't then, and I don't now—but that doesn't mean I didn't respond to people who needed me. There was one little girl who needed me a lot in the early days: Josephine Baker.

Josephine came to Paris in the fall of 1925. She came with a whole bunch of American Negroes for a colored revue produced by André Devan called *La Revue Nègre*. By 1925 Paris was having its own version of the Harlem Renaissance. It was called *Le Tumulte Noir*. I may have benefitted from this great interest in Negro things, but Josephine be-came a star overnight.

Maude de Forrest was the original star of the revue, but Maude's voice was tricky. It could fail completely without a moment's warning. On the ship to Paris, Josephine was rehearsed secretly to take over from Maude, because the company was afraid Maude wouldn't make the important Paris opening. A hit in Paris opened the way to bookings all over the Continent.

Well, Maude's voice did fail, and Josephine Baker got her chance. She made her Paris debut wearing practically nothing, and the theater turned into a circus. Paris had never seen anything like Josephine. She was still a teenager, and the ovation scared her so that she ran off the stage.

Overnight, she was a star. Within a few nights after that, she was be-ing dressed by Paul Poiret—and, oh, how she could wear clothes, al-though her fame would rest a lot on her ability to perform without them.

107

Her reputation for performing nude too often overshadowed the fact that she was born to wear couturier styles, or the fact that she had a live, wonderful, natural talent.

Also overshadowed was the fact that she was still a kid, and she was one of the most vulnerable stars I've ever met. At the time, Negro female entertainers were still a rarity in Paris. Naturally, Josephine and I got together.

She was only about seventeen years old. She brought out the mother instinct in me, just as Scott Fitzgerald had. Only, Scott had a lot more going for him when I met him than Josephine had.

She hadn't had much schooling. She could hardly write her name and, suddenly, everyone wanted her autograph. I said, "Baby, get a stamp." I talked her into writing her name once, in the clearest and best script she could manage, and having it made into a rubber stamp. That saved her a lot of embarrassment.

She didn't know how to take care of nice things. She didn't know how to appreciate them. I arrived at her hotel room one day and found the floor covered with stacks of couturier clothes, mostly Poiret's. I'd been given couturier clothes, too, but I'd never piled them on the floor. I said, "Hang these dresses up, or have your maid do it." Josephine said, "But, Bricky, they're going to take them away tomorrow and bring me another pile." Everything was for the moment with Josephine. She couldn't see past today.

However, she was scared—and who wouldn't be? She was a star before she was even full grown. She could put on couturier clothes and not know what she was wearing—but she had sense enough to know she was in over her head.

I became her big sister. She'd come into Le Grand Duc and ask me about everything. She'd say, "Bricky, tell me what to do." She wouldn't go around the corner without asking my advice.

A big sister doesn't get far when she gives advice about men, however, and when Josephine needed advice the most, I couldn't do much good.

She used to come into Le Grand Duc with a fellow named Zito, a caricaturist who worked at Zelli's across the street. Zito wasn't much of a date, but there are always times when a woman in the spotlight doesn't have much choice. Many boys who might have asked her out were too shy, and too frightened by all the publicity she was getting. When a gal hits the top, it's taken for granted that she's being wined and dined by some rich, handsome guy—and maybe a different one every night. The Josephine legend supports that idea about her, even though everyone knew she mostly went around with Zito.

One night Zito was sick. He got his cousin Pepito to take Josephine around. It turned out to be a fateful night.

Pepito had just arrived from Rome. His real name was Giuseppe Abatino and he was working as a gigolo at Zelli's. He and the others preferred to call themselves "dance instructors." He was good-looking, in his late thirties, and it hadn't taken him long to figure out that there were a lot of lonely women with money in Paris. In no time at all he was calling himself Count Pepito de Abatino. I called him the no-account count.

The night Josephine showed up at Le Grand Duc with Pepito, I couldn't believe my eyes. I didn't hesitate to tell Josephine how I felt. "What are you doing with this bum? He can't even pay for a glass of beer." Josephine explained that Zito was sick, but I didn't like the looks of things. I knew what Pepito was.

Zito may have seen Josephine again, but it was never the same between them. Pepito took over. He flattered Josephine, wrote her love notes, followed her around like a puppy. But he was slick. He had a plan, and part of it was to cut Josephine off from her old friends.

Being a kid and not knowing any better, Josephine told Pepito what I'd said about him. He started steering her away from the club and me. He kept her away from all the blacks in Paris. Pretty soon Spencer Williams, the musician, was the only old pal still allowed around. I guess he didn't present any threat.

With Pepito's encouragement, Josephine opened her own club, Chez Joséphine, on the Rue Fontaine in December 1926. It was an immediate success. That Christmas they came into the club and Pepito showed me the platinum watch studded with diamonds that Josephine had just given him. It was exactly like the watch I'd just given my "man of the moment." I blew up. In front of Pepito, I lit into Josephine and told her what a fool she'd become.

For some time afterward, whenever we met on the street, I found myself saying hello to her back.

Pepito came to control more and more of Josephine's life. He put a kind of guard around her. You couldn't get near her. Pepito especially didn't want Josephine to have anything to do with Bricktop, because I'd told her what he was from the beginning.

He talked her into putting all of her money in his name, in case she was ever sued. I have to give him credit for what he did for Josephine, though. She wasn't a hit in her second Paris show, and without Pepito she might have become a nobody. Pepito turned out to have a sharp business know-how. He manipulated her back into stardom. At the same time, he practically put her through school. He saw that she learned to read and write and speak proper French. He educated her in music and art and the social graces. Josephine was a smart kid, though. She could have picked a lot of that up on her own, or from someone else who wasn't so interested in using her.

I didn't lose complete contact with Josephine. We saw each other every once in a while. Since she was always in the papers, I couldn't help knowing about the progress of her career. Pepito made her a star, internationally famous, but Josephine always remained what she was—a great, great actress—and she played it, and she lived in another world. She had to live in another world. How else can you take a shirtwaist and skirt and make it into a Paris gown overnight? But she acted as if she'd been born to that gown. There was never anything vulgar about Josephine. If there had been, I would have been the first one to see it.

I spent the summer of 1926 with Cole and Linda Porter in Venice. They had a palazzo overlooking the Grand Canal, and it was as huge and magnificently furnished as their house at 13 Rue Monsieur in Paris. All their friends were there, enjoying the usual large parties. However, something was missing: no Charleston lessons. So Cole said, "Why don't we send for Bricktop?"

It was typical of Cole to think up an idea one minute and act on it the next, and it was perfect timing as far as I was concerned. I was free and had never been to Venice. I knew Cole and Linda had made arrangements for Leslie Hutchinson's Negro band to play at their parties, and it helped that I'd worked with the boys several times.

When I arrived, I learned that I had another job to do besides give Charleston lessons. I was put in charge of staging for the annual benefit for the Tubercular Children of Italy. The benefit was organized by

Princess Jane di San Faustino, one of the first American women to marry into Italian nobility.

Princess Jane was a tall, white-haired woman who'd worn widow's weeds ever since her husband had died, but that didn't keep her from putting on the best show of the Venice season every year. It was probably the best because everyone involved was absolutely terrified of Princess Jane.

Normally, she was a perfectly charming woman, but when it was called for, she could be so nasty that she could frighten people half to death. It was the secret of how she got things done.

My job was to stage the dance numbers. My "chorus girls" were some of the top names in society. They were all good enough dancers, but, like all society people, they had their own notions about punctuality. They'd drift into rehearsal when they had the time, and I couldn't seem to get them all together at any one point. I complained to Princess Jane.

She said, "Cuss 'em out."

I told her, "I don't swear, and I never cuss out my clients."

That got a rare laugh from Princess Jane. "Okay," she said, "I'll do it for you." She did. My ladies started showing up on time.

The show was presented at the Excelsior Lido, and it was one of the most successful in the history of the charity ball. Elsa Maxwell wore a blond wig and a short dress and sang "I'm a Little Old Lido Lady." The chorus "girls" did their numbers beautifully. I closed out the show, with the chorus behind me, dancing the Charleston.

For me, however, the highlight of the show came before it was over. I was seated with the band when, suddenly, the lights went out. Then a single spotlight found me. Count Andrea Robilant emerged from the crowd, carrying a birthday cake. It was August 14, 1926, and it was my birthday.

I burst into tears. Before I knew it, everyone else seemed to be crying as well. One by one, the people in the audience wished me happy birthday. All the while Cole Porter beamed. "Well," he said, "at last something has gotten to her. Something has impressed Brick."

He had it right. That night in Venice way back in 1926 remains one of the most memorable moments of my life.

That's one reason why I came to regard the Porters as among my real friends. They were really interested in me. Bringing me to Venice was one way that Cole helped me to make my way as an entertainer, to create an identification with his set of people. There wasn't anything of the sponsor-protégé relationship in our friendship, however. He wasn't trying to groom me to sing his songs. My style was pretty well set—and it wasn't his. Of course, when it came to singing his songs, I appreciated the directions he gave, but you could count on one hand the number of Cole Porter songs I'd sing, especially when he was there. He never told me what not to sing, but I knew Cole Porter and I knew his songs, and I knew better than to sing some of them. He was very funny about his songs. I knew that even before I met him.

Cole Porter was interested in me, first, because I could dance. Later, I like to think, he was interested me as a person. He wanted me to be beautifully dressed. Whenever we went out together, he bought me gorgeous clothes. One time he bought me a set of silver-fox furs that I insisted made me look like a madame. I didn't wear them very often—I didn't feel I was the fur type.

Linda Porter was a great lady. When Cole first started doing things for me, she didn't try to put any blocks in the way. She was a Southern woman, and early on she asked me a question that was probably important to her. Would I rather be white than Negro? I answered, "I don't want to offend you, Mrs. Porter, but to be white and poor? Never!" She seemed satisfied with that answer.

A lot of people thought that Cole was a strange man—cold, indifferent, rude. But I didn't know that Cole Porter. He was shy, and shy people have problems—especially if they're prominent. He wasn't very good at dealing with hurly-burly newspapermen or with other people who weren't well mannered, as he was. If you were going to be pushy with Cole, you had to do it with flair, like Elsa Maxwell did. He couldn't stand plain snobs or social climbers, and, as I've said, he'd go out of his way not to be rude. He could have told off a lot of singers, but he preferred to leave by the back way.

Cole's shyness may have been one reason why he liked me. He admired how easily I got along with people, how I fitted in with his friends and still managed always to be myself. I don't care to speculate about what made Cole Porter tick. I only know he was a good friend to me— one of the best friends I've ever had.

BRICKTOP'S

IN THE FALL we all went back to Paris and I returned to Le Grand Duc. While in Venice, I'd received a letter from a colored boy named Gerald Hall. Someone had given him a nightclub in the hotel where he was living, right across the street from my apartment. He didn't know about the nightclub business and was worried that he wouldn't have any customers. Would I help him out when I got back? I answered sure, and when the season started up again, I began taking some of the clients I knew well over to Gerald's.

One was Gene Bankhead, Tallulah's sister. Her name was Eugenia, but we called her Gene, or Sis. I met her when I was giving Charleston lessons, and she became a regular at the club. Whenever she came to Paris, she brought her friends there.

In those same years Tallulah was making theatrical history in London. One weekend she came across the Channel to visit her sister, and Gene brought her to Le Grand Duc.

Tallulah was really someone special. She had everything—beauty, grace, wit, personality, and intelligence. When Tallulah walked into the club, she was the center of attention, and she expected to be. When the entertainment began, however, you could hear her "shushing" any customer who kept talking.

Tallulah in Europe and Tallulah in America were two different people. I think when she came back to the United States she came up against the resentment that many artists who've made it in Europe feel. The minute they come back, people want to bring them down. They just can't accept an American making a hit abroad, but they'll pay fabulous salaries to French singers who are a dime a dozen in Paris.

Maybe Tallulah started becoming an exhibitionist because she could feel that resentment. The Tallulah of my day wasn't the loud woman always attracting attention to herself that she later became, although she certainly was theatrical.

She loved Hutch—Leslie Hutchinson, the pianist—who was working at Gerald's club. She was there the night Hutch's wife gave birth to their first child. As the champagne went to work, Tallulah got all emotional about "that beautiful child and her mother being in some lonely hospital room away from those who loved her." Nothing would do but that she visit the child herself.

I didn't go along, but I heard about it the next night. Tallulah waved away the doctors and nurses who tried to prevent her from visiting in the small hours of the morning. She got into the room and woke up Hutch's wife and the baby.

After "oohing and ahhing," Tallulah dramatically took off her pearls and held them out to the baby. "They are for you, darling. Keep them and remember me always." Then she placed them on the pillow.

The next night, Gene Bankhead came in very early. "Now, Brick," she said, coming right to the point, "you get back those pearls."

I wanted to know why it was my business to get the pearls when I hadn't had anything to do with Tallulah giving them away. I hadn't even been there.

Time passed, Gerald's filled up. Every little while Gene would bring up the pearls again. I was just about to lose patience when one night Tallulah walked in. I decided to get things out in the open.

I said to her, nice and loud, "Gene wants me to get back the pearls."

Tallulah looked daggers at Gene, who stuttered, "I was telling Brick we must get back the pearls you gave Hutch's baby."

Tallulah got ready for one of her balcony projections. "Darling, I definitely don't want them back. No, no, no. I gave the pearls to that precious little baby. I want her to have them."

Satisfied that everyone in the place had heard her, Tallulah let me take her to a table. On the way, she whispered in my ear, "Brick, I do wish you'd get the pearls back. I'd like to have them."

She never got them.

Gerald's Bar was really owned by a man named Arch. He noticed how I was helping out by bringing in some of my regular customers. One night he said, "Brick, you're so great at this business. Why don't you open your own place?"

I laughed and said, "But I'm doing all right at the Duc. Besides, I don't know anything about running a bar."

"That's because you've never thought about it," said Arch. "If you'd look at it from all the angles, you'd be surprised to find out how much you know."

I thought about what Arch said and I realized that it was true. I did know a lot about the bar business—not everything, of course, but more than a little. The idea appealed to me. I started looking around for a place, talking to people.

I talked to Louis Mitchell. He was kind of down and out at the time. Not long after Florence Jones had gone over to his place, he'd let her talk him into renaming it Chez Florence—then Florence and Palmer Jones had gone back to New York.

He'd been forced to close his place. I never found out exactly why. It may have been because Florence left. Also, Louis was a big gambler, and he probably got in so deep he lost the club. He would later open a new Chez Florence, even though there was no Florence, and Chez Florence would be around for years and years and years. When I was looking for a place, however, Louis had a closed-up club.

115

It wasn't long before we started talking business. I went to George Jamerson and he said he wouldn't stand in my way. I started setting up the Music Box.

It was down the Rue Pigalle from the Duc, right on the corner of a cul-de-sac where one of Van Gogh's sisters had once lived. Since that time the house had become a brothel—you knew which were the brothels because the blinds were always closed—and one of the most famous in Paris.

Opening the club wasn't any big thing, really, except that I was new at it. Setting up in Paris at that time was easy. All I needed was the place. The furniture was already there. Just the rumor that a new club was opening up brought all the champagne wholesalers I could ever do business with.

I stayed on at Le Grand Duc until everything was ready. One of the regulars was Amos Lawrence, a Boston millionaire who was a delightful fellow to know and entertain. A few days before the Music Box opening he said, "Brick, I'd like you to come to my house. I'm going to have a party and I think His Royal Highness the Prince of Wales is going to be there."

The world never knew a more popular person than the Prince of Wales. Everyone loved him, and so did I, even though I had never met him. I wasn't going to miss the chance and agreed to entertain at Amos's party on October 29, 1926.

Amos Lawrence's house had several salons, and things were arranged so that there would be entertainment in one, and a buffet in another, and dancing in still another. Hutch and the boys and I set up in one and performed our show. I was doing some numbers with Hutch when someone asked me to join the Prince in another room. A servant led me to the Marquise de Polignac, who presented me to His Royal Highness. I curtsied. The Prince shook my hand.

The Marquise said, "His Royal Highness knows how to dance the Charleston, but he would like to learn the Black Bottom. Could you teach him?" I answered that I'd be delighted.

The Black Bottom followed the Charleston. By 1926 it was the "in" dance. The Prince and I went out onto the floor and I showed him some of the steps. It didn't take long for him to catch on. He was a very good dancer.

Later on a Mr. Bate, or Bates—a distant cousin of the royal family, I think—came over and said, "His Royal Highness wants to give a party—"

Before he could finish, Hutch spoke up. "Bricky, it would be great if the Prince would give his party in that new place you're going to open."

The man looked at Hutch and me. "I'll ask the Prince," he said. Pretty soon he came back. "Bricky, he said all right, but come tomorrow, because he wants a private dance lesson at my house."

That's how I added the Prince of Wales to my list of high-society dancing pupils.

I went to the house the next day and gave the lesson. I asked what he wanted at the party, and afterward I went right up to Montmartre and got Mitchell and he saw to everything. And so before my first club ever opened to the public, it hosted a party given by the Prince of Wales.

That was all we needed to put the Music Box over. I had him and I had Cole Porter, and that was enough to pack the place every night. Spencer Williams, who wrote "Everybody Loves My Baby," and Hutch took turns at the piano. Mitchell and I were together at the door, except when I took the floor. The club was a fantastic success.

The Music Box had a short life, however. We didn't have a regular license. We had what was called a *provisoire*, a temporary license that was good until someone complained about us. I never found out for sure, but I believe the complaints about us came from other club owners who were jealous. When we applied for a permanent license, we were turned down. They said it was out of the zone, which wasn't true, because Chez Florence used to be just across the street.

The closing of the Music Box was the first lesson in my lifelong education as a barkeep—try as you might, you can never figure out all the unpredictables that make up the nightclub business.

Although it bothered me to see the club close, I knew it wasn't my fault. It had been a smash, and I'd gotten my feet wet in the business.

George and Madame Jamerson welcomed me back to Le Grand Duc. Madame told me he'd been inconsolable while I was away. Once she'd found him with his head in the toilet bowl, crying, "Oh, get back my little baby girl. Please get back my little baby girl."

George was a strange man, a silent drinker who sat at the counter all night, drinking away. He would rarely look up unless someone spoke to him. Both George and Madame were tired, and fed up with running a nightclub. They often talked about retiring to their home in the country, and my coming back after running my own place must have caused them to make up their minds to do it.

I was only back about a week when George said, "Brick, take this place for yourself. You can run it. You're getting two hundred francs a night. You give us two hundred francs a night and we'll be satisfied." I told Cole about the offer. He said, "Take it." George and Madame went to the country, and I became the owner of the club.

The whole arrangement was perfect. I knew that club as if it were my own home. I knew the waiters and the cook and the musicians. Mitchell was still with me, and that was a comfort, too. The only sour note in the changeover came from Gene Bullard.

He had never gotten along too well with George and Madame, and they'd often thought of firing him. One of those times was when the Jamersons and I went to the embassy to sign a new contract. Gene stood outside shouting at me to be careful about what I was signing. It was very embarrassing for me. He was the last person I wanted advice from.

Gene and I hadn't had much to do with each other since my first days in Paris. I appreciated what he'd done for me when I'd had my attack of appendicitis, but I didn't like his temper. Talk about a trigger temper— he had it, and the fists to go with it.

He'd been a boxer. I once saw him beat up three sailors with absolutely no help. He was drunk, but when one of the sailors knocked him down, he sobered up the instant he hit the floor. One of the sailors was about to kick him, and he said, "I'm sure you wouldn't hit a guy when he was down." The sailor said, "On your feet, nigger." Gene jumped up swinging. It took five cops to break up the fight.

Gene deliberately used bad language in front of me because he knew how that annoyed me. Once when he did this, I whistled in his face. A musician saw what happened and hustled me downstairs and into the street. We were in one of those second-floor billiard halls, and the musician probably saved me from being skulled with a billiard ball.

However, I was still spoiling for a fight. I went home, got my pistol, and went back to the pool hall. Luckily, Gene was gone by then. I don't know what I would have done if I'd found him.

I haven't the slightest idea why I had that pistol. I'd bought it in New York, probably to protect myself. I never did get around to shooting it.

Anyway, Gene didn't take too well to my being the boss, but he stuck it out, and I stuck it out, and after a while we became friends. I guess that since neither of us was willing to give an inch, we started to respect each other. With all my new responsibilities, I was glad to have a big, tough man like Gene around to take care of any problems.

I soon found out that I had a lot to learn about the nightclub business. One thing I had to learn about was money. It was hard to worry about money in those days. Like Scott Fitzgerald said, there was so much of it around that even those who didn't have it didn't worry about it. It came in such quantities that I was careless. At times I had four musicians playing—didn't care at all what I was having to pay them. Once I told the leader of a combo, "I'll pay you tonight." He looked surprised. "Brick," he said, "you paid me *last* night."

Incidents like that made me realize I should start attending to business. I wasn't worried about the money, but I was worried about not being taken seriously as a businesswoman. There was nothing I could do about all the wild waste and extravagance that was going on around me. I wasn't running a boarding school. However, I could do something about how money was handled at Le Grand Duc. I'd often seen waiters collecting checks from four or five members of the same party. When I became proprietor, I stopped that. I put my foot down on that kind of bookkeeping and improvised my own system of checking bills. I would use it successfully for many years.

I stayed at Le Grand Duc for a year or so before I decided I wanted a better-looking place. I made plans to move across the street, and when I talked to Cole Porter about it, he said I shouldn't call it something like the Music Box.

"What should I call it?" I wanted to know.

"Bricktop's," he said. "That's the only thing you should call it. It's your place, it's you. You're the reason why people come."

How right he was! When hard times hit in the Forties and I had to move from place to place, I carried the name, and people knew where to find me because of it.

Bricktop's was a lovely room. The lighting came from underneath, illuminating a magnificent glass floor laid out in big panels. The walls were lined with banquettes lit from behind. There were only about twelve to fourteen tables. It was a warm, intimate place where I could entertain my friends the way I wanted to.

Bricktop's was the first club in Paris to serve whiskey at the tables. The other club owners said it wouldn't work, that I'd lose the chic of the exclusive champagne service at the tables. Whiskey should only be served at the bar. I tried it anyhow, though, and heard no grumbling. The whiskey drinkers were delighted. The other clubs, like Casanova, had to follow suit.

Bricktop's also featured American music. It was all the rage in Paris in those middle Twenties. A new sound in American music had been born because of the Harlem Renaissance and all the great bands, like Duke Ellington's, that had gotten a chance for some exposure. It even changed things on Broadway, where the musical comedy was starting to push out the schmaltzy vaudeville dramas.

Producer Jake Shubert, whom I dearly loved and who never missed coming to Bricktop's on his annual trips to Europe, eventually played a big part in the musical revolution. Whenever Jake came in, I could always depend on one of the American show people in the club to mutter the prayer of the Shubert chorus boys and girls:

> Now I lay me down to sleep,
> I pray the Lord my soul to keep,
> If I should die before I wake,
> Give my regards to Lee and Jake.

As far as music was concerned, we had the best of two seasons. We could hear previews of the next year's hits and the clients always brought over the latest sheet music. Sammy, a sax player with Florence Jones, used to go to New York every year and pick up music. We were in tune with the Hit Parade long before it was ever heard of.

There was a lot of coming and going by musicians and singers. They were always showing up at Bricktop's, and if they were good, I'd hire them. They were always Americans, though.

French singers wouldn't have been comfortable at Bricktop's, but I always let them audition. It would have been rude not to, and anyway I had connections and might be able to steer them someplace else. Once someone brought me a girl who was thrilling to hear. She was singing in a place little better than a brothel. I told her to wait, her time would come. It did. Her name was Lucienne Boyer.

After she became a star, she got to be so temperamental that you couldn't so much as light a match while she was singing. That was quite a different girl from the one who came begging to Bricktop's.

I never attempted to sing French songs. Sometimes guests who didn't know me well would request them. When that happened, I'd tell them to go see Suzi Salador or Lucienne Boyer. However, French phrases began to drift into some of my American songs, especially the light ones.

Take a song like "Manhattan." I'd say, "We went to Coney to *mange baloney*." "Thank you, Father, thank you, Mother" became *"Merci, Papa, merci, Mama."* "Baby carriage" came out as *"infant voiture."*

This was years before Hildegarde came out with "Darling, *je vous aime beaucoup*," and the Fractured French vogue. I originated Fractured French, and when I sang it, I fractured the audience.

It never failed to surprise me that people actually enjoyed hearing me sing. They would stop whatever they were doing to listen. I wasn't temperamental about it, but I did expect my entertainers to be given respect when they were out on the floor. If customers were acting up, I'd tell them to keep quiet, that Bricktop's was a place of entertainment, and that if they didn't want to see the show, they should buy a bottle and go home—it was cheaper. That didn't happen very often. I operated a high-class place.

Within a year Bricktop's was widely known as one of the most elegant and chic clubs in Paris. I never advertised—didn't have to. The clients did it for me. They traveled a great deal, and wherever they went, they recommended my place.

We were the last place to close in Paris. People would say, "Let's stop and see Brick before we go home." Whole groups would often show up after leaving private parties.

There were times when I stood apart from myself and said, "Now, how could all this have happened to me?" Most of the time, though, I didn't have to ask why. I knew. I made people feel welcome and at home. They enjoyed my entertaining, but that wasn't the main reason why they came. They liked the atmosphere I created.

Cole Porter had the most to do with my success, but even he took pains to understand it. One night he was talking about a singer he thought was terrific. I agreed, but said she was not my style. Cole laughed, "Your style? What is it? It's hard to put into words. I've told everyone that Bricktop is Bricktop. Without Bricktop, this place wouldn't make sense. She has the genius of an Elsa Maxwell. She can feel a place slipping, walk across the room and say something to someone, and pick it up again."

At the time, I didn't pay much attention. But, looking back, I realize they spent a lot of thought trying to figure out what made me so successful. Elsa once said to Cole, "You know, I think Brick must have been a queen in some former life." Cole replied, "No, an empress. You can't take anybody else and throw them in the middle of all this royalty and all these famous people and have her not turn a hair, like Bricky. She has not changed one iota. She had to have been an empress before."

I never thought of myself as an empress or a queen. I thought of myself only as the hostess to a very select group of people. There was a time, in those early years after Bricktop's began, that hardly anyone who came to the club was a stranger. Everyone who was there knew Cole Porter. In a way, Bricktop's was Cole Porter's club.

It was a wonderful time. My small place was filled every night with Cole Porter and his friends, or Cole Porter's friends, or friends of Cole Porter's friends. I never took reservations, not even on New Year's Eve, because I knew who would be coming in and when they would be there. There were choice tables, special treatment to make the regulars feel more comfortable. There were favorites. The "friends of the house" demanded very little in the way of special treatment, however. You didn't have to pretend in my place, you could just be yourself.

Everybody in that room knew each other. They belonged there. Noel Coward would hit the door, and then he'd hit the piano. He'd say, "This is my latest song," and he'd sit down and play it. He was a funny, funny, funny guy. He'd say, "How'm I doin'? How'm I doin', Bricky?" He was always trying to make somebody.

Cole would try out his new tunes, too, but never when there were a lot of people around. He'd come in once in a while when there was nobody around but me and the musicians and the waiters, and he would sit down at the piano and say, "What do you think about this tune?" Then he'd pick it out with that one finger of his. I always knew the songs from Cole's shows before the shows were ever produced—songs like "Begin the Beguine."

Dwight Fiske was the naughty entertainer of the 1920s. He'd sit all night at the piano playing and singing *double entendre* songs that became classics. He performed an endless repertoire, and when he sat down to entertain, he just took over Bricktop's. I could not have afforded to pay him for all the entertaining he did just because he enjoyed the audience he found at my place.

Dwight and Helen Morgan were great friends. For a solid week they came in together every night, stayed until we closed, and finally left. Helen always got up and sang her heart out. I never failed to be at the door when she left, so I could thank her for singing all those wonderful songs.

One night she came in alone, just before midnight. It was early for Bricktop's and early for her. They'd all go down to a place like Harry's New York Bar before coming to me. I was at the door when she came in.

"Where's Brick?" she wanted to know.

I couldn't believe it. "*I'm* Brick."

"That's fine," she said. "I'm Helen Morgan. I wanted to get a good look at you."

"But you've been looking at me all week."

"Yes, I know that. But I figured before I got started on the juice, I ought to come in and see what you really look like."

Very few American entertainers were part of the "in" crowd. There were some theatrical people from England, but the ordinary actor or actress from America just didn't belong. Most of those who did had something to do with Cole. When Cole was writing shows, he would meet American show people, and if he entertained them in Paris, they were accepted.

One of them was Marilyn Miller. She was a very sweet little girl, and when she started coming to Bricktop's, she got to fooling around with Michael Farmer. Michael was rich, the best-looking guy in town, and one of "the set." He was also a real cut-up. There was the night I'd like to forget, when he ordered plate after plate of spaghetti and dumped them all over Dolly O'Brien's white dress and diamonds. Pretty soon Dolly got into the act, and the two of them started trying to see how much spaghetti they could make stick to the ceiling.

Michael used to get some of the boys from Chez Florence and they'd all get on the long-distance telephone to Hollywood and play music and sing to Marilyn. Those were the days when you didn't usually pick up the phone in Paris and call Hollywood—not like today when it's the same as calling across the street. She was blond and pretty, and what a dancer! When she came to Bricktop's, she loved to get up and dance, and people loved to watch her.

Billy Reardon wasn't an entertainer, he was a socialite—but he loved to entertain. He'd get out on the floor and strut with a cane while he sang "My Hair Is Curly." I'd do it behind him. Snow Fisher had created that routine in *Shuffle Along*, but everybody at Bricktop's got to thinking it was Billy's routine. Snow came to Paris once. He came to Bricktop's and started doing his famous routine, and Michael Farmer shouted, "You can't do that. It's Billy's song!" I had to tell everyone who Snow was.

Jascha Heifetz would often borrow a violin from one of the musicians and play. I'll never forget the night he was in the club and I had a new girl violinist named Angelina.

I liked changing the acts around. I hired Angelina because she played the violin very well and it was something a little bit different. She wasn't exactly right for Bricktop's, and I made it my business to introduce her myself.

That night she couldn't help noticing that there was a very distinguished gentleman at a front table who applauded longer and more loudly than anyone else when she played. She finally signaled me to meet her in the ladies' room.

"Who is that man?" she wanted to know.

"Jascha Heifetz," I answered. I watched Angelina faint dead away.

Mary McCormic and Grace Moore were regulars in those early years. They were both great opera singers, and they battled to be the top prima donna of Bricktop's. They'd come in and one would go "OOOOOOO-aaaaa," and the other one would say, "I can beat that—OOOOOOOOO-OOOOOOOOOaaaaaaaaaaaaaaaa."

There were some quiet ones. There were entertainers who didn't entertain, like Irving Berlin. He was very quiet, very polite, very nice.

There were socialites who didn't entertain, such as the Prince of Wales. Why should he want to entertain? All he had to do was just be there. He was so easy, so relaxed. Of course, other people found it hard to be casual around someone like the Prince—even those who otherwise belonged. Some people waited at the bar for hours just to catch a glimpse of him. Others arranged to get the table next to him. Then they'd request a photographer, hoping the Prince would be included in the shot. The Prince never complained. Instead, he pulled a neat little trick. Just before the camera clicked, he'd bend down to pick up some imaginary object on the floor. He'd look up at me and laugh that little royal laugh.

There were some bores: people who ran from table to table, butting in on people's conversations. Elsa Maxwell could be a bore sometimes. But if they belonged, they belonged.

Everybody belonged, or else they didn't bother coming to Bricktop's more than once. When people came to Bricktop's and belonged, it was as if they were coming to one of their own salons. They could just come and be themselves, and that's what they wanted. They never worried about being embarrassed. They were among friends. Otherwise, they wouldn't dare get up and do the things they did. They were performing before their friends, their peers.

They felt at home at Bricktop's. They didn't mind borrowing money when they were short of cash—or charging their drinks on my tab. Len Hanna, of the Cleveland, Ohio, Hannas, was always saying, "Send the bill over to my concierge—she'll pay it." They left messages for each other with me, and always knew I'd relay them. I think it was Michael Farmer who said that Bricktop's was a combination mail-drop, bank, rehearsal hall, clubhouse—even a neighborhood bar. But it was always chic.

SALOONKEEPER
PAR EXCELLENCE

RUNNING A CABARET was not an easy business. I had to keep my clients happy but make sure they didn't go too far with their antics, watch the waiters so they didn't cheat the customers, make change, tally the receipts, hire and fire the entertainers. Every night there was something new, and I loved every minute of it. The writer Kay Boyle said, in *Being Geniuses Together*, that I had perfect coordination of faculties and reflexes. She ought to know. She and Robert McAlmon, another writer, spent many nights in my places, starting back in the Grand Duc days with Scott Fitzgerald and Man Ray and that crowd. She described in the book what happened on a typical night at Bricktop's:

One drunken Frenchman wanted to get away without paying his bill. At another table a French actress in her cups was giving her boy friend hell and throwing champagne into his face. In the back room several Negroes were having an argument. Brick sat at the cashier's desk keeping things in order. With a wisecrack she halted the actress in her temper, cajolingly made the Frenchman pay his bill, and all the while she was adding up accounts, calling out to the orchestra to play this or that requested number, indicating to the waiters that this or that table needed service; and, when asked, she began to sing "Love for Sale," while still adding up accounts. Halfway through the song there was a commotion in the back room where the argument was taking place, which meant that the colored boys had now come to blows. Brick skipped down from her stool, glided across the room, still singing. She jerked aside the curtain and stopped singing long enough to say, "Hey, you guys, get out in the street if you want to fight. This ain't that kind of a joint!" Then she continued the song, having missed but two phrases, and was back at her desk again adding accounts.

I *was* good at my job, and it was paying off. I was getting successful in the nightclub business, and a lot of it had to do with someone I really didn't even know—someone named Bricktop. Ada Smith would sometimes step back and say, "Who is this Bricktop? What's so great about her?"

For the life of me, I still can't answer that. There are some things I know. I know that without Cole Porter I wouldn't have been anything. He created Bricktop, and he and his friends formed a sort of protective cocoon around me. I got so used to it that I sometimes forgot about what the outside world was like, although from time to time I would be reminded of it. Usually, the reminding had to do with racial prejudice.

There was very little racial discrimination in Paris. In fact, there was a strong pro-Negro prejudice. There had been a lot of colored soldiers in Europe during the war, and the Parisians welcomed colored Americans as heroes. Also, of course, the Parisians identified the new jazz with Negroes. If there had been a lot of average white Americans around, *they* might have influenced the Parisians, but there weren't. White Americans in Paris who were not rich and sophisticated and well traveled were pretty rare. Anyway, the Americans didn't mix much with the Parisians. However, just across the Channel, things were very different —maybe because of the way things were across the Atlantic, in America.

Paul Robeson arrived in London in 1928 with the musical *Show Boat*. He was a smash in London and became one of the darlings of the British upper class. His wife, Essie, went to London with him, and with her stunning clothes, she was written up in the society columns almost as often as he was. However, Paul had a great appeal to white women in London, and I guess one of them had a great appeal to him. That started to cause problems, not just between him and Essie, but for his English producer, C. B. Cochran.

Charles B. Cochran was a friend of Cole's and the producer of many of his London shows. He'd started out as an actor and gone to the United States around 1890, when he was eighteen, to make it on the New York stage. He didn't, and he ended up doing everything from operating a flea circus and a medicine show to selling fountain pens when they were the newest rage. He later turned to producing shows, and that's where he made his big success. He brought to producing all the things he'd learned in the flea-circus and medicine-show business; people said he was a cross between Ziegfeld and P. T. Barnum.

C.B. never did things halfway; it was all or nothing. He made and lost I don't know how many fortunes over the years, and it didn't surprise me at all to read that he died from taking a bath in water that was so hot it scalded him. Cole liked characters like C.B., and so he stuck by him after C.B. had a nervous breakdown in 1925 and lost over a million dollars. C.B. was trying to get back on his feet when he brought Paul Robeson to London, and the last thing he needed was a big scandal. Since C.B. was going to produce *Wake Up and Dream* the next year, for which Cole had written the score, Cole also had a business reason for not wanting to see C.B. involved in any unpleasantness.

One night in Bricktop's, Cole told me he was going to take me to London especially to see C.B. I wanted to know why, but Cole wouldn't tell me, and I knew better than to ask Cole twice about anything. So the next day we took a boat across the Channel and went straight to C.B.'s office.

C.B. said, "Bricky, you've got to talk to Paul Robeson."

"About what?" I wanted to know.

"You've got to tell him that he can't divorce Essie and marry this white woman."

"What's that got to do with me?" I demanded. I was furious. I wasn't the keeper of the race. They'd already had me over to London once to talk to Hutch, the piano player, over the same situation. I thought that was enough.

C.B. kept talking. "Paul Robeson is the greatest Negro in England. He's the greatest Negro in *America!* You know what prejudice is, Bricky. You're a girl and you haven't felt it—we see to it that prejudiced people don't get near you. You are for the private few. Paul is a man, and he's on the stage. He's a *public* figure. If he divorces his wife and marries this Englishwoman, it's gonna ruin him. He's got to be talked out of this."

I said, "Well, I don't know, that's a big job . . ." but they wore me down and I did wind up talking to Paul.

I didn't do it just because C.B. and Cole wanted me to. I had my own strong feelings on that issue of interracial marriage. Sure, I'd had white men, but I certainly never intended to marry one. He might care very much, but he doesn't want to—he doesn't *mean* to care.

So I talked to Paul. Even though it was his life and I'd tried never to butt in on other people's lives, I talked to him, because C.B. and Cole wanted me to, and because I personally thought he was making a mistake. I don't know if I influenced him or not. He and Essie separated in 1930, but later they got back together. He never did marry that white woman.

The woman came to Bricktop's once, not long after I had talked to Paul. She walked right over to me and said, "I'm going to marry Paul Robeson."

"You are not," I said.

"Yes I am," she said.

By this time I was angry. "Did you hear what I said? You *are not* going to marry Paul Robeson." As everyone there said, "Well, Bricky, *s'appelle d'accord.*"

Years later I met Essie. I don't remember where. She said, "Bricky, thanks so much. You saved my life." I pooh-poohed all that, of course, but inside I was pleased, because I think C. B. Cochran was right—Paul would have been ruined if he'd married that white Englishwoman.

C.B. was also right about how my friends shielded me from prejudice. Though friends made Bricktop, there had to be something about

Bricktop that attracted those friends. I know I had style. Thanks to Jean Patou and Eddie Molyneux and Schiaparelli, I dressed beautifully. At that time I still had my figure and those beautiful legs and feet.

Elsa Maxwell once said that of all the celebrities she'd known—and she knew plenty in her life—I was one of the greatest because I was always correct. I think that was the key. I knew how to act, and it didn't matter what the situation was. I always had good manners, thanks to Mama, and what Mama didn't teach me, I picked up right away quick on my own. I remember when Cole asked me, "Brick, where did you learn to curtsy?" My answer was simple: "I watched how other people did it." That's how I learned how to behave around royalty—how to address them, how not to speak to them unless spoken to, and all that.

Mostly, though, I just naturally knew how to act. I never got confused about who I was. I always knew my place. People today think that's a terrible thing to say. I get criticized for it. I don't mean I thought I was any less than anyone else, or that anyone was better than me. The rich and famous, royalty, they're just people—they go to the bathroom just like you and me. But that doesn't mean there aren't certain rules to go by in life. I was a saloonkeeper, a hostess. My job was to make my clients feel at home. That meant being their friend in Bricktop's, but I usually didn't see them outside the club—and didn't want to.

It also meant not gossiping about them. I'd hear things and see things, of course, but I put them out of my mind. I told my employees to do the same thing, although I know they often didn't. I was trustworthy, I was sympathetic, I cared about my clients having a good time. And I had a clientele who all knew and cared about each other. These, I guess, were the main ingredients of Bricktop's success.

One other thing: I never fooled around with any of my male clients. I could have. They were sure after me, and I'll say it myself, I was a pretty fast little girl, and very well made. I didn't want to be a back-street mistress to any of those big clients of mine, however, and that's all I could have been. What would we have talked about when we got out of bed? I don't know nothing about polo!

Once in a while some stupid girl would go after one of these men, but she would soon be put down by the women in that high-class way they had: "But, dahling, you can't *afford* to do what I do."

It wasn't in my best interests to mix business with pleasure, or to be some sort of threat to wives and girlfriends of my clients. I also kept my private life private. My clients didn't know who my lovers were. It wasn't any of their business. They wondered, of course; someone was always trying to figure out what I was doing. Cole used to say, "We know that Bricky's doing something, but catch her!"

I was doing plenty in those days. It was always with men, and always with one at a time, of course, but in those early Paris years I had a lot of men—a whole passel of men—and I did it up and down alleys, in taxi cabs, in the bed, out of the bed, all around the bed.

I never in my life met a man and went right to bed with him. I always got to know him first. I had to know how he acted when he was drunk, and when he was sober. However, that didn't mean I had to know him for a lifetime and all that messy stuff.

Sometimes I'd get attracted to someone, a taxi driver or something. I'd say, "Now, what in hell do I want with him? I want him, though." And then one morning I'd wake up, turn over, and say, "What are you doing here? Get outta here!"

Everybody was sleeping around. It was the thing to do. In those days you'd see a guy and say to yourself, "I'm gonna knock you off that pedestal. You think you're so big and so great." And you'd bring him down a little bit. I never considered myself promiscuous. As Mama used to say, "If you do it once, you might as well keep it up, 'cause it's gone."

I didn't hold with talking about it, though, or writing about it. Henry Miller gave me a copy of *Tropic of Cancer* when it was first published. I picked it up and started reading and was so disgusted I put it right back down. I couldn't believe how everyone else could say it was so good, and I told them so. Henry heard about that and came to see me, and as soon as I saw him, I said, "How dare you give me a book like that!"

"Well, it's true, Brick," he said.

"I know that's the way it goes," I said. "I'm grown up. But you don't write about it." In those days you didn't, and, in my opinion, you still shouldn't.

I slept with white men and black men. *Women's Wear Daily* interviewed me once, and I told them I could dispel that myth about Negro men being the only ones who knew how to make love. I've known some white boys who could make some awful good love, straight up and down, too—no funny business. But you draw the line. Ralph Bunche once asked me, "Brick, what do you tell those Negroes when they say you want to be white?" I said, "I tell them I'm one of the few successful Negro women they've got who never married a white man. And I never lived with one."

I'd say to those other successful women—the ones with white men—"What do you want with him?"

"Well, he's my manager," they'd say.

"I never had no white man for a manager," I'd say.

"Yes, but you had all those famous people—"

I'd interrupt. "They came looking for me. I never looked for them."

If I haven't said a lot about my lovers, it's because most of them weren't important. I've talked about Chappie and Walter. When I'd been in Paris for a while, I got to fooling around with a colored musician named Bobby Jones, who had really been around Europe by the time I met him—Brussels, Berlin, London, as well as Paris. He had his own band, could play both cornet and alto saxophone, and was a superb musician. People said he could have become a great musician in America, but he preferred to stay in Europe. I went with him a couple of years before I got to fooling around with a colored French boy. And then there was Peter.

I met Peter Ducongé in 1927. He was a saxophonist from New Orleans. He and Louis Armstrong had been kids together there. Peter came to Paris with Leon Abbey's band, one of the early Negro jazz bands in Europe, and since all the Negro musicians came to Bricktop's in the morning, it was natural that Peter should come, too. They would drift into Bricktop's after the other spots closed, and by seven o'clock in the morning the place would be filled. I'd set up the drinks myself.

Peter was good-looking, of medium height. He dressed immaculately and smoked a pipe. He was quiet. I was drawn to him right away, and he was to me. It was a comfortable relationship that just grew quietly and naturally. We never really talked about how we felt—we just took it for granted.

We gave each other a lot of leeway. I had my club and Peter had his music, and neither of us had any desire to interfere in the other's business. He'd go off to some other country to play a gig, and in the summer months, when Bricktop's closed, I'd go off traveling by myself. I loved to travel, and whenever I could, I visited some European city where I'd never been. I went to Rome, Capri, Biarritz, Monte Carlo, Budapest, Berlin.

One of my nicest memories is of a Hungarian man I met in Budapest. I met him through two rich Hungarians who came to Paris regularly. They found out I was appearing in Budapest and brought him and his brother along. His name was Kalman Kovacs. Neither he nor his brother could speak English, and I certainly wasn't up to Hungarian, but we got along in that wonderful way you learn in Europe—by signals, acting, looking up words, asking someone to translate. I got stuck on him, and he got stuck on me. He came to the club night after night, his beautiful puppy-dog eyes followed me all around. When it came time for me to leave, I found that pretty hard to do.

Actually, I had several Hungarians after me. Two or three of them were rich. Naturally, the one I picked up with was the broke one. For some reason, I hadn't a penny to get out of Hungary. Peter sent me some money. Lady Mendl supplied the rest, which I lost on a stopover at Monte Carlo.

Back in Paris, I thought I'd heard the last of Kalman, but I guess I didn't know Hungarians. He wrote long, passionate letters—and they were translated to my blushing ears by some Hungarian friends. When spring came to Paris, so did Kalman. He looked me up, and there we were again. His company had given him a trip to Paris. *Blackbirds* was playing, and I took him to see it. Until then he had never seen another Negro woman. He told me that he had never in his life seen so many beautiful girls. I said, "Try one." He looked hurt: "Brick, I already have one."

His vacation was about to come to an end when he showed up in my club looking sad and thoughtful. He told me he was going back to Budapest. "What would I do in your life, Brick? Just hang around the sidelines and watch. I am going home and I will get married to a girl I know who understands me and my station in life. It's safe."

I hope that Kalman found a happy life. It was a sweet interlude—one of those things you can look back upon with a smile. Like Budapest—

133

those beautiful men in the band and all those glorious children with dark, dark eyes.

One of my worst experiences happened in Germany. I went there on vacation in the summer of 1927 and spent most of the time in Berlin, because I loved that city. Its nightlife in those days was the most exciting I'd ever seen. It was like a circus. Compared to it, Montmartre, even at two o'clock in the morning, was a sleepy little town. Friedrichstrasse, Behrenstrasse, the Jäger were so packed with night spots—sometimes two or three in a single building—that you wondered how there could be enough customers to fill them all. But there were. At night the sounds of music and singing and laughing made a steady, joyful din, and there were so many lights that you could hardly see the sky. Anything went in Berlin, and I mean anything. All the dope-taking and homosexuality that was done in a light-hearted sort of way in Paris was serious business in Berlin. Some people said it was depraved, but I think it was just a way to forget the humiliating war defeat, to block out what you couldn't help seeing when the sun came up in the morning.

In the daytime the whole mood changed. Everything seemed grim and gray and, well, like you would expect a war-torn city to look. That's when you saw the crippled and maimed veterans begging on the streetcorners, and the crowds of street children. Even when the sun was at its highest, it felt cold in Berlin. I preferred the city at night, and since I was a night person anyway, I didn't get to see that much of the ugliness.

While I was in Berlin, I met the secretary to the Ambassador from Italy and he said, "Bricky, why don't you come here and open up a nightclub?" That sounded like a good idea to me, so I returned to Paris and talked to some musicians. Then I went back to Berlin and talked to several people with nightclubs, and finally made a deal with some fellows to be with them in their club and to bring these certain musicians.

They were colored musicians, of course. Negroes were quite a novelty in Germany, even in Berlin. I remember a German girl got stuck on one of my musicians, and one thing led to another. Because I was so light-skinned, they didn't really think of me as colored. *She* sure didn't. She came running to me and said, "They don't smell bad."

I said, "What are you talking about?"

She said, "We had been brought up to think that all black people smell bad. He smells good." And she went on fooling around with him.

Anyway, came the time I was to go to Berlin with the band, and two or three of the musicians backed down. It was awfully hard to get a musician out of Paris in those days. I went on with the others, but when my German partners heard them, they didn't want them. They did have awfully good music in Berlin—those Germans could really play. So they sued me.

I was living in a private home with some German people. Agents of these two nightclub fellows showed up there and seized my belongings— locked up my trunks and put seals on them, tore my diamond ring off my finger.

The people I was living with were really high-class people. They helped me get a lawyer, did everything they could to help me. Meanwhile, Florence Mills was in Germany—in Hamburg, I think. I sent her a wire and told her what was happening, and right away quick she sent some money, and she came herself on the next plane. She couldn't stay long, but it was so good to see her again; she gave me the moral support I needed. I felt very alone in a strange city, trying to communicate in a strange language, trying to figure out a strange legal system. I was so grateful to Florence. I didn't know it then, and neither did she, but it was the last time we were to see each other. In a matter of months she was dead of appendicitis.

The case came to trial. One of the first things the judge said to me was, "Why, you are not even Bricktop. Not only did you misrepresent the musicians, you are impersonating Bricktop."

I said, "But I *am* Bricktop."

He said, "Bricktop is a *black* woman." (In Germany in those days you had to have kinky hair and all that; I didn't fit the image.)

"But I *am* Negro," I said. "*I* am Bricktop." Well, the whole courtroom went into laughter, and it was in all the papers. Too bad it didn't help my case.

The judge ruled against me. The only thing to do was decide what I was to pay. I didn't feel like waiting around for that. At the risk of getting themselves into a lot of trouble, the people I was staying with undertook to get me out. I don't know how they did it, but somehow they got me and all my trunks—the ones that the two nightclub men had sealed up—to Potsdamer Station and onto the Berlin-Paris express train.

I lost my jewelry, however. It had been taken as bond. I had an assortment, but I remember that diamond ring best. It was nine carats—a beautiful, pure white diamond. Peter had given it to me. He'd given me a four-carat ring first, and then on my birthday had exchanged it for a nine-carat. It was pure-perfect, set by Cartier—Cartier doesn't fool with imitations—and I had the certificate and all. It was worth a hell of a lot of money, but I was young. I had the world in front of me. A little thing like a lost diamond wasn't going to worry me. I wasn't going to moan about yesterday. To heck with yesterday! What are we gonna do tomorrow?

I was in my prime. Life was so good that such things just sort of slid off my back. T. S. Eliot expressed my life in those days better than I can.

I wish I could remember the exact year he said it—it must have been around 1929 or 1930. It was fall and Bricktop's was open and my clients were celebrating my birthday. Since my birthday was in August, when many of them were away, they celebrated my birthday late, and ever since then I've always celebrated my birthday for at least two months straight. Somebody would usually ask me, "Where were you born, Brick?" and I had this stock answer:

"On the fourteenth day of August 1894, in the little town of Alderson, West-by-God-Virginia, the doctor said, 'Another little split-tail,' and on that day Bricktop was born."

T. S. Eliot was at this particular celebration, and he added a line of his own:

> . . . and on that day Bricktop was born,
> And to her thorn, she gave a rose.

I've never forgotten that.

With life so rosy, I started looking for a larger apartment. I'd long thought about getting a bigger place so Mama could come and stay, and it just sort of happened that I wound up with a place that was big enough for Mama and me—and Peter. Our affair got a big lift when I moved into that new apartment.

It was on the Rue Pigalle—one flight up instead of the three I was used to climbing. It had three bedrooms, a living room, a kitchen, and a couple of bathrooms—two bathrooms with a bidet in each. I'd never thought about having my own very private special bathroom until I moved into that apartment. Maybe I didn't want to—until I had one.

It was there that I got down to the business of being the fanatical, fussy old Bricktop I am today. From then on, whether I was in the money or not, I saw to it that I had an apartment or a hotel suite with two baths—one for me and one for other people.

Mama had walloped cleanliness into us kids, but it had taken special talent to keep up her standards once I hit the road and those American roominghouses. I learned to keep clean with sponge baths, or what performers used to call "whore baths." That's because I refused to sit in any of the tubs—heaven knows what germs were hidden in all that grime.

This is as good a place as any to say something about the bidet. If Americans would install and use it, instead of making crude jokes about it, we'd have more right to our claims of being such super-clean people.

Sending for Mama was a much bigger occasion than shacking up with Peter. As I said, Peter and I just naturally got together, but it was a proud Ada Smith who sent to the United States for her mother. Blonzetta had been so successful with her real-estate ventures. Now I was successful enough in the club business to send Mama passage to Paris, France.

Boats from the United States always docked early in the morning, whether it was at Le Havre or Cherbourg. Both Peter and I were working, so I sent a friend to meet Mama and bring her back on the train to the Gare St. Lazare, the main train station in Montmartre. We were waiting there at the station—along with half the musicians and entertainers in Paris.

We cheered when the locomotive emerged from the gray mists, its stacks belching out steam, and when I saw that beautiful head poke out of a window, it was the thrill of my life. I felt like a kid—and in seconds Mama reminded me that she was still Mama.

As she climbed down from the train, I looked around for my friend, but he was nowhere to be seen. "Mama, where is the colored man I sent to meet you?" I wanted to know.

She didn't know what I was talking about.

"But how did you get through customs?"

She gave me one of those now-aren't-you-a-silly-girl looks. "Like everyone else, of course. I've been traveling all my life. Maybe not in these foreign countries, but I *have* been around."

The welcoming committee moved in a fleet of open-cockpit taxis to my apartment, where the opening of Mama's trunks was an event we'd all looked forward to as much as seeing Mama. I'd written what to bring —things that Americans take for granted until they leave America: American cigarettes, American whiskey, hair straightener, aspirin tablets, the latest records. Fletcher Henderson and Duke Ellington records were pure gold in Paris; you could buy them, but once the tax had been slapped on them, you had to pay an outrageous price. And if aspirin seems an odd request, you've never met up with European pills; they came in horse size and no other.

When I marveled at how Mama had gotten so much loot past the French customs officials, who were really tough on things like whiskey and records, Mama got that look on her face again. "Ada, I think you've forgotten everything about your mama. Why, when that nice man asked me if I was bringing in any cigarettes or liquor, I just looked straight at him and said, 'What kind of woman do you take me for? Do you think I would ever smoke or take a drink?' That sweet fellow just marked my trunks and let me walk right through to the train."

Of course Mama wanted to take in the sights, and when I confessed how little I had seen, she huffed, "Wouldn't you know? Ada's been here for five years and hasn't even been up the Eiffel Tower."

Well, a person couldn't work all night, sleep much of the day, and handle sightseeing with any energy. Besides, I've never pretended to be something I'm not. A grade-school education doesn't make you a connoisseur of art, and a saloon singer doesn't qualify as an expert on great music. I found my own way of absorbing the cities I lived in—through the people and by reading.

My friends did most of the sightseeing with Mama, but there was no way for me to escape the Eiffel Tower. Mama was determined to get me up there, so one day we set off for the Place du Trocadéro, and after we'd walked around the gardens a little while, we joined the crowd of tourists on their way to the most famous sight in Paris. We rode the elevator up, but Mama insisted on walking down. She made it all right, but about a quarter of the way down I fainted. Mama loved to tell about that.

Having Mama close to me again was good. We'd never failed to write regularly, and her letters were always full of wit and common sense, but there was nothing like Mama in person, and I was proud to have her with me when I was beginning to enjoy the rewards of being at the top.

Of course, I kept that kind of thought to myself, because the idea of my name being in lights was the last thing to impress Hattie E. Smith— or at least that's what she'd tell me. Nothing impressed Mama. Sometimes when we were at home in the apartment I'd hear the door slam and I'd say, "Mama, who was that?"

"Some fool who couldn't speak American."

"You mean English?"

"No, I mean American."

Mama wasn't in Paris long before she fell ill and had to be taken to the American hospital, where she was treated by a Dr. Jackson. The first morning she was there, I went to the hospital after work to find her sitting up and in a real state. First, she was furious that Peter and I had arranged for a private room. Second, she didn't like being in any hospital.

Fortunately, Dr. Jackson walked in, and he had a will as strong as Mama's. He forced her to stay put, and we managed to get her through the examinations. She eventually had her way, though. She left the hospital before she should have. Two months later she was back in it. I was in Biarritz; Peter wired the news to me. He met me at the station with "Ada, your ma is really something. She won't stay in a private room. She's got herself into one with six beds."

I raced to the hospital. When the receptionist saw me, she said, "Madame Bricktop, your mother has this hospital upside down."

Mama was ready for me. "Ada, don't be mad. I'm not going to stay in a private room. Besides the cost, I don't have anyone to talk to."

Then she started complaining about the service. "These foreign fools bring the pan around before visiting time when I don't want to use it. Then when I need it, they want to know why I didn't use it the first time. I tell them, 'Don't talk to me that way. I'm American. This *is* an American hospital, isn't it? My daughter Blonzetta is one of the biggest taxpayers in Chicago, and it's her taxes that are keeping this hospital going.' "

After a few days Mama was released from the hospital, and after a few months she went home, promising to come back. She didn't say anything to me about how well I was doing in Paris, but I knew she was itching to tell everybody else. When I put her on the boat train to Le Havre, I said, "Now, Mama, don't go telling perfect strangers your whole history," but I knew that by the time the boat left the dock she'd be saying, "My daughter this and that" and someone would ask, "Who is your daughter?" and Mama would be on.

Before she left, she cleaned out my closets. I knew she never intended to wear all the things she took, but I didn't question her. They were no longer of any use to me. Cole kept me beautifully dressed. About two or three times a year the entertainers changed wardrobes, and I was no exception. Besides my things, Mama had a whole trunkful of items she'd picked up during her Sunday excursions to the Flea Market.

Years later I found out what she'd done with all those things. In spite of her illness, which was cancer, those were the good years for Mama. With me doing well in Paris and Blonzetta doing well in Chicago, Mama was well taken care of. She didn't have to worry about supporting either her children or herself. She kept busy and continued to run small boardinghouses, but she was able to take as many trips as she wanted to, and she loved to travel. Most of all she liked traveling back to Alderson to see old friends and visit the family graves, and then she'd go over to Washington, D.C., to visit other friends.

On one of her trips Mama heard about a minstrel show playing in a nearby town. It was the owner who told me, "Your mother came to see the show. She told all the girls, 'I'm Bricktop's mother and brought over a lot of beautiful clothes from Paris. If you'll come to Alderson, I'll sell them to you.' " Of course, Mama literally gave them away, but she enjoyed it, and that's what counted.

I had a nervous breakdown not long after Mama left. I don't think the two things were connected. I broke down because I was working too hard, trying to please too many people.

When it happened, I couldn't understand it. I'd been a nervous child ever since that fall from the porch in Alderson, but I thought I'd outgrown all that years before. Suddenly, though, I was jittery, bad-tempered, depressed. I went to a doctor, who said I was suffering from repressed nerves, that I was holding myself in. It came from saying yes to everybody for so many hours each day. "You've got something inside that you have to let out," he said.

"Do you mean I should scream at my clients?" I wanted to know.

"You'll be in a straitjacket if you don't. The top of your head is about to come off."

I didn't take his advice, and things got worse. When I went to the club, I felt like bawling everybody out. Even when there was nothing wrong, I found some reason to yell at the waiters or the entertainers. Sometimes I couldn't believe I was acting like that. I honestly thought I was going crazy.

That's how it is with nerves. When they start racing, you can't stop them. I had sense enough to realize the problem was with me, not with those around me, so I decided not to go to the club every night. I had been off a couple of nights when Louis Cole, my piano player, told me that the Dolly Sisters had come in and, on hearing that I wasn't there, got the wrong idea. "Oh, well," they'd said, "Brick's rich now. She doesn't need to work." (You see, I was *Bricktop* and could handle everything and anything.)

Rosie and Jenny Dolly were legends. Their real names were Roszicka and Yancsi and they had been born in Hungary but brought to the United States when they were children. They grew up in Rockaway, New York, and it wasn't long before they were discovered. Not only were they two dark-haired beauties who could dance, but they were also identical twins. That was a winning combination for vaudeville. They were only sixteen when they made their debut on the Keith circuit, and two years later they were in Ziegfeld's *Follies of 1911.* In the next fourteen years they did both Broadway shows and movies in Holly-wood, and they almost always appeared together. When you talked about the Dolly Sisters, you didn't talk about their careers but about their career.

They retired when they were in their early thirties—mostly, I think, because they were very vain about their looks—but they continued to

141

be celebrities. Practically from the moment they entered vaudeville, their lives were followed closely in the gossip columns. They made good copy. If you think the Gabor sisters were famous for their husbands and jewels, you should have seen these Hungarian twin sisters in their prime. It was always being reported that one or the other of them was marrying a millionaire, and between them they had five husbands, all millionaires.

After they retired from the stage, they took up residence on the Riviera because of all the casinos. They were both confirmed gamblers, and they played for real. Once they broke the bank at the Cannes casino, winning four million francs. A couple of years later Jenny by herself won $280,000 playing baccarat at the Casino de la Forêt at Le Touquet. As the Depression started showing its effects in Europe, things started going downhill for the Dollys, especially Jenny. She was seriously injured in an automobile accident near Bordeaux in 1935 and had to have I don't know how many plastic-surgery operations. She had to auction off her jewel collection to pay for them. The Dollys returned to the United States in 1935 and both got married and settled in Chicago. Jenny's marriage didn't work out, though, and I think she really felt lost. Then one day she opened the door of her Lake Shore Drive apartment and some strange man threw white pepper in her face, blinding her for several weeks. In 1941, while on a visit to Hollywood, she formed a noose from the heavy drapes in her apartment and hanged herself. Rosie, I think, lived to old age and died a natural death.

I met the Dollys through Cole, naturally. He'd written the score for *Greenwich Village Follies*, their last Broadway show. They never came to Bricktop's separately—always together—and I was always a little bit uncomfortable greeting them because they looked so much alike I couldn't tell them apart. I wasn't the only one who had that trouble. For most people, it was easier to just think of them as the Dollys and not worry about who was who.

Everyone loved the Dollys, including me, and so their remark to Louis Cole hurt. I started going to the club every night, waiting for them to show up. It wasn't long. When they walked in, I went right over to their table and said, "I heard you made a pretty mean remark about me."

"Oh, Brick," one of them, I think it was Jenny, said, "we didn't mean anything by it. Forget it. We only said that because we love you, and when you're not here, people just don't stay. Bricktop's is just not Bricktop's without you."

I calmed down a bit. "Well, I'm sick. I'm having a nervous breakdown."

Suddenly, the whole room went quiet. Someone said, "Why didn't you tell us?"

"What am I supposed to do? Go around telling everyone I'm having a nervous breakdown?" I demanded.

After that, my breakdown became a big joke, and that may have helped speed my recovery. My clients would say, "Don't annoy Brick, she's having a nervous breakdown."

To me, it was serious, though, so the first doctor sent me to a nerve specialist—the same specialist who treated the president of France. He told me the same thing the first doctor had: I had repressed nerves from wanting to fire back at people and not doing it, holding it in. "You've been saying *'Oui'* and *'Merci beaucoup'* and 'Yes, yes, yes,'" he said. "Start saying 'No, go to hell.'"

"I don't swear," I said.

Then he gave me some really good advice. "When it's raining, walk in the rain and just scream out loud whatever you feel."

Well, it rains a lot in Paris, especially in the mornings, and it was in the mornings after a night of running Bricktop's that I'd go out onto the wet cobblestones of the Rue Pigalle and start walking and muttering to myself, up to the Place Pigalle and down the other side of the triangle along the Rue Frochot, then down the Rue Henri Monnier or back across the Rue Victor Massé, and by this time I'd be screaming very nicely and my face would be all wet and the rain streaming down over my cheeks, and I'd feel much better. I didn't always take the same route. Sometimes I'd go down the Rue Pigalle and along the little curved Rue de La Trinité, up the Rue de Clichy, and back across the Rue Moncey. Those little, narrow, winding streets with their houses jumbled together, all gray and soft-looking in the drizzle, were good places to work out problems, and early morning was a good time to be reminded that everyday life went on, no matter how you were feeling. I'd watch the window shutters open, the concierges come out and start sweeping the sidewalks, the flower and fruit vendors opening their stalls. They didn't pay any attention to the crazy little woman walking along screaming at the top of her voice. The people of Montmartre understood and never complained. Once in a while a stranger would hear me and inquire of one of the gendarmes, and he'd answer, "Oh, that's just Madame Bricktop getting rid of her nerves."

After walking down the street and screaming for a while, I'd feel fine, and in a few months I didn't have to scream anymore. Except for a much milder attack in 1939, I never had any more trouble. I still have my nerves, but I'm a lot older now and I don't mind saying my piece whenever I feel like it.

It wasn't long after I had my personal breakdown that over in the United States the stock market crashed and a lot of people started jumping out the windows. I read about the crisis in the papers, and I heard my clients talking about the market, but it was all a big, complicated mystery to me. Mine was a cash business. I didn't even have a checking account, still don't. I don't trust myself. I know that I would sit down and write checks to buy things I didn't need, or give away more money than I could afford. I didn't understand about these pieces of paper called stocks, and how they could be worth millions one day and nothing the next.

Only a handful of my clients were affected immediately and suddenly disappeared from Paris. Others who hadn't been wiped out kept telling one another that it was only a temporary crisis, and that in a few weeks there would be a turn for the better. Many had good reason for their confidence. Like the Europeans, they'd made investments in real estate, coal mines, tangible things that took more time to feel the pinch. The artists who'd had heavy investments in the stock market had their talent to fall back on. George Jessel, one of my favorite comedians, teamed up with Eddie Cantor, another victim of the crash, and hit the vaudeville circuit. Clifton Webb, Beatrice Lillie, and the Astaires all had shows to go home to. My business didn't suffer at all. At my place it was so packed that the ropes were up nearly every night. It took several years for the crisis really to be felt in Europe.

It must have been within a week or so of the crash that Jeff Crane came in. Peter was there. I said, "Mr. Crane, I'd like you to meet my husband." Peter didn't say anything about the slip until later. "You introduced me as your husband, you know," he said. I started to laugh it off, but Peter interrupted, "Maybe we should get married, Brick." I thought a second. "Why, sure," I said, "let's get married."

That was all there was to it. Getting married was just making legal what we'd been doing anyway. We were married at City Hall on December 29, 1929. Gene Bullard was the best man. He guided us through the intricacies of a French marriage ceremony and prompted us when to say *"Oui."*

The reception was held at Bricktop's, and the only thing missing among all the presents we received was a Rolls Royce. All the musicians were there, and as many of the clients as could crowd in. They brought me furs, jewelry, beautiful things. Michael Farmer broke three of my glass floor panels that night, which was his way of celebrating things.

Being married didn't affect the pattern of our lives. We were used to each other. Peter kept busy playing at the clubs and gambling. He gambled a lot, but there were as many big wins as losing streaks. That was his life, and I never interfered. I had the club. Peter dropped in like everybody else, but he chose to stay in the background. When I wanted to introduce him to people, he'd laugh, "Brick, they're *your* clients. *You* entertain them." When someone suggested he could be a big help in managing the place, he really howled. "When I met my wife, her name was outside that door. She won't let anyone else do it. She does it herself, and I think she's right."

The dream of every performer, at least in my day, was to have a place in the country. Maybe it was a need to have roots, because the performer's life was basically rootless. We were typical. In 1930, a year when lots of entertainers were having the mortgages on their country homes foreclosed, we bought an estate in Bougival, outside of Paris. It was a lovely, wooded area where Mistinguett, Maurice Chevalier, and a number of other French artists owned homes. Some of the American musicians lived there, too. Arthur Briggs, the trumpet player, lived about two hundred yards away and was over at our place all the time. The villa had three stories and a surprise for me—a billiard room. Peter wanted to raise chickens, and there was plenty of room—five thousand meters of gardens. There was also a tennis court.

We bought all kinds of chicken-raising paraphernalia. It wasn't just a hobby. We had a built-in market at Bricktop's and the other Montmartre clubs that followed the custom of serving chicken fricassee or bacon and eggs or chicken sandwiches in the morning.

Peter turned out to be a good chicken farmer. We had Rhode Island Reds and other prize breeds. However, I laid down some rules: no chicken could be killed while I was in the house, and when I gave a party, I'd buy my chickens from a place down the road. The eggs were great, and I brought them to the club every night.

Mama came back from America, and we fixed up a beautiful room for her. Louis Cole, who was working at the club, lived on the top floor. He had come to Paris a couple of years earlier with a Negro revue that had gotten stranded. He was a chic, elegant little boy. He drove a red racing car that was one of the sights of Paris. Peter and I bought a car once we'd moved to the country—an elegant Citroën.

After we'd settled into the villa, Louis Cole suggested a party there for the whole Bricktop's crowd. "What? Me give a party for my clients? Why?"

"Why not?" Cole answered, and the way he said it told me that it was something I'd never get out of.

Everybody came—Cole and Mrs. Porter, Elsa Maxwell, Billy Reardon, I can't remember all of them. They wanted to see Brick's home in the country. They were proud of the "monster" they had created.

That was the first of many great parties Peter and I gave at the villa, including a barbecue that lasted three days. On the first day I looked across the garden and spotted six men I'd never seen before. I asked them who they were. One answered that they were from New York, which didn't exactly explain their presence in my garden. "Who invited you?" I wanted to know. The fellow who was doing the talking said, "Bill Henley."

Bill had worked for years at Harry's New York Bar and he owned a roadhouse not far from the villa. He was working the barbecue pit and I went over to him and asked about those men.

"Oh," he said casually, "that's Dutch Schultz and some of his pals."

The last thing I needed, as an American living abroad, was a bigtime gangster in my home. I was furious. "Why did you ask him?" I wanted to know. "And without even telling me?" I was ready to ask them to leave, but Bill talked me out of it. Still, I refused to have anything to do with those gangsters.

Life at the villa wasn't all parties. There were quiet weekends when I could prowl the garden and tell the gardener not to pay any attention to Mama's meddling. Mama insisted that "those foreign fools don't know a rose from a petunia." She and Peter were as thick as thieves, so it was a happy home, and the quiet days were a relief from the busy nights.

THE GOLDEN ERA

AS THE 1920s drew to a close and the 1930s came in, Paris was as wild and gay as ever. There was an *awful* lot of money. Judging by who came to Bricktop's, everybody had money and everybody was spending it. It's unbelievable, the life and the ease with which they lived it. If you'd never belonged, you found yourself *trying* to belong. There was an attitude of total abandon that I don't think anyone who wasn't there could really understand—and it wasn't all concentrated in Bricktop's.

The biggest playboys in Paris were the Argentine millionaires. They spent money like it was going out of style. They didn't usually come to my club—they weren't in "the set." They hung out down the street at a club called El Garon. They said it was a custom in their country to break a dinner plate after someone made a speech, and they'd get full of champagne and pretty soon they'd be breaking plates. They'd order a hundred dollars' worth of plates, smash them all, and when they had a satisfactory pile they'd sweep them away and then order another hundred dollars' worth. *My* South American millionaire was a man named Macoco. He preferred to smash glasses. He'd load up a table with champagne glasses, then turn the whole thing over. He didn't do that in my place very often—I'd tell him to get over to El Garon and do it.

Some of my guests—and it had to be Michael Farmer who started it—discovered that if you dropped a bottle of champagne at a certain angle, it would break one of the glass floor panels in my club. Each panel cost about two thousand francs to replace, but he didn't mind paying, and as long as he didn't mind paying, I really didn't mind if he did it. I had a soft spot in my heart for Michael.

Michael Farmer was one of those famous big spenders who are all but extinct now. Big spenders today usually figure out a way to take it off their income taxes. They pay with an American Express card and make sure they get a copy of the itemized bill. In those days, though, you paid so little in income tax that you didn't even worry about it. You just spent, period. Needless to say, big spenders were always welcome at Bricktop's.

At the same time, I never looked down my nose at the good spender, or even the medium spender. It was always my policy to treat them with courtesy and respect. I consider a good spender someone who runs up a pretty good bill, knows what he's doing, and doesn't squawk when he has to pay it. For every good spender, though, you have the other kind, too: the show-off who buys round after round, gets the bill, goes over it item by item, and complains, "I didn't have this, I didn't have that."

A medium spender is the fellow who brings in a party of four and orders six or eight whiskeys apiece. That's pretty good drinking.

Sometimes the spenders will order a round for the entertainers, but that custom is disappearing. Nowadays only a few Texans entertain like that.

Of course, sometimes you get someone who's a big spender mostly because he's drunk. They were not taken advantage of at Bricktop's. The first thing I told a new waiter was: "If I find you putting so much as half a drink on the bill that doesn't belong on it, I'm going to fire you right in front of the client." And I'd do it. If they wanted to work in a gyp joint, let 'em work in a gyp joint, but not in my place. I wanted people to know that even if they came in drunk, they weren't going to be ripped off.

I had some real big spenders. Ralph Beaver Strassburger was one. He'd inherited about ten million dollars from his father back in Pennsylvania, but he wasn't one of those idle rich. He served as U.S. Consul General in Romania before World War I and later volunteered for service in the war. After that he was Consul General in Serbia and Bulgaria. He was also the publisher of the Norristown, Pennsylvania, *Times-Herald*, which he'd bought in 1921, when he was in his late thirties. His biggest love was horse racing, though, and when I met him it was as a horse-racing tycoon. He had stables back in Pennsylvania and in England and Ireland, where he raised thoroughbreds and hunting horses, but France was his favorite country. He had both a home and an office in Paris and a summer place in Deauville. He died in Paris in 1959.

Every time Ralph walked through the door at Bricktop's, I knew it was going to be a good night. He lived like a tycoon, and I never could picture him in those stuffy diplomatic circles. He would come into my place, look around, and call me over. "Brick," he'd say, "close the door. This is going to be my party tonight," and he'd pick up the tab for the whole place. He was one of the all-time big tippers. He usually tipped me a hundred dollars, and he would tip all the musicians and entertainers and waiters. I can still see him folding those franc notes and going up to each person individually. He knew better than to leave the job to the headwaiter.

Even Nicky de Gunzburg would pick up the whole tab sometimes. He was Russian, a baron, and very gentlemanly and quiet. With his quiet little self, he would sometimes come in and say "Bricky, it's kind of slow around here. Come on, let's give everybody some bottles." He never bought a drink—he bought a bottle.

Jeff Crane, who got his millions from the family business—National Cash Register—was a big spender who never carried money. He'd run up huge tabs, sometimes ten thousand francs a night. At the end of the night I'd present him with an itemized bill, and he'd always tear it up without even looking at it. "I don't need to check the bill," he'd say, "just tell me the total." Then he'd tell me to send the total to his concierge. She'd pay it.

There were always a few big spenders who were mystery men. At Bricktop's no one ever asked who anybody else was, but, as a rule, I found out eventually. Still, there were some people, especially after I moved into my bigger place, that nobody *ever* found out anything about.

The one I remember best would show up most nights, and always with the same girl—and the two of them would drink more champagne than the average party of four. I was always a little bit suspicious of these mystery men, because most of them came to Paris for a fling, spent their money too fast trying to show off, and wound up owing me. This one seemed typical—he always wore the same suit, and it looked as if he only owned two shirts. I predicted to myself that he'd run out of money pretty soon, and, sure enough, one night he did.

I was ready for the usual line: "Brick, I'm short. Do you mind if I pay this tab tomorrow?" And I was ready to say okay. After all, these fellows spent a lot of money in my place, and I could afford a little charity. This mystery man was different, however. He *was* short of cash, but he had collateral for me to hold against his tab. He pulled out a letter of credit worth ten thousand dollars!

I didn't like holding that kind of negotiable note overnight, but I was curious and agreed to take it, meet him the next morning, and go with him to the bank. The letter of credit was worth just what it was supposed to be worth. The man paid me, came back that night, and was at Bricktop's for many nights afterward. I knew nothing more about him the last night I saw him than I'd found out the first. I figured he simply came to Paris with ten thousand dollars, spent it, and left when he was broke.

Next year, he was back—one suit, two shirts, another ten-thousand-dollar letter of credit, different girl. Once the waiters found out about that letter, they'd try to distract me. "You're wanted on the telephone," they'd say, then they'd put another bottle of champagne on his table, with a view toward pocketing the cost of that bottle. I got wise to that pretty soon, though. No cne, not even a mystery man, was going to be cheated in my club.

Every year for several years this man would arrive—always in the spring when the Paris season was really on, and always with that letter of credit. Years later I heard or read that Howard Hughes said he'd been to Bricktop's "many, many times," and I've always wondered if he was that mystery man. I certainly don't remember any Howard Hughes being in my club.

Another mystery man was named Walsh. He was a banker from Alabama, among other things, and he came to Paris with a girl. I didn't like him because he was very common. He spit on my floor once, and I felt like throwing him out. He also used bad language. He was a professional gambler, too. Some of the boys set up a game for him, and he beat the hell out of all the other players. One night he came out to Bougival, stood outside the gate, and hollered, "Brick, come down, open the gate." Peter was out, Mama was asleep, and I was just about to catch the train to Paris. I really worried about leaving the house when he was in the neighborhood. I just didn't trust him. Later it came out that he had embezzled a lot of money from his bank, and that the girl he had brought to Paris with him was a teller who had helped him. He was finally murdered back in the States; I think it had to do with a car-stealing ring somehow.

Michael Farmer was my favorite mystery man. What made him a mystery man was that no one knew for sure where he came from or how he got his money. The rumor was that he got it from some old woman in Ireland, but he had such a great personality that nobody really cared. As I said, he was always doing crazy things—like calling Marilyn Miller in Hollywood just to play music to her. Then there was his champagne-bottle trick—all those broken floor panels!

If I had on a dress that he didn't like, he'd just tear it down the front and say, "Bricky, go down to Schiaparelli and get a new dress! I'll pay for it." That always got a laugh, and sometimes I'd deliberately wear something I knew he wouldn't like because when he did it he livened up the whole place.

It was hard to get angry at Michael. He was like an overgrown kid. I felt the same way about him as I did about Scott Fitzgerald, and he felt the same way about Bricktop's. A night was just lost if he didn't spend at least part of it at Bricktop's.

People like Michael Farmer didn't have to play by the same rules as ordinary people. They did what they wanted when they wanted. If they wanted to smoke opium or sniff cocaine, they did it. There were maybe ten or fifteen among the real crowd who smoked opium, including a very rich marquise in Paris. Others carried cocaine in little jeweled boxes. They always did it in a classy way, though. There was something light-hearted and elegant about the way those people did everything. As Anita Loos put it, they were just letting off steam in the brightest kind of way.

They were all fooling around with each other. When people ask me, "Who was fooling around with whom?" I say, "Who *wasn't* fooling around with whom?" It was all very incestuous, but of course that was the thing to do. They were having affairs and doing the same things people do now, but they had a more elegant way of doing it, my dear. They all knew who was fooling around, and whom with, and it was all right as long as you didn't step out of your clique or go outside the set.

If they did step out of the set, it was just for a lark. I have seen some real *ladies* from England come to France or Rome to pick up a gigolo. I remember once, before I knew better, I saw one of these Englishwomen in the club with a man. The next night she came in with some friends, and I was naïve enough to ask her if she was going with the man. "Bricky, dear," she said, "that was *last* night." I'll never forget the way she looked at me. Right away quick, I learned to stop asking such questions.

They went to bed, but by the next morning they'd forgotten they'd even had an affair. That's a good way to live.

That reminds me of one of the differences between European royalty and American "stars," at least in those days. The Americans didn't know a gigolo from the real thing. Europeans always did.

Peggy Hopkins Joyce and Mabel Ball used to come to Paris for two or three weeks every year. They'd been showgirls with Ziegfeld and collected many admirers and lots of diamonds. They called themselves the "Diamond Queens."

Of course, their diamonds weren't any better than a lot of other people's. Everyone had diamonds, emeralds, and rubies. The most beautiful set of diamonds I ever saw belonged to Lady Mountbatten. She always wore white evening gowns that showed them off to perfection. Nobody paid all that much attention, though, because everybody was bedecked with jewels.

Peggy and Mabel were successful to a point. They never got to the

Rothschilds, but they managed to be part of Cole's show-business set. You see, Cole had three or four sets. One of them I used to call the "Who's Who," and it included the Rothschilds and Lady Mountbatten and Nicky de Gunzburg and Lady Mendl. Peggy and Mabel hadn't a prayer of getting into that set. One reason is that they were too showy, besides the fact that they weren't royalty and weren't very good at recognizing it when they saw it.

Peggy Hopkins Joyce was a good example of the "rags to riches through marriage" story. She had been born in Virginia to an average family, but she was blond and pretty and ambitious, and she didn't stay in Virginia long. At fifteen, she ran away with a vaudeville bicyclist, got as far as Denver with him, then left him for her first husband, a man named Archibald. Her family caught up with her and had the marriage annulled and sent her off to a private school in Washington, D.C.

There she met and married a man named Hopkins. This next marriage was a further step up the ladder. Hopkins was from one of the real social families in Washington. Peggy didn't just want social acceptance, however, she wanted to be a star. That ambition probably didn't sit well with the Hopkins family, and pretty soon she was divorced from Mr. Hopkins. She went to New York, started a stage career, and pretty soon she was married to Mr. Joyce. As a Chicago lumberman, he was a few steps down the social ladder, but he had lots of money and apparently was happy to help Peggy with her career. It was as Peggy Hopkins Joyce that she became a Ziegfeld girl. After that, she was in a couple of movies and plays.

Peggy became a star not so much because of what she did onstage as what she did off it. Her divorce from Mr. Joyce made all the papers. There was a big court suit, and it came out that during their marriage he'd given her a million and a half dollars' worth of jewels. That's probably how she came to be called a "Diamond Queen." After that, it seemed as if every time I picked up the *International Herald Tribune*, I read that Peggy was either getting another divorce or contemplating another marriage—and of course the reporters asked every man she went out with how many diamonds he'd given her.

I suppose one reason why Peggy came to Paris every year was to look for a noble husband. She had money and fame, but she didn't have a title. The trouble was, at least at first, that she didn't know a real title from a phony one, or real nobility from the bogus variety. I remember she came in one night with a very good-looking French fellow, and she whispered to me how he was a big whatever, and we were all laughing behind her back because we knew he wasn't nothing but a gigolo. That guy was well known as nothing.

Finally, I told her, "Darling, stop trying to build this guy up. Everybody knows what he is."

"Oh, but he told me . . ." she started.

"Sure, sure," I said, "he'll tell you anything." Peggy thought she was going to get something from him, but he was out to get a whole lot more from her.

I'll say one thing for Peggy, she learned quickly. She got herself a Swedish count—Count Gosta Mornet—but that didn't last long. She got rid of him and his name, too. I think she might have liked to have kept the name, because of its Continental sound, but there are only so many names you can carry. She was to marry six men altogether, but she always went by the names of the second and third, Hopkins and Joyce.

After the Swedish count, there was an English engineer named Easton and a banker named Meyer. She was still married to Mr. Meyer when she died of cancer in 1957 at the age of sixty-three. Marriage never did more for anyone than for Peggy Hopkins Joyce. Her wide experience even got her a job as a lovelorn columnist for a while. None of her experiences ever soured her on the institution; she always praised marriage as the foundation of society.

Once in a while there would be a scene in Bricktop's. Somebody's jealousy would get out of hand, or people would have words. They all knew each other, though, and someone would usually step right in and say, "Come on." It was almost like being in someone's parlor or living room.

I remember when Horace Dodge, of the Dodge automobile family, was separated from his wife, Lois. She was going around with a fellow, and Horace came in one night and tried to pick a fight with the guy. It wasn't the first time he'd tried to pick a fight in Bricktop's. He was a very testy sort of guy even then, and at the time he was only in his early thirties and hadn't gone through all those divorce suits and other court battles that would make him so well known.

Horace's father, Horace, Sr., and his Uncle John were blacksmiths in Detroit who went into partnership with Henry Ford making cars. They later sold their share of the business to Ford and started making their own cars, Dodges. Then they sold that business to Chrysler and ended up with a pile of money. Horace, Jr., grew up in a 127-room mansion. He never had to struggle for anything, but he had a strong desire to be on top. He loved speedboat racing, and in the summertime, when everyone went to Deauville and Biarritz, he'd be there looking for people to race him. Later on he'd hire a whole train to transport all his boats from one place to another. In 1949 he won all four of the big international races.

Horace liked to win. If he didn't win, then somebody else wasn't playing fair. It seemed as if he was always in court for one thing or another—usually about racing or divorcing. Lois was only his first wife. He had four others, and four divorces that were really sensational and written up in all the papers. The only one I had any experience of was his divorce from Lois, and fortunately I didn't see any of the really nasty stuff. When Horace tried to make trouble that night in Bricktop's, his and Lois's friends jumped right in and put a stop to it.

Of course, when that kind of thing happened, I could always say, "You can't do that in here, because this is Bricktop's." Starting a fight at Bricktop's was like starting a fight in somebody's house.

Everybody has arguments, of course, and these people were no different. There were no permanent rifts. Somebody'd get drunk and say to somebody else, "I've wanted to tell you this for a long time . . . ," but there were never any knockdown, drag-out fights. Those people were too close.

As I've said, everybody was fooling around with everyone else. There was homosexuality, but it was pretty discreet. Most of it was done outside the set. I'd have gay men come into the club and say, "Bricky, I don't want to see the little boy that I gave five hundred francs to last night in here tonight. I know where to find him. I might come in with my wife or somebody."

You know those little boys, they'll tell you right away quick: "What's the matter? You don't know me tonight? You knew me last night."

In later years gay and straight people mixed more—I noticed it especially when I returned to America—but back in Paris before the war that kind of stuff was kept pretty much separate. There was a place in Paris called Le Boeuf sur le Toit. The name means The Cow on the Roof, and it came from a popular Brazilian tune of the early Twenties. Darius Milhaud, one of the avant-garde composers of the period who were called "Les Six," based one of his pieces on that tune, and it became the name of the bar. In the early Twenties, when it was on the Rue Boissy d'Anglas, Le Boeuf was a center for French writers and artists— Jean Cocteau, Erik Satie, René Clair, and many others—but by the late Twenties most of that crowd had drifted away. In 1928 the owner, Louis Moyses, moved the place to Rue de Penthièvre, and it became known as a gay hangout, but very elegant. One of Moyses's managers in the second place was named Jacobi, and he later went to the United States and opened up a place with Bobby Short.

I went to Le Boeuf sur le Toit sometimes. They were nice people, well-mannered people. It wasn't like some of those gay bars they have now.

Looking back, I know that a lot went on, but I really can't remember many specifics. I probably would have seen more if I didn't like Rémy Martin so much. I never got drunk. I was never too drunk to add up the receipts, or to catch a waiter double-billing a customer, or to make sure the entertainers were doing their job, but when you're drinking, things have a habit of passing over the top of your head. When you're sober, you sort of catch them and take them inside. Sometimes I'd announce, "I'm gonna stay sober tonight, because I want to find out what the hell's going on around here."

I'd stand at the bar as usual, and as usual the clients would say, "Have a drink, Bricky, have a drink," but the barman would give me water, or take away the champagne when the client wasn't looking. Then, when I closed up in the morning, I could say, "Gee, I didn't know that was going on." The barman and waiters and entertainers would say, "We could have told you, but we know you don't like us to carry tales."

Even so, I'd forget what I'd heard and seen right away quick. Mama used to say, "Anything you don't want to hear again, don't even tell your-self." It wasn't my business to know these things. It was my business to make my clients feel at home.

Speaking of Rémy Martin, it was partly the fault of that champagne that I started putting on so much weight around 1929 and 1930. I hadn't been skinny since I'd been a teenager, and since my teens my weight had run around 135. I was what I'd call well made. After a few years in Paris, though, my life-style began to take its toll. We drank an *awful* lot of champagne. We also had dinner very late at night, then went and lay down, and *then* got up and went to work. No exercise. Then we worked until six or seven o'clock in the morning, and then we went to the bistros until nine or ten o'clock, had another big meal, then went home and went to bed. In no time at all I shot up from about 135 to about 175. I still had those "singing legs and feet," but the rest of me got to be almost too much for them to carry around.

I cared about losing my figure, but I didn't worry about it all that much. Life was too good. I had a husband and a big apartment and a house in the country. I had a thriving business. In fact, business was so good I was looking around for a bigger club.

With the times what they were, with the economy across the Atlantic so rocky, I should have cut down—hoarded my francs and behaved like a normal businesswoman with cash on her hands instead of bills. But *I* decided to open a bigger club.

It was at 66 Rue Pigalle—a great big room that could seat about a hundred people, with a couple of smaller rooms, a bar and a kitchen. I had Hoyningen-Huené do the lighting—he did lighting for a lot of theaters, but he was most famous as a society photographer. Neil Martin did the decorating. The walls were lined with banquettes, and Hoyningen-Huené lit them from behind and created a cozy, kind of mysterious atmosphere. There were heavy patent-leather curtains across the door, and as you approached you could see only shadows—the silhouettes of people's heads. The carpet was red, the banquettes were red and black, everything was done in red and black—and with that lighting, well, when it opened in November 1931, it was the talk of Paris.

A few people cautioned me about taking such a big step. Eddie Molyneux said, "Bricky, are you sure you're making the right move, leaving this place and going into a larger one? The word to us in England is stay at home and save your money." However, it didn't seem to me that very many people were taking that advice. I had lots of English people, lots of Americans, lots of all those special people who would say to each other, "Where shall I see you?" "Well, tonight you'll see me at Brick's." That was the place everybody was supposed to be. My smaller place was packed every night. A bigger place would just let more people get in.

I did have sense enough to realize I would need some help, however. After all, the new place would be three times as big as the old one. Peter didn't want to be my partner in the club business. I had to find someone else, and my first and only choice was Mabel Mercer.

I'd known about Mabel Mercer almost as long as I'd been in Paris. In those days there were so few colored women in Paris—so few colored *people* in Paris—that we all noticed each other immediately. I was with a boy and I looked across the street and saw this woman, and he saw her, too. He called out, "Hi, Mabel."

"Who's that?" I asked, and he said, "That's Mabel Mercer—she's an English girl, a soprano." I filed that away in my mind for the time being, but of course the Negro colony in Paris was so small that it wasn't long before I knew all about her.

She had been born in Staffordshire, England. Her mother was a white woman, a show-business woman, her father a Negro musician. Mabel never knew him. I think he died just before she was born, or else he left her mother. Then, right after Mabel was born, her mother left Mabel.

Mabel spent I don't know how many years looking for her mother. She had all her friends and all the reporters she met and, later, even CBS looking for her. It wasn't until Mabel came to the United States, however, that she finally located that woman. She'd moved to America years before and married an American.

Mabel was raised by her relatives—*all* her relatives, the colored and the white. They put her in Catholic schools, and I suppose the nuns really raised her. They brought her up to be a real lady. She is English, dahling, and don't you ever forget it—but she didn't have any mother and father and she had to go out to work. She was born singing, with a beautiful soprano voice, but of course with her background and in her station the only place for her to go was vaudeville. She'd been in vaudeville many years by 1931.

She had come to Paris with an act that had broken up after a few weeks, and she'd decided to stay. In Paris she usually got into the chorus line of one of the Negro revues that were so popular in France in the Twenties. In between, she worked in the clubs, usually as a last-minute replacement. Once in a while she'd get to do one of her superb male impersonations, but she had never received any real recognition. Because she was a soprano, it was hard for her, and when I announced that I wanted to hire her to help in the new place, people said, "Bricky, who wants to hear a soprano at twelve o'clock at night?"

I didn't really want her for her singing, however. I wanted her because she was very well-met—very shy and reserved, a lady. Beautifully friendly, but never familiar. I knew I could sit her down at a table and know that she wouldn't use any bad language or tell any dirty jokes, and that she'd laugh at the right times. She also drank nothing but champagne. Mabel was someone I knew I could trust—and an entertainer besides. It was a decision I made as a businesswoman.

I sent for her at the little club where she was working. She came over to my place and I said, "Mabel, how would you like to come and work with me?" Right away, she said, "Oh, great, Bricky, I'd love to." Then, however, she said she'd give me definite word in a couple of days. She probably wanted to discuss it with Harvey.

At that time she was going with Harvey White, a big black fellow who'd made a name for himself as an entertainer in New York and was quite rich. I don't know how much he influenced her, but when she came back a couple nights later and I asked her how much she wanted, she said two hundred francs. That was big money, good money. She really couldn't have gotten it anywhere else, but as a businesswoman I was willing to pay her that much because I knew how much help she would be to me. As it turned out, I was a big help to her, too. Mabel is the first to say it, and has said it many times: "I became a star at Bricktop's."

At first, though, I couldn't even get her to go out on the floor. Night after night I would arrive to hear the bandleader complain, "Mabel hasn't sung yet." When I told her that she simply had to get on the floor and sing, Mabel's answer was always the same: "Do you think they really want to hear me?"

"I don't know about them," I'd say, "but *I* want to hear you."

The clients really didn't take to her voice. After she'd sung, I'd go over to the tables and say, "Well, what did you think?" and the clients would say, "Wellllll, Bricky . . ." And I'd say, "But she's an awfully nice girl."

She was, and they found that out, and pretty soon when the clients came to the club, they'd say, "Tell Mabel hello" or "Tell Mabel to come and have a drink." And that's how she made her reputation—with me. She didn't make her reputation singing, that's for sure.

It took some prodding, but eventually Mabel gained the confidence that had been missing in her work and started to become the great stylist she is today. She's got great timing, and if her voice isn't what it used to be, she certainly knows how to put over a number.

We were a good team. She was about six years younger than me, but she had poise and those beautiful English manners. We complemented each other. Cole used to say, "If you want to talk social, talk to Mabel; if you want to talk money, talk to Brick." Mabel will tell you even today, "If I know anything about taking care of people, I got it from Brick."

By 1932 the Depression was sweeping the United States, but it still hadn't really hit Europe. There were no soup kitchens, no long lines of unemployed people, no one selling apples on the street. At Bricktop's it was as if nothing in the world had changed. The rich and powerful played and loved just as they had before.

Bricktop's cradled any number of romances, and one that pleased me very much was that of Gloria Swanson and Michael Farmer. Michael's romance may not have started at Bricktop's, but I think it blossomed there.

Gloria was one of the few American movie stars who were accepted by the Bricktop's crowd. She had probably gotten in with that set because of her marriage in 1925 to the Marquis de la Falaise de la Coudraye (whom everybody called Hank). She deserved it on her own, however. What a lady—and cooool. I was so pleased to see her and Michael get together, and the last thing I ever expected was for her to be jealous of me.

They were married in August 1931, after her divorce from the Marquis came through, and when they came back to Paris, they spent the first night at Bricktop's. When I greeted them, Michael gave me a big smile. "I'm having trouble with Gloria about you," he said. I didn't pay much attention to the remark at the time, but later I realized she hadn't seemed very pleased to see me.

I found Michael alone a couple of nights later, and I asked, "What do you mean about trouble with Gloria because of me? I don't understand." He only repeated that there had been trouble, and that I was the reason.

A night or two later a waiter said, "Mrs. Farmer would like to see you." I went to her table, and as I sat down Gloria said, "Have you noticed I've been a little upset with you?" I said I certainly had and wanted to know why. "Well," she said, "how would you like to go on a honeymoon and have your husband say, 'I'll be so happy to get back to Brick's'?" Gloria was icy calm. "I've heard a lot of rumors," she added.

I wanted to laugh, but I didn't, because in Gloria's mind this was a serious situation. I assured her there was nothing between Michael and me and never had been, but I don't think she was convinced.

It really bothered me that I was the cause of any trouble between them. I thought about it a lot. Finally, I figured it out, and it was so simple. Michael hadn't been saying he wanted to get back to Brick, but to *Brick's*. There's a big difference between a woman and a nightclub that anyone except a gal on her honeymoon would know. I explained all this to Michael, and then separately we both explained it to Gloria. To-day Gloria and I are still friends. I'm very fond of her.

Gloria and Michael were divorced in 1934. I saw Michael after that—he came to Bricktop's after the war—but eventually I lost touch with him. A few years ago I saw a clipping from the London *Times* that said he'd gone there to be the manager of a pub. I was going to write to him, but kept putting it off. In the meantime I ran into Gloria. She said she'd seen him, and that if I did, I'd cry. His looks were gone, he was old and heavy and had lots of gold teeth. After that, I decided it was best to remember the sweet cut-up I'd loved.

So many people felt about Bricktop's as Michael Farmer did. I re-member Jimmy Walker, who used to come over every spring when he was mayor of New York City. The last time he came over as mayor—I think it was in 1932—there were street repairs being done in the Place Pigalle, and he got confused and didn't know where the club was. He started climbing over the rubble, muttering, "Where's my gal? I've got to find her." There were about twenty-five clubs in the neighborhood, and Jimmy must have opened many doors before he found me.

Whenever Jimmy came in, the piano player would launch into "East Side, West Side" and then slip into "Melancholy Baby," as Jimmy would break into a dance and remind the crowd that he could still do a soft-shoe.

Frank Shields, the tennis champion, came to the club every night when he was in Paris. Often he'd come out to the country for breakfast with Peter and me. He swore he was playing better because of my food. One time the whole tennis team was on the train, ready to leave Paris, but nobody could find Frank Shields. The train left without him, and so did the boat back to America. The police got into the affair of the missing tennis star, and after they heard that he'd had breakfast with us that very morning, they came dashing out to the villa. I knew less than they did and wasn't aware of what had happened until I read it in the newspapers. Frank had simply left the villa one morning, boarded a tramp steamer, and gone home to the girl he was in love with.

There was Monty Woolley, who had to wait many years before his talents and his beard were fully recognized in *The Man Who Came to Dinner*. He was the most well-known obscure man I've ever come across. He was one of those professional socialites, always in the chic places during the "in" seasons, always well dressed and charming. He came from a well-to-do hotel-owning family in New York and had gone to Yale, where he got into dramatics. He'd always dabbled in things, however, and never really set his mind on any single one. After he got out of Yale, his father died and left him enough money so he could just go on dabbling in things.

I've always thought that a little money is dangerous. It's just enough to make you weak. You're better off having either a lot of money or no money at all. With his personality and his connections from Yale and all, Monty didn't have to put much energy into being a success on the stage. He just put it into being charming. Of course, it also helped that he didn't care very much about possessions. He always lived in hotel rooms—never had an apartment—and didn't even care about making his rooms look like a home. His friends once complained that he should do something to make his room look like he lived in it, so he went out

163

to some art store and bought three copies of the *same* print and hung them on the walls.

The only thing he cared about was his beard, which was perfectly shaped and pure white from a relatively early age. When he was still a nowhere actor, Paramount offered him a part in a film. The only condition was that he shave off his beard. Monty said he'd do it if Paramount paid him a two-thousand-dollar bonus and five hundred dollars a week until it grew back. He didn't get the part.

Monty and Cole were classmates at Yale (along with Gerald Murphy, who, with his wife, was later such a leader of the American intellectual colony in Paris), and Monty was a member in good standing in the Cole Porter–Elsa Maxwell–Noel Coward set. At some point he must have been feeling "unaccomplished" or something, because Cole came to me and said Monty thought he ought to be doing something for a living and would I pay Monty ten dollars a night to be a sort of charmer-in-residence? I'd do anything for Cole, so I didn't mind paying Monty the ten dollars a night, but I did mind the fact that Monty often went out and spent that ten dollars at another club.

Cole also talked producer Ray Goetz into giving Monty his first professional job directing Cole's *Fifty Million Frenchmen* on Broadway (Monty's earlier directing experience was in little-theater productions). From there he went on to direct other things, including Dwight Wiman's *Second Little Show*. A few years after that, Wiman talked him into leaving Hollywood, where he hadn't had much success, to return to New York and play the ballet impresario in Wiman's *On Your Toes*. Finally, he ended up in *The Man Who Came to Dinner*, and from then on he was set for life. He could go on with his little bit of money and his many social connections and live just as before, but now he also had an accomplishment on which to rest. Accomplished or unaccomplished, he was one of the most charming men I've ever met.

Ray Goetz was also a Bricktop's regular and one of the people to whom I felt especially close. He was a friend of Cole's, of course. He first came to my place with his wife, Irene Bordoni, a French singer who went to the United States before World War I and was quite a smash there as the epitome of the French cutie. Ray and Irene were married after the war, and he produced the shows that made her really big in the

Twenties. Although they lived in the States, they came to Paris a lot, and after they split up, around 1929, Ray kept coming back anyway. He and Herbert Fields were great friends, and the two of them usually came together—to see Cole and come to Bricktop's.

Herbie was also part of that "set." He wrote for several of Cole's Broadway musicals, including *Fifty Million Frenchmen*. Herbie always seemed to be paired with his songwriting sister, Dorothy, but he did plenty on his own. When he and Ray Goetz got together in Paris, I don't know which one was crazier than the other. They never slept a wink, as far as I could tell, and they were regulars at both my places in Paris.

For a time I had two places. There was the big club, Bricktop's and then, down the street, a little bistro called the Band Box. My partner was a Chinese man, who did the cooking, and I had a cashier representing me. It was mostly for the musicians, a place where they could go after they had finished work and drink and hang out together. I charged them low prices, and often I would go there and set up the drinks myself.

Ray and Herbie and their friends would come to Bricktop's for a while, then they'd say, "Good night, Bricky," and go hang around some other club until all the nightclubs closed. Then they'd go find the cook and waiters and their musician friends and open up the small place and start the night over again.

In the spring of 1932 one of my *best* old friends came back to Paris. Miss Sophie Tucker—blond, big, and booming (Sophie never talked if she could boom)—walked in. I was thrilled.

"Good evening, Miss Sophie," was the best I could manage. She gave me one of those Tucker looks that could kill you if you didn't know her. "Miss Sophie!" she boomed. "I'm Sophie to you. No one could forget you from the Palace Theatre in Chicago. That hair. Those freckles. And you were as fresh as everything."

After Sophie had made her entrance and everyone knew she was there, she called me to the table. "Brick, do you know where I can get a black piano player? None of these French boys know what I'm doing."

I believe that I made some recommendations that helped. I hope so, because Sophie had played London for the first time a couple of years before and had been a sensation—then come to Paris and flopped. In her autobiography she blamed it on a wave of anti-Semitism, but I don't remember anything like that. At any rate, Sophie was determined to make it big the second time around, and she did.

Sophie lived at Bricktop's during that second trip to Paris, and one night the manager of Chez Florence came in to ask if he might present her with a bottle of champagne. I took him to her table. "We feel a little hurt that you haven't been to Chez Florence, Miss Tucker," he said.

Sophie could never resist a compliment. She threw back her head and laughed one of her deep, roaring laughs. "Let me tell you something," she said. "You see that little redhead standing there? I can see her now at the stage door in Chicago waiting to say hello to me. She's pretty famous now, but if being in her place means anything, that's where I belong. And that's why I'm here. But I'm grateful for the invitation and I'll come to Chez Florence tomorrow."

Of course, she went to Chez Florence the next night. Sophie's word was her bond and her punctuality was awesome. The only time I came close to a third nervous breakdown was when I had a date with her just a few years before she died. It was in New York, and all day long I prayed, "Please God, don't let me be late."

Sophie went to Chez Florence, applauded the show in her usual style, and, when the show was over, said, "Excuse me," in her big, booming voice, "now I'm going over to Bricktop's." Needless to say, everybody followed.

The only unpleasant thing I remember about that first season in the new club was the Baron and the way he tried to muscle in on my business.

No one in the saloon business can avoid gangsters, hoods, petty crooks, and other types of criminals. They seem to be a built-in nuisance. Meeting up with gangsters never surprised me, but the differences in their characters did. Back in the days of Barron's in New York, Jack Diamond seemed like such a quiet, serious man that he could have been taken for a bookworm. One of the handsomest and most debonair fellows I ever met was a racketeer, Scarface Joe. And the only French underworld figure with whom I ever had a run-in was an aristocrat by birth, appropriately called the Baron. He really was a baron and came from a highly respected family in Monte Carlo.

The Baron was a little guy, lithe and slender—he looked something like Alan Ladd. Way back in the Grand Duc days the Baron took a liking to me, either because his interest was personal or because he was surprised at finding an American woman running a bar in Paris. If it was personal, his first appearance at the club wasn't exactly calculated to win a girl's heart. He ordered chicken sandwiches for himself and the fellow he was with. He'd barely tasted his before he started complaining that the sandwiches were no good. My trigger-Irish temper started to flare and I could feel my cheeks getting red, but I kept quiet until the two men left.

Still, the more I thought about it, the angrier I got. After we closed, I decided to find him and have it out with him. Luckily, I didn't find him, but word got around that Bricktop was after the Baron, and Gene Bullard showed up at my apartment, fit to be tied. "Are you crazy?" he demanded. "No one but an idiot would go looking for the Baron. He'd take you on just as easily as he would a man."

Well, the Baron must have heard about how I'd gone looking for him, and must have become curious about me. He started coming in regularly. Sometimes he complained, sometimes he was just tough, sometimes he didn't open his mouth. As the months went on, however, he softened and even gave me a pet name—*mon petit oiseau*. This "little bird" was not touched, but it was better than being snarled at.

By the time I opened the big club, the French underworld was beginning to take some cues from American gangsters. They got them from American gangster movies, and in my opinion they were seeing too many—though I have to admit they weren't the only people in Paris who were hooked on them. When Edward G. Robinson came to Bricktop's, we all went crazy over him. The Bricktop's set didn't include many American film stars, but Edward G. Robinson was *Little Caesar!*

Anyway, probably as a result of seeing these movies, the French gangsters started organizing protection rackets. Businesses, whether they were laundries, greengrocers, butcher shops or nightclubs, either paid a percentage of their receipts to the hoods or risked damage to their property. When the gangsters decided to get nasty, those who protested found themselves at the wrong end of a bullet or a switchblade.

I heard what was going on in Montmartre businesses, and I fully expected to be approached about paying protection money, too. I had an idea that it would be the Baron who would approach me and that my "little bird" days were numbered. It was a surprise, then, when he suggested, not protection, but prostitution. The Baron wanted to put some women in my club to hustle Billy Leeds and all the other rich men I had coming into my place.

The proposition came one morning after the Baron had finished his ham and eggs. He walked over to the bar, where I was in my usual place at the end, tallying receipts. "How come you don't have any girls in here?" he wanted to know.

"Who needs them?" I answered. "I don't need any hostesses, and you know I don't even allow women alone into my place."

The Baron had a weak smile he used when he tried to be nice. "They wouldn't have to be out-and-out whores. They could be beautifully dressed, attractive girls."

"But they'd be hustling just the same. That's not my kind of thing."

Having played his first card, the Baron left, but he came back again and again, sometimes alone, mostly with other hoods. Each time they were more sinister, more threatening, but they didn't actually do anything. Still, I knew there'd be a showdown before long.

It came early one morning, shortly before Christmas. Two men came in whom I'd never seen before, then pretty soon in came the Baron with two of his boys.

"Are those your friends?" I said, pointing to the first two men.

The Baron didn't turn his head. "You talk awful fast and awful big," he said. "I think you've been in France too long."

"So what?" I said.

"You don't cooperate. You don't run your place like the other places."

"Of course I don't cooperate. Not with you. You want me to have whores in here, maybe even sell dope. That's not my line. I sell champagne."

The Baron pulled out a pistol. There was a huge bottle of cologne on the bar, a Christmas present from a client. As I started to reach for it, the Baron said, "Suppose I shoot that bottle?"

I didn't answer him. Instead, I pulled out a pad and started jotting down some figures. The two strangers got up and left, leaving just the Baron and his two goons. Four of my waiters stood by helplessly, which was the smart thing to do. My Chinese cook was in the kitchen.

I didn't look up from the pad. "Go ahead, Baron, shoot it."

A shot rang out and the bar flowed with cologne. It spilled over onto my evening gown. It was a couturier gown, and it just about killed me not to jump up and start wiping the cologne off, but I was furious, and when I'm furious I get very, very calm and very, very cold. I signaled a waiter. "Bring a serviette and wipe up this stuff."

Then I looked at the Baron. "Listen, my husband is not a fellow to fool around with. When he hears about this, you're going to be in trouble. I wouldn't want to be in your shoes."

My calm must have thrown the Baron off guard, because I don't think the threat would have. The Baron sputtered something, and I couldn't understand a word of it, but his goons did. They walked into the kitchen.

About two seconds later they scooted back out and didn't stop until they were out on the street. Without his henchmen, the Baron wasn't so brave. "I'm going to put you out of France!" he yelled as he followed them out the door.

By this time my Chinese cook had come out from the kitchen into the bar—quiet and serene as a Buddha. Confronted by the goons with their guns, he'd pulled out one of his razor-sharp carving knives—and that's all the prodding they'd needed to get out real quick.

Within minutes, it seemed, everyone in Montmartre had heard about me and the Baron, including Peter, who was mad as a hornet. He went right out and bought a pistol, and I had a hard time talking him out of using it. A police inspector came by and asked if we wanted protection —Jimmy, my headwaiter, had told the police; he was a stool pigeon for the police at that time, though I didn't know it. I said no thank you, I didn't need protection. The inspector said, "Very well, madame, but if they cause trouble, just shoot them."

Since the police inspector had given me permission, I started bringing my revolver to the club.

Not many of the nightclub owners stood up to the Baron as I had, and it must have bothered him, but he had sense enough not to tackle me personally again. Instead, he worked through a third party—one of my waiters told me the Baron wanted one hundred thousand francs or there would be trouble. I told him I wouldn't pay one sou. "Give the Baron a message," I said. "You tell him that if he sends anybody around again, he's gonna get shot. And I'm gonna do the shooting. The police told me to shoot anyone who gave me trouble, and I'll do it. My husband isn't going to do the shooting. *I'm* going to do the shooting."

I walked over to the bar, pulled out the pistol, and pointed it at him. "Now you tell the Baron that you saw me with this gun in my hand and you know I'm not fooling around."

I must have had the nerve of the Devil. I still can't believe I did that. But it worked. That was the end of the pressure on Bricktop's from the French gangsters. The "little bird" was left alone, while others, like the haberdasher nearby, came to business one morning to find their places shot up.

When Jack "Legs" Diamond and his wife, Alice, came to Paris, they stopped at the club because they remembered me from Barron's in New York. I heard from others that Jack was in town to pick up a piece of the Paris action and was trying to negotiate a deal with the Baron. The French-American merger didn't come off. The Baron didn't like Jack trying to poach on his territory. I heard that Jack got so mad he challenged the Baron to meet him in the Bois de Boulogne. The duel, or whatever it was supposed to have been, never happened. If it had, I wonder who would have won. Probably not the Baron. Being born to good family, he probably wasn't as tough as an American gangster.

With the years the Baron was seen less and less around Paris. The last time we met was in Monte Carlo. I was at the bar when the Baron walked in. His fish eyes lit up and he walked toward me, exclaiming, *"Mon petit oiseau!"*

He invited me to have a drink. I said, "You know I don't drink with you."

He looked disappointed and slid away. He wasn't much of a tough guy by that time. He was no longer the king of the rackets in Paris, and the gossip on the Riviera was that his family was supporting him in return for his promise that he stay quiet and out of their sight.

AND WE ALL
PLAYED ON

SUMMER WAS A MIXED time for me. Bricktop's closed for the hot-weather months exactly like all the other Montmartre bars. There wasn't any business to speak of, and the French, certainly the Parisians, took the vacation month of August seriously. They swarmed to the country, the mountains, the sea. If today's tourist is dismayed by the fact that it's almost impossible to get a dress cleaned or shirt laundered during the month of August, he should have known Paris in 1932 when we had to locate new butchers and bakers.

The villa in the country was beautiful in the summertime, and for the first few weeks after we closed I enjoyed the peace and serenity, the gardens, and just getting away from things. I suppose I had become a warhorse, however, indifferent to and honestly incapable of enjoying leisure. I didn't care for the resort routine. The cocktail parties, the round of dinners, the lounging around all day, and the business of thinking up things to do at night just weren't my idea of a good time. I think what bothered me most were the nights—I always needed a place to go to at eleven o'clock, and, frankly, I still do.

Julie and Charlie Wacker of Chicago were wonderful clients of Bricktop's and equally wonderful personal friends. Knowing how I felt about summers, they wondered why I couldn't move Bricktop's to Biarritz, where they lived all year round. They suggested that it would be perfect for me and for Biarritz, a resort that had become famous because Edward VII, grandfather of the Prince of Wales, used to spend his summers there. Now that the Prince was a young man and more or less on his own, he was doing the same thing. Biarritz was an hour's drive from San Sebastian, where Spanish royalty spent the summer, so I would be right at home.

The Biarritz season was very short, only five or six weeks from the first of August to around the middle of September. Before that, most of the crowd went to Deauville. Gloria Swanson, Michael Farmer, and others went to Nice first, then to Cannes; they started Cannes as a summer resort. However, almost everyone landed in Biarritz as the summer came to an end.

I went to Biarritz and found a place a block from the Grand Casino, right on the Mediterranean. The Merry Sol was a terrace, divided by the dance floor and the band. When it rained, we simply went indoors. The deal was all put together in a matter of hours. All I had to do was move the Paris Bricktop's to Biarritz, which I did—from dishes and glasses to cooks, waiters, and artists. Peter was also with me.

Once things were put together and the place in Biarritz opened, we settled down to one of the most successful and beautiful seasons of my career. The Prince of Wales came opening night and every night thereafter. Beth Leary, a rich New York woman, a close friend of Lady Thelma Furness, entertained a party of thirty or forty many nights. There was Spanish nobility from San Sebastian, and of course the top social figures of Biarritz. Lady Furness was the Prince's constant companion, and the tongues wagged about how their friendship would end up.

Nineteen thirty-two was the year of the red pullover shirt, a style that I think originated with the Prince of Wales, who was a brilliant and imaginative innovator in men's clothes. I always loved the story—and it might have been just a legend—that the Prince was so fastidious about his tailoring that his suit jackets were tailored in London and his trousers in New York because he felt each city had the perfectionists in one of the two arts.

When the Prince, wearing his red pullover shirt, tried to get into the Casino one night, the doorman, who didn't recognize him, told him he couldn't enter because he wasn't properly dressed. Because the Prince wandered around alone a great deal, there was no one there to tell the doorman who he was barring from the Casino. Just as the Prince was about to go away, the manager ran up and started apologizing, at the same time bawling out the doorman and threatening to fire him. The Prince cut the manager short. "If you fire this man, I'll never come back to this place again. I have no business coming in dressed like this. I have no right to take advantage."

That was the sort of thing that made me admire him. He rarely made reservations except when he was entertaining. When he saw there wasn't a good table available, he would always say, "Put me behind anything. It doesn't matter." He was never fussy or formal. The door would bounce open and there would be the Prince—a joy to see and to entertain.

I never had any problem feeling comfortable around the royalty that came to the club. That, too, probably came from Mama. She was there in Biarritz with me once when I was expecting the Prince. I went upstairs and said, "Mama, if you watch the road, you'll see His Royal Highness the Prince of Wales arrive."

After he came, I went back upstairs. "Well, Mama, what do you think of the Prince of Wales?"

"What? That little man?"

"What did you expect?"

"As a prince, I thought he was going to be tall," was all she said.

Mabel Mercer had an entirely different attitude. Mabel by now was really going to town as an entertainer. No longer the wallflower who had to be pushed out on the floor, she had become a complete professional. Every time the Prince came, however, he just stunned her. When he entered the club, she stood at attention as strict as a member of the

173

Royal Guard. There was no relaxing Mabel. The Prince represented *her* royalty. She was interested but never swayed by other members of the nobility who filled the place night after night.

Among the other nobility was Prince George, younger brother of the Prince of Wales. I had met him earlier in the year in Paris when the Marquise de Polignac had driven to my apartment building on the Rue Pigalle one day and sent her chauffeur to ask me if I would come downstairs. There had been three young men in the car. She'd asked me if I wanted to go to Rheims and entertain at a party. She hadn't introduced me to the young men. I'd been wearing house shoes and an apron. I'd said, "Oh, yes, certainly," and then later I'd heard that the party was for His Royal Highness Prince George.

I went down to Rheims on the train, and that was the first time I stayed in a hotel where you could lie on the bed and just press buttons and doors would open and close. As I've said, in those days we entertainers were treated as acquaintances—not friends, but good acquaintances. If you were asked to entertain at a party, you didn't go through the back door or the side door, you went in the same door they did.

When I got to the party, the Marquise de Polignac said, "I want you to meet Prince George, brother of the Prince of Wales. That's why you're here."

We walked over to him. "This can't be the same woman!" he said, remembering me in my apron and house shoes, and looking at me now in my couturier gown.

The Marquise said, "Oh, yes, that's Bricky. She's two different people—one at night and a different one by day."

After a while someone said, "Maybe you should go in the next room, since His Highness wants to learn some dance steps." So we went to another room, just him and me. At that time American records were rare in Europe. Most people had to go through the black market to get them. The Prince had a whole stack of records and an old-fashioned wind-up gramophone.

"Sit down, Bricky," he said. Meanwhile the people outside were listening for the dancing to start. When they didn't hear anything but music, they peeped in, and there was the Prince serving me champagne and playing records for me, and no dancing going on at all.

That's how the royalty were. They'd put you right at your ease—but you knew, if you had any sense, right where you belonged. And if you didn't know, you'd soon enough find out, because they'd put you there.

Another time a stray dog followed Mabel and me to the club. We were soaking wet—Mabel, me, and the dog—from one of those sudden Biarritz showers. The Prince and Edith Baker were there. We all sat on the floor, dried out the dog, played with her, and drank champagne.

The Prince never paid a bill until I had checked it—a joke, of course, because by that time I had my waiters well trained. I'd pass him the check and say, "It's all right, darling." Once there was an Englishman at the bar who objected to my informality. "Don't you think you should say 'Your Highness' to the King's son?" he said. I told him that that wasn't the first time I had been in his presence, and that since the Prince wasn't offended, I didn't see why he should be. "I can address royalty properly under any circumstances," I added.

Two nights later I went to entertain at a formal party. I curtsied to the Prince of Wales. Prince George came forward with his hand extended, but I gave him a deep curtsy. The same Englishman was at this party, and I looked out of the corner of my eye at him. Later he came over and said, "Well, you certainly know what to do at the right time. I'm going to buy you a bottle of champagne when we get back to Bricktop's." The fellow and I became good friends.

Prince George was known as a playboy, but I think he was just trying to follow in the footsteps of his brother, whom he adored. He fell hard for a couple of girls, as I remember. The first was one of the most famous singers we had in France—Yvonne George. She took the name from him. Unfortunately, she used dope and died young.

Then there was Edith Baker, an American girl—very good pianist. During my first summer in Biarritz he was hanging around her so much that the tongues were really wagging, and his mother ordered him back to England right in the middle of the season. The next we heard, he was engaged to Princess Marina of Greece.

He was very nice. His favorite song was "Blue Room":

> We'll have a blue room,
> A new room,
> For two room . . .

I used to sing it for him.

175

Another famous romance was cradled at Bricktop's that summer, in the Biarritz Bricktop's. Barbara Hutton may even have met Prince Alexis Mdivani there—I don't remember—but I do know they did a lot of their courting at Bricktop's in both Biarritz and Paris.

Barbara, the Woolworth heiress, was only nineteen at the time. She still had some baby fat on her, but she had beautiful, white, white skin and that sparkle that comes with youth—and money. She was very shy, very quiet and retiring, but that didn't stop the men from being interested in her. With her fortune, she could have had two heads and some of those climbers would still have insisted she was the most beautiful, vivacious woman in the world. Alex wasn't one of those men, however. He was later called a fortune-hunter, just after Barbara's millions, but he was already married to millionairess Louise Van Allen when he met Barbara.

Alex and his brothers were Georgian princes. One was married to Pola Negri. I don't know how much family money they had, but they had that breeding, and so women with money were attracted to them. Alex was a charming man, and he really loved Barbara. They came to my place in Paris a lot, and they'd sit at their own table and just look at each other, the way people in love do. They were married right out of my place. It was the early summer of 1933, and Barbara was just twenty years old.

They were divorced in 1935. I don't know what led to it. All I know is that Alex didn't stop loving her. Not long after the divorce I met Alex at a Paris party given by Jimmy Donahue, Barbara's cousin. He was alone and looking so unhappy. I went over to him and said, "Don't look so sad, Alex." He just shook his head. "You still love Barbara, don't you?" I said. "Yes, I do, Brick," he said. "When you see her, please tell her that I love her with all my heart and soul."

Later that night he came into the club with a German girl. He took me aside and said that in a few weeks he was going to give a party in Venice and he wanted me to come and entertain. Then he went outside and got into his car. Suddenly, he was back. "Don't forget to tell Barbara I love her. If any one can make her believe it, it's you, Brick."

Just a few weeks later he was killed in an auto accident. I hadn't seen Barbara, and so hadn't been able to give her the message before he died.

As a matter of fact, it was some fifteen years before I gave that message to Barbara Hutton.

It was 1950 and I had returned to Paris after the war to reopen Bricktop's. I'd taken a place with an apartment upstairs, where I lived, and one night I was upstairs dressing when one of the maids came in to tell me, "Barbara Hutton is downstairs." As soon as I was dressed, I went down. She was with Baron Alexis de Rédé, but as soon as I appeared he walked away, leaving us alone.

"Barbara," I said, "I've been carrying a message around for you for many years."

She smiled softly. "I'll bet I know who sent it."

When I told her what Alex had said, she cried. She and Alexis de Rédé stayed for a while. Sometime after they left, I was on the floor singing when the hat-check girl caught my eye between numbers. I went over to her. "Princess Troubetzkoy is on the phone." The name meant nothing to me, so I said, "Ask her to hold on. I'm doing a song."

When I got to the telephone, I found that it was Barbara. I had forgotten her new name. She said, "Bricky, let's start from the beginning. Tell me again just what happened, just what Alex said." So I repeated Alex's words—slowly and quietly, because I had a feeling that's the way she wanted to hear them. As I put down the receiver, I sensed that Barbara was weeping.

The hat-check girl wanted to know who Princess Troubetzkoy was. "Barbara Hutton," I said. The girl started to laugh. It seems that while she waited for me to come to the phone, the Princess had asked the girl what was going on at the club. "And you know, madame," said the girl, "I told her that Barbara Hutton had just been in!"

Jimmy Donahue was another of my big fans. When he came to Paris, he would be at Bricktop's every night, and when it came time to return to the United States, he couldn't go cold-turkey—so he'd call from the ship every single night. The band would play and Mabel would sing, and Jimmy would go to bed happy. The same thing would happen when he left New York to come to Paris: the telephone would ring and it would be a shipboard call from Jimmy wanting to hear Mabel sing "My Belle." And there'd be a call every night after that until he showed up at the club in the flesh.

After that first season in Biarritz we returned to Paris and rested up for about a month before reopening Bricktop's. Paris still wasn't showing the effects of the Depression across the Atlantic. A few people didn't show up anymore, and when I asked about them, I was told that they'd suffered financial reverses. It was a time when I was especially glad to be in Europe and not in America. There was a lot of talk about what was going on there. Most of it was about money and business, but every so often someone would mention racial strife, which seemed to get worse in a bad economy.

One day, in the fall of 1932, I think it was, Cole walked in and said, "Baby, I got a song for you." I said, "What!?"

Cole never asked me to sing his songs, because he knew I was no singer. As I've said, he was very funny about people singing his songs, and so when he was around I wouldn't sing "Love for Sale" or "Night and Day" or "Begin the Beguine."

Cole said, "It's called 'Miss Otis Regrets She's Unable to Lunch Today.'"

"Where on earth did you get that title?" I said.

He said, "From you. Don't you remember the other day we were talking about a lynching down South, and you said, 'Well, that man won't lunch tomorrow.' I just went home and wrote this tune. Now I'm going to teach it to you."

"Miss Otis Regrets" is a song about a woman whose lover has deserted her. She tracks him down and shoots him with a gun she pulls from beneath a velvet gown, and then she's hanged for it. It's a tragic song, and very few people do it correctly. The pronunciation, the pauses and things are very important. Cole himself came up to the club several afternoons to teach it to me, but he wasn't the kind of writer who insisted that singers do it his way. He encouraged us to use our imaginations. When I first heard "Miss Otis Regrets," I saw the singer as a maid. I put in the bow at the end and raised my hand in a cut across my neck to suggest a lynching.

To sing it correctly, you need a good pianist, and I always have had a terrible time getting pianists, even the best ones, to put in the bam . . . bam . . . bam . . . after the opening lines.

I can't remember whether I sang it first at the club or at one of Cole's parties. I regret this, because picking me for "Miss Otis Regrets" was a remarkable thing for him to do. Knowing Cole, I'm pretty sure he didn't throw it my way simply because I'd inspired the title. I'd never done more than a handful of serious songs—and even during those songs I sometimes kidded. "Miss Otis" was real casting against type.

Once the song caught on, there were nights when I must have sung it ten times. There were other nights when I deliberately skipped it. The audience wasn't right for it. "Miss Otis" was the only song I ever announced, and it has always been my signature song because Cole Porter wrote it for me.

Although I only inspired one Cole Porter song myself, I know for a fact that three of his biggest hits—"Night and Day," "Begin the Beguine," and "Love for Sale"—started their rise to the all-time hit parade at Bricktop's. The idea for "Love for Sale" came out of an experience Cole had at Zelli's on the Rue Fontaine. About fifty percent of the girls there worked as taxi dancers. They weren't whores. When Cole asked one of them what she did, she answered, "I've got love for sale." It was a great title. Mabel Mercer brought it to Bricktop's.

Cole had such a great sense of humor—very quiet and dry. He lived on the Rue Monsieur, as I've said. Not far away was a street called Rue Madame. Once I was joking with him about how rich he must be getting from all his big hit songs, and he said, "Yes, and now I'll be able to afford Rue Madame."

I realize I haven't said much about Cole for a while. That isn't because he wasn't still a very great and good friend. He'd done what he'd set out to do—he'd launched me as a successful saloonkeeper—and so a great number of other people had come into my life, people who are worth talking about. But Cole was still my special friend. He was the only person who had a special table reserved for him at Bricktop's. Not even the Prince of Wales had a reserved table at my place, but Cole Porter did.

When you walked into the club, you walked into the big room. The bar was to the right, and right there at the beginning of the bar were two tables, and one of them belonged to Cole. No one sat at that table, even when Cole was in New York, without my permission. Everyone knew that was Cole's table. If somebody happened to "back in" to that table when the room was full, a waiter would come and say, "Madame, someone is sitting at Mr. Cole Porter's table." I'd go right over. If they said, "Bricky, we're friends of Cole's and we know he's not in town," I'd usually say okay—but they had to be his friends.

I wish I could say that my relationship with Peter remained as constant and as satisfying as my relationship with Cole Porter—but of course they were two different kinds of relationships, and I think it's always easier to maintain friendship than love. What still bothered me years later, though, was that I was practically a mother to the girl Peter took up with.

Hazel (the first name is enough—I don't want to give her too much credit) was a very pretty Negro girl who somehow came under my wing, just as Josephine had years before. Hazel had come to Paris with a Negro revue that had gotten stranded. She found her way to me and brought out my mother instinct. I took her to the theater a few times and gave her advice about clothes and behavior. She was a dizzy sort of gal, and I felt protective toward her.

I was especially afraid that she would take up with the wrong man, and so I set about finding a man who would be good to her. A rich man who'd been stuck on me for years came to Paris, and things started to work out very well.

He was from Philadelphia—a big department-store man, very attractive. A few years earlier he'd been very persistent, telling me he wanted to "take me away from all this" to exotic places like the Virgin Islands. I'd held firm to my rule about not being intimate with clients, though, and after I'd married Peter he simmered down. We became good friends. He used to come out to the villa and play tennis with my husband. He arrived in Paris about the time I was worrying about Hazel, and when he saw us together at the theater and asked me to introduce him to her, I was pleased.

It was one of those whirlwind courtships. He really went for her. He wanted to give her everything, and I found myself right in the thick of it. He asked me to take her to dressmakers and help pick out clothes for her, and I agreed to that. However, I didn't go for his suggestion that I handle the money he gave her. She had to take some responsibility herself.

180

She did a lousy job at that. I kept warning her not to get too smart, but she wouldn't listen. She screamed at him and then refused to talk to him when he didn't come through, on the dot, with some promised furs. I said, "Hazel, you're acting like a two-dollar whore." She went right on behaving that way. They fought and made up more times than I could count. A man with money doesn't have to put up with that sort of non-sense—one day he just didn't come back. He eventually married some white American girl.

Of course, it didn't take long for Hazel to spend all the money he'd given her. Meanwhile she hadn't found a new man. I felt responsible, although I don't know why I should have: I'd introduced her to a rich man and she'd messed up. When she was kicked out of her hotel because she couldn't pay for her room, however, I brought her to the country, thinking I might still get some common sense into her.

She didn't leave for a long, long time.

After a while I started getting calls: "You know, Peter and Hazel are fooling around." I'd say, "Who is this?" but the caller wouldn't tell me. I didn't say anything about it to Peter for almost a year. I didn't see anything going on between Peter and Hazel. He went out a lot to gamble, but every time I called, he was where he was supposed to be. I kept hearing rumors, though. Finally, one day I said to him, "You know, people keep telling me you're fooling around. I don't believe gossip, but if I ever become convinced that it's true, that's the end for you and me."

One night he didn't come home for dinner and neither did Hazel. When he showed up, I asked, "Peter, where did you eat your dinner?" He said that he'd been gambling all night and had dropped by at the home of friends to eat.

That didn't sound right to me. Peter was a fastidious, fussy man, and it just wasn't like him not to come home for one of the good meals there. I said to myself, "Isn't he stupid, trying to fool me?"

I asked who else was there, and Peter reeled off a list of names. Along near the end he mumbled, "Hazel."

Peter knew there was no use protesting when I said calmly, "You know how I feel about fooling around. We're through."

I waited for Hazel to come home. She didn't have to be told what was going on—she could see it in my eyes. I told her to get out. I went up to my room.

A few hours later I went down to the kitchen. Hazel was still there, talking to the cook. I said, "I told you to get out—and that means get out. I don't want you here. When the next train leaves, I want you out of here."

Hazel packed and left, and I thought I'd heard the last of her until a friend telephoned a few days later. "I know you don't like tales, Brick, but we were playing cards the other night and one of the crowd was Hazel. She was laughing and carrying on, and she said, 'I don't care if I lose. I know someone who'll pay.' "

That did it. I went looking for her, and when I found her, I used bad language for one of the few times in my life. "You bitch, you get out of Paris or I'll kill you."

Hazel not only got out of Paris, she got out of France. Years later, in 1949, I was in Chicago visiting Blonzetta. Hazel was working in town, but she disappeared for the couple of weeks I was there.

Although we lived together for several months afterward, I kept my word and never slept with Peter again. I wasn't so hard-hearted that I wanted to throw him out, however. The Depression was finally beginning to hit Europe. The French government had introduced a quota system restricting the number of foreign musicians who could play in a band, and at the time the blow-up with Hazel happened, Peter was working at Bricktop's. He stayed on until he could make other arrangements. Louis Armstrong was playing in London. Peter got in touch with him, and we split.

We remained friends and helped each other, though. He sent me money when I needed it, and years later I helped him open a club in Harlem. We even stayed together in the same hotel room for three days once, but we never made love.

Peter was seriously ill in the 1960s and needed help. I did what I could, but my conscience bothered me. Should I try even harder? I wondered if God wanted me to pick up with this man after all those years. Peter's family kept assuring me that I shouldn't, but still my conscience bothered me. I went to my confessor, who said, "God doesn't expect you to do that. Just do what you can to help."

Peter died in 1967. We never got divorced. I still use the name Ada Smith Ducongé—but the whole thing never should have happened. I got married all by mistake. I hadn't meant to get married, and certainly not to a musician. Ever since I'd been eight years old and heard my mother cry, I'd said, "No man's ever going to make me cry." I had broken my own promise to myself, and I think I was angrier at myself than I was at Peter.

I knew at the time that I should have felt differently. It would have been so simple to forgive him. Nobody should be that rigid. If the same thing had happened to a friend, I would have said, "Come on, kid, forget it," but when it happened to me, I couldn't.

As I said, the Depression was beginning to affect France by this time, but it mostly affected the little people. Most of the big people still didn't feel it. The band musicians, like Peter, were having trouble, but the stars were doing just fine.

I remember Ethel Waters's first trip to Paris. She was the talk of the town, but she took me aside and confided, "Brick, I'm starving to death." It wasn't a matter of money, but of food. Right in the middle of Paris, with all those fabulous restaurants, Ethel was starving for some real American food, so I let her move into my place for about three weeks and she cooked greens to her heart's content. Ethel was never one to stay out or to drink. I was able to turn Paris for her from a nightmare into a place where she could really enjoy herself in her own way. They talk a lot about people "doing their thing" today. Well, I was on that side of the fence a thousand years ago. You can't tell people what to put in their stomachs, where to pray, or in which bed to sleep.

Bricktop's still had plenty of European celebrities in those days. Emil Jannings, the great German actor, would come in looking dour and serious. By the time he left, he'd be smiling like a kid. Grock, the famous French clown, turned down the Palace in New York, but he performed free at my place.

Then there was Georges Carpentier, the boxer. He always came with a group of Americans. They adored him. No Frenchman was ever better liked—not even Chevalier. Women were mad about him. I think athletes are more worldly than actors and know how to get along better with people. I often wished there had been a fight between him and Jack Johnson. What an attraction that would have been.

Speaking of Jack Johnson, one night in 1933 there he was at Bricktop's, and the way we all greeted him, you would have thought he'd just won back the championship.

You had to come up a flight of stairs to get to Bricktop's, but you still weren't inside once you got there. First, the big patent-leather curtains had to be parted. Whenever they did, everyone in the room would turn to see who it was. On the night that they parted and Jack Johnson stood there with his last wife—a white woman named Irene Pineau—the room went into an uproar. There was no mistaking those broad shoulders and that big wonderful smile of the Champ. I flew over to him and threw my arms around him.

What an evening that was! There have been many exciting evenings at Bricktop's, but that night was exceptional. Among those present was Jean Patou. He came over to me and said, "Bricktop, *chérie*, let me send Monsieur Johnson a bottle of champagne." I said, "But certainly," and soon everyone else was doing the same thing. The Champ just sat there taking it all in like the king he was—with me standing close by, looking at him and crying for joy.

He came in night after night. No one ever created the commotion that Jack Johnson did when the curtains parted and he stood there. His prestige in the world at large may have dropped, but Jack the Champ still stopped traffic out on the street and up in Bricktop's. People like Josephine Baker, Maurice Chevalier and Mistinguett would come into my place asking if Jack Johnson was coming in that night. Even Cole Porter, who never got excited over nothing or no one, watched those curtains every night to see if Jack Johnson was coming through them.

I was so very happy to see Jack again. I couldn't allow him and his wife to be anyplace but with me, and with Mama, who was visiting me then. The first time we sat down to dinner together at my house, Jack leaned over to Mama and said, "Your little girl told me that when she got to my age she was going to be bigger than me. I can truthfully say she is."

Jack and his wife came to my house nearly every night for dinner. He raved about the house, and the food. One night during dinner my butler called me aside and said, "Madame Bricktop, Monsieur Johnson is on his fourth or fifth chicken." I told him to tell the cook to give the Champ fourteen chickens if he wanted them.

Those great nights were the last I was to see of Jack Johnson, but I love him to this very day. If anybody ever made me feel proud of being who and what I am, it was Jack. He bowed to no one, yet everything was "yes," "no," "please," and "thank you." His behavior only made stronger my belief that you're either born with "it" or you're not. Greatness comes from a person knowing who he is, being satisfied with nothing but the best, and still behaving like a warm, gracious human being.

I never will believe that he married his white women just to spite white people. It could have been that in my admiration for him I overlooked a lot of things concerning racial prejudice, and reactions to that prejudice; but I just think he did what he wanted to do because he wanted to do it.

The newspaper reporters wrote that the Champ was down and out when he died in an automobile accident in 1946. He was driving a Lincoln Zephyr, hardly a car that would be owned by a person who had hit the skids. He was on his way back to New York from an engagement with a small Texas circus, driving through the same part of the South he had traveled forty years before, when they warned him he would be lynched if he appeared publicly with his white wife at his side. But he had said, "Where I go, she goes," and no one had laid a hand on him.

Let them write all they want about Jack Johnson. He knew how to take the blows in the ring and turn them into a victory, and he did the same thing when he walked through this world as the Champ.

In 1969 I went to see James Earl Jones give his magnificent performance in *The Great White Hope* on Broadway. I had heard about the play, but hadn't realized that it was the story of Jack Johnson. A public-relations man for the play called me and offered me tickets because I was one of the few people around who had known and worked for Jack, and I couldn't wait to get to the theater.

The play was far beyond my expectations—it deserved every single award it received. During the intermission the PR man asked if I would like to go backstage to meet Mr. Jones. I was so filled up with emotion that I couldn't right then, but I told him I'd like to go after the final curtain.

I was so carried away by the play that I could hardly keep my balance as I walked backstage. I just fell into the big, outstretched arms of James Earl Jones. "You just took fifty years off my life," I said. "Standing here beside you, I almost sense that Jack is here, too. He was a champion. So are you!"

Duke Ellington and his band came to Paris in the spring of 1933, and it was practically a national holiday. Although Europeans tried their best, few were able to duplicate the uniquely American sound the French called *le jazz hot*. The Duke was an idol, even though the French knew him only through those expensive black-market records, and when he came to play at the Champs-Elysée Theatre, all of Paris was there, including every American musician and performer.

At the concert Pepito, Josephine Baker's manager, took me aside. He asked me if I would take him backstage and introduce him to the Duke. I thought he had a nerve, considering how he had reduced my warm friendship with Josephine to formal politeness, but holding grudges gets you nowhere, so I introduced him to the Duke and left. Josephine was appearing in a revue at the Casino de Paris, and as I left the dressing room I heard Pepito blurt out, "Miss Baker would like to invite you and the whole band to the matinee tomorrow."

Ellington, being the Duke, accepted, but probably half the members of the band refused to go. Josephine had a bad reputation for avoiding Negroes when they came to Paris. The fault was Pepito's, because he kept Josephine locked away in an ivory tower, but how could the band boys be expected to know that?

A couple of nights later I had the Duke and all his troupe as guests at the club. The party was really swinging when Josephine, who hadn't been in Bricktop's for years, walked in with Spencer Williams. It seems Pepito was ill. She was wearing an organdy dress and an organdy hat and she looked absolutely beautiful.

A few minutes earlier I had noticed a party of young Americans. I enjoyed seeing kids at Bricktop's. I got a kick out of watching their fresh, eager faces as they nudged each other and tried to appear sophisticated among all the celebrities. Privately, I felt they were better off at my place than at many others in Paris, but I knew young people couldn't always afford Bricktop's prices. It was club policy to have them pay the tab round by round. That way there was no embarrassment. The kids knew right away how far they could go.

Only one boy at this particular table hadn't paid his check. The others were on the floor dancing. I sent the waiter over to ask if he'd mind taking care of his check. I could hear him say, "Not at all," as he paid up and tipped the waiter. A few seconds later the waiter took me aside. "Madame, that young man is Franklin D. Roosevelt, Jr.," he said. "Fine," I shot back, "and I'm Galli-Curci."

Well, it turned out that the good-looking young man was indeed the President's son. When he was introduced, he said, "Please do me a favor. Forget I'm the President's son. I want to have a good time." Then, very shyly, he said, "Brick, could you introduce me to Duke Ellington?"

I brought Franklin, Jr., to the Duke's table, and there he sat with Josephine on one side and the President's son on the other, having the time of his life and creating one of those spontaneous nights that could only have happened at Bricktop's.

Franklin, Jr., and I became instant friends. Like so many others, he made Bricktop's his second home.

In the summer of 1933 Mabel and I went to Biarritz again. At least, we'd planned to have a second Bricktop's season at Biarritz, but when we got there, we found that the Merry Sol had been taken by Jimmy Mussolini, my former headwaiter; he'd decided to go into management, as so many headwaiters do.

So we had to look for another place, and though we finally found one, the location was not nearly as good. As it turned out, no location in Biarritz would have been good enough that season. A lot of the regulars didn't come, and it must have been because of the Depression. After a couple of weeks of half-empty clubs, Jimmy and I put our heads together and decided to join forces. He was in the better location, so Mabel and I went over to Jimmy's, but even our combined forces couldn't make that summer a success.

The one bright spot in that whole Biarritz season was when Franklin Roosevelt, Jr., came to see me. One morning, at some unearthly hour, I heard the loud, insistent honking of an automobile horn below my bedroom window. I looked down and there was a car filled with a bunch of college kids all dressed in toreador hats and matador shawls. "Who's that?" I hollered. "It's me, Franklin, Jr. We had to stop by and say hello."

They'd been to Spain and, driving back to Paris, found out that I was in Biarritz. I went down and cooked breakfast for them.

Franklin came to Paris on his honeymoon after his marriage to

Ethel du Pont. He asked me to give a party for him "just like the one for Duke Ellington." Of course I was delighted, and the party turned out beautifully.

A newspaperman who I knew was prejudiced asked Franklin, "Who shall I say gave the party?"

Franklin looked surprised. "Why, Bricktop, of course." However, I wasn't at all surprised when there was no mention of me in the man's newspaper.

The next time Franklin came to the club, he was very upset. "Brick, you were standing right there when I told him who was throwing the party."

I patted his hand. "It doesn't matter. I know him. He's so prejudiced he couldn't bring himself to write that a Negro saloonkeeper gave a party for the son of the President of the United States."

Mabel and I did a few private parties in Biarritz after the Merry Sol closed. There was time to kill before the Paris season began, and, besides, it was a way to make some money, which we were pretty short of after that lousy Biarritz season. With time on our hands, we started going to the Casino. The last time we went was the night before we were to go back to Paris. We won like crazy. I was at baccarat and Mabel was at *chemin de fer*. For a gal who gambled very little, Mabel was winning so fast she couldn't keep track. She was a regular Nick the Greek. I quit playing to help her count her winnings.

We went back to the hotel suite, finally. It was a relief to feel that we could go back to Paris in something resembling style. I was really counting francs that season. We weren't there a minute when Mabel said, "Bricky, let's go back to the Casino."

I couldn't believe it. "Mabel, you don't know what you're talking about. Quit while you're ahead. I've got the money here for Mama's ticket to America, and I'm buying that ticket tomorrow at the American Express before I have a chance to lose the money."

Mabel went back anyway. Two or three hours later I heard her coming back. I had been reading. I put out the light. I waited until she was in bed before I hollered across the connecting bath to her room, "Mabel, how did it go?" There was a long pause. "Forget it, Brick. Go to sleep." Of course she had lost everything.

Fortunately, we were on one of those milk-and-banana diets, so the twelve-hour train trip to Paris didn't kill us. At the station Mabel started looking around for a porter. Then she stopped. We didn't have the money to pay him. It was hard to believe, but we hadn't a sou between us. We carried our own bags to the taxi rack, and at Mabel's apartment the concierge had to pick up the taxi fare.

I did have Mama's ticket, though, and that was the most important thing. If I had had to go without eating to pay for Mama's ticket, I would have been willing to do it, and, as it happened, she in turn was able to help me when I needed it most.

Somehow, we managed to reopen the big place that fall, but it was a spotty season. Some nights the club was less than half full. People who never had a prayer of getting into Bricktop's in the big years had no trouble getting in now. I didn't relax my rules, though. Women still couldn't come in without an escort, no one was admitted who wasn't in evening dress, and if anyone acted up, they found themselves out on the street.

THE CRISIS

EVEN LETTING in those new people didn't help my business very much. That Paris season was the worst I'd had since I'd been in business. It wasn't just the clubs, either. Parties had become fewer, and I could probably count on the fingers of two hands the number of parties I worked in the fall of 1933 and the spring of 1934.

In fact, things were so bad that I started being invited to parties as a guest so they wouldn't have to pay me. Always before, if people had asked me to come to a party, they paid me, because they expected me to sing. After everybody got broke, however, people started just plain inviting me, assuming that I'd sing for nothing.

Well, I'd never been much on parties just for social reasons. As a matter of fact, I hated parties. You'd see people come into a nightclub and order one drink and nurse it all night long, but they'd go to a party and drink up the place. If you'd spent your entire life catering to people when you wanted to punch some of them right in the nose, why should you go to parties? Bobby Short is the same way. When people say, "Bobby, I saw you at such-and-such a party," he says, "Did you see me later? I was on my way to the bank."

Most people knew how I felt about parties, and so I had a good excuse. "Well, you know I never go to parties," I'd say, and I'd be off the hook. Cole would laugh when I told him about these invitations. "You know what Brick is for," he'd say. "Brick is for the *rich* rich."

Not being as busy as I was used to being, I found myself with a lot of time to think. All sorts of ideas raced through my head, including one that seldom occurred to me—going back to America. I didn't think about it long. I'd heard that even big-name American stars were in trouble. What would Americans make of someone like me? I just wasn't known outside the small, select circle that had cultivated me and kept me going.

I could look for bookings around Europe, but that's not why I had fought so hard to be in business for myself. Also, from the experiences of other entertainers, I knew that you could get a date in Amsterdam, for instance, and show up to discover that the place had closed down the night before. That's how tough things were in the nightclub business.

However, I'd learned one thing: the key to surviving in the cabaret business was not to despair. Only a fool would have decided to go back to Biarritz, which I'd left the year before without even the fare for a taxi home. Only a fool or a confirmed optimist.

Whatever I was, I was right. The summer turned out to be better than I had any right to expect. I couldn't find a place right in Biarritz. Instead, I took a spot at the Yacht Club, right at the waterfront of St. Jean-de-Luz, next to Biarritz.

It was there at St. Jean-de-Luz that I met Wallis Simpson. The Prince of Wales had been going around with Thelma Furness for a long, long time, but early in 1934 Thelma had been called back to New York unexpectedly. She'd said to her good friend Wally Simpson, "Don't let him get lonely." Wallis Simpson took her responsibility seriously. By the time Thelma Furness had returned to Europe, about six weeks later, Mrs. Simpson was the Prince's closest friend.

I'd heard all the gossip, of course. They had been seen together con-

stantly since the previous winter. From the moment the Prince introduced me to Wallis, she struck me as being a real, real gal. The Prince's
attitude toward her was different from the way he acted with the other
women he'd brought into Bricktop's. There was none of that roving-eye
business that you couldn't miss when he escorted other women. The
Prince had eyes for no one but Wallis. I felt then, and still do, that
Wallis wasn't impressed by his title or importance. I think she just
ignored the fact that he was heir to the British throne and treated him
as a human being. That was something new for him, and you could see
he was enjoying the experience.

I wonder what kind of first impression I made on Wallis. The first
night they came in together, the Prince headed for a table by the water.
I said, "Your Highness, I wouldn't take that table there if I were you."

The Prince looked surprised. "Why not?"

I explained, "Well, there are rats coming out of the water."

He grinned. "Brick, what are you doing with rats?"

"Well, they're not my rats," I answered. They took the table anyhow,
and it became theirs for the rest of the season.

You could see that the Prince was totally absorbed in her. I felt she
had to have been the only woman in the world who had ever said "no"
to him—but of course with exquisite taste. She just wasn't excited. She
wasn't loud, didn't put on airs, didn't try too hard to impress him. She
was just herself, a natural woman.

People had many opinions about why the Prince chose to give up the
throne for Mrs. Simpson after he had become King. I heard them all,
and the most common assumption was that, as King, the Prince wanted
a more active role in government, that he didn't want just to be a figure-
head and wanted to work for the people. I can believe that he cared about
people; I saw that side of him many times. However, I didn't then have
an opinion about why he abdicated, and still don't. It was all way over
my head.

I do have an opinion about Wallis Simpson's motives. I don't believe
she ever set out to become the Queen of England. If she had, I think she
would have been more awed by him, more respectful of him. She wasn't
awed at all. She was always saying, "No, I don't think it's that way, boy.
No, that's not right, boy." If you wanted to become the Queen of England, would you call the future King "boy"?

The night the King and Wally were married, Lady Mendl was in my place. She hadn't attended the wedding because of Sir Charles Mendl's official capacity. Although I did not know this to be a fact, the word was that Britishers in high positions were not supposed to attend the wedding. Even Prince George didn't go, and that was a sad day for that nice, nice man.

What seemed to preoccupy people most, at least in the Bricktop's crowd, was how to behave with Wallis Simpson once she had become the Duchess of Windsor. There was much speculation among American women about whether it was correct to curtsy to her. Grace Moore, though she was a lovely woman, still had her Southern prejudices, even if she generally managed to keep them under control in Bricktop's. She tried to needle me by asking, "Brick, how do you feel about this? After all, Mrs. Simpson is from Baltimore and a Southerner. How do you feel about curtsying to her?"

I looked straight at Grace. "The King is one of my favorite people. I intend to respect the woman he has decided to marry. If it is correct to curtsy to the Duchess, I know His Royal Highness would want me to do it, and I most certainly will."

I suppose that it's because of the Prince and Wallis Simpson that I look back on that summer of 1934 as such a big success. Lord knows, it wasn't successful enough financially to make me feel very secure when I got back to Paris. Mama was coming back, and I didn't know how I was going to keep up the villa, much less that big club.

I had to give up the villa after I returned from St. Jean-de-Luz. Nineteen thirty-four was a tough year, and everyone was saying that things would get lots worse before they got better. I could never be that pessimistic about anything, but even extravagant, optimistic me knew I couldn't afford that grand-style country living.

I remember the last couple of times I drove out to the villa, knowing I wouldn't be there much longer. The villa represented a triumph for me —it was proof of how successful I'd been in the club business. More than that, it had been a real home, and for a brief, happy time there had been a real family in it—me and Peter and Mama. I didn't brood over losing it, however. When the time came, I just packed up, closed the door, and didn't look back. I was going on to something new.

I still had a lot of spunk. That's probably why the apartment I took in

Paris was much larger than I really needed—even when Mama came to visit. I still had faith, and, frankly, I was used to thinking big.

Somehow, I even managed to reopen Bricktop's. I had to give up the big place and move into a smaller place, but it was still Bricktop's and I was still on the Rue Pigalle, and the regulars still came because it was me they wanted to see and the atmosphere I created that they wanted to enjoy.

It was a sad time in many ways, though. There was no question that the Depression had hit Europe full force, and to watch those grand, gay people go down made me cry.

It didn't happen all at once. They dropped off sort of one by one. Come spring, So-and-so, who came *every* spring, didn't come around. Come fall, So-and-so, who *always* came to Paris in the fall, wasn't there. It was all so gradual . . . until the day you sat up straight and said to yourself, "It's like somebody took a broom and just swept out all those millionaires." And still they didn't all go. The Duke and Duchess of Windsor, Lady Mendl, and others stayed on until the very end.

I really don't remember who left when. Just a few incidents stay in my memory.

One night a banker came in, walked straight up to me, and said, "Let's celebrate. We'll have a big party. Everything's on me." The place was full, and he ordered bottle after bottle of champagne. At the end of the evening he paid the tab, tipped the musicians, waiters, me. As he left, he said, "Goodbye, Brick. This is the last tab I'll be picking up in a long time. I'm going home tomorrow, and when I get there I'm going to be sent to jail." I read about it months later.

Some of my best clients wrote little notes marked "Personal" asking to borrow three thousand or five thousand francs. It was hard for me to understand this, because, while I was in their world, I wasn't part of it. I could understand me being broke, but it seemed strange that people who used to have all the money in the world were suddenly pressed for just a few dollars. I lent the money gladly, because I realized it represented only a very small part of what they had spent at Bricktop's through the years.

From time to time the steamship companies called and asked if I would guarantee someone's passage. I never hesitated, and there were more than a few very important people who got back to the States on my say-so. Maybe I had to back up a guarantee a couple of times, but I didn't think twice about it—then or now. Most people paid me back as soon as they could, but I didn't feel the others owed me a nickel.

I was having my own troubles, meanwhile. Mama would tell people, "I know my baby's broke, because she used to lay down thousands of francs and never say anything. Now she lays down ten francs, and when I come back from shopping, she says, 'Mama, where's the change?' " It seemed best to send Mama home. Just before she left, I was having a problem finding the money to pay the electric-light bill. Peter was at the apartment on a weekend from London, and I mentioned it to him, but he was short of cash, too.

The next morning Mama said, "Ada, I can let you have the money for the light bill." Since I hadn't confided in her, I wanted to know how she knew about it. "I heard you and Peter talking last night," she said. That wonderful mama of mine not only paid the light bill but quite a few others, enough to make things a lot less difficult both at home and at the club. I asked Mama where she got her money.

"Ada, when you came home early in the morning, flying so high, you'd throw your purse on the dresser. When you went to sleep, I'd come into your bedroom and take half the money in your purse. I knew you'd never miss it and someday you'd come down to earth."

After I'd sent Mama back to Chicago, I found in my trunks at the American Express a hundred pairs of silk stockings and gangs of silver coins she had hidden. That seemed more exciting to me than one of those weeks at Bricktop's when we would have four big spenders on four different nights.

Besides "bringing me down to earth," as Mama put it, the Depression accomplished something else. It brought the people of Montmartre closer together than they'd ever been before. The entertainers, most of whom lived there, got to know the French better, and we found out more about one another than we'd ever learned in the days when we'd lived it up as if there were no tomorrow. There was a surprising lack of bitterness. The most commonly heard sentence wasn't "I wish things were the way they used to be." No, it was "Have you got any money?"

We all shared what we had and looked out for one another. I went to the movies one afternoon and returned to find I'd been locked out of my apartment. The police helped me get inside, where I found my clothes and valuables intact, but not the money I'd saved for the rent. I wired Peter in London, who cabled the money, but couldn't resist the message: "Not the great Bricktop!" After my experience, the artists and musicians in Montmartre started keeping an eye on each other's apartments.

It was a scrounging existence. I can't begin to count the times I went in and out of the hock shop with my furs and my one diamond. I scrounged from my friends, and when I had money, they scrounged from me.

There was a lot of hurt connected with the Depression—for me, it was mostly wounded pride at being forced into a situation I couldn't control. What did I know about economics or the stock market? All I could see was a gal who'd made her own way since she was sixteen suddenly forced to live from hand to mouth. It hurt that I couldn't take care of Mama as I'd been doing, and I thanked God for Blonzetta, who was doing the job for the two of us. Once I weakened and asked Blonzetta for the fare back to America. She didn't have it—of course the Depression had affected the real-estate market, too—and by the time her letter arrived, I'd realized that, no matter how bad things were in Europe, I was still better off where I had friends and a reputation. At home I'd be a nobody when even the somebodies were finding things tough.

Every little while I was reminded about how lucky I was, in a way. I'd been big, sure, but I'd also been nothing. When the great tumble came, I didn't have so far to fall. Some people had a real long way to drop—like Jeff Crane, whose family fortune had come from the National Cash Register Company.

Jeff had been one of the big spenders, but always a real gentleman. I remember the time he came to Paris with his whole family from Toledo —even the maid. Her name was Della, and she had been raised up with that family. Jeff said to me, "Brick, I hate to ask you this, but would you mind taking Della around?" He was really embarrassed about asking.

I didn't try to analyze his reasons. I don't know what he would have done if the rest of the family hadn't been there. Probably nothing. After all, in his position, he couldn't very well be seen taking his maid around.

Della was "the family nigger," and that's not quite like being part of the family. I didn't take offense. I told him, "If I can show around a colored person who comes to Paris, I'll be glad to do it." He was a good client, and Della turned out to be a very nice woman.

During the Depression—it was probably some time in 1935—I came into the club and was surprised to see Jeff at the bar. He had a *stinger* in front of him, and that was downright astonishing. The Jeff I remembered never drank anything but champagne. Someone came in and Jeff, who was a great talker, turned from the bar to greet him. While his back was turned, I told the barman to get rid of the stinger and serve up a bottle of Cordon Rouge. Joe, the barman, was very diplomatic. He got a bottle in front of Jeff without making a big thing of it. When Jeff turned around and saw the bottle, he looked at me at the end of the bar. "Thank you, Brick, that's one of the nicest things that's ever happened to me."

I said, "Mr. Crane, you spent thousands of dollars with me over the years, and I couldn't see you drinking a stinger. You don't like anything but Cordon Rouge. I don't know how many cases I have downstairs, but as long as there's champagne in this place, you and your friends are welcome to drink it."

I think it was also around 1935 that Nicky de Gunzburg left Paris. I don't know this for a fact, but I heard that he took all the money he had left and bought a ticket to New York. He did well in New York at first, became an editor at *Vogue* or *Women's Wear Daily*, but I hear he died broke. It wasn't all that long ago that he died, almost blind and just about destitute. I never saw him after the pre-war years in Paris, and I prefer to remember him as the quiet, classy man I knew then. He was an aristocrat right down to the bones.

There were some happy evenings. I'll never forget the night Paul Robeson walked through the door. I'd met him in Brentano's bookshop on the Rue de Rivoli the day before, and I'd said, "Paul, what's the matter? You're in Paris and you haven't been to Bricktop's?" He explained that he had been busy, but he'd be sure to come the next night. I said I was counting on it.

The next night came, and he came, with Essie. Paul was a huge man, and he had to stoop a little just to get through the door. I had my back turned when I heard a French woman say, *"Oh, un nègre. Quel nègre!"*

I turned around immediately, because I knew it could only be Paul. I went over and said, "Paul, this way," because I had reserved a table for him. Two tables away was Prince George, by now the Duke of Kent and married to Princess Marina of Greece.

After a while the Duke sent for me. I went over to the table and Marina said, "Brick, ask Paul Robeson to sing something." I said, "Darling, you know I never do that." I never asked another artist to perform for free. She said, "Tell him that your baby boy here would like it," and I said, "That I can't refuse." So I went over to Paul and explained the situation.

He said, "Bricky, go back and tell those people that I *would* sing, for *you*, but I've just come back from location"—he was making *Sanders of the River* with Nina Mae McKinney—"and my throat is still full of gravel."

I went back and told them, and then the band started playing a dance tune, and Paul got up to dance with Essie, and the Duke got up to dance with Marina. When they met on the floor, they stopped—and since when royalty stops, everybody stops, all the dancers froze. Both Paul and the Duke were tall, but Paul was a little taller and had to look down on the Duke a bit. It's an image that has stayed in my mind all these years—everyone frozen in position on the dance floor and Paul looking down on the Duke.

I was at the door, with Mabel at my side, and we both started crying. Mabel said, "What are you crying about?" and I said it was because I was so proud of Paul Robeson. "What are *you* crying about?" I wanted to know, and Mabel said it was because she was so proud of "her Duke."

In the fall of 1936 I realized there was just no way I could open up Bricktop's. I just didn't have the money. Nowadays people ask me, "Well, why didn't you go to your friends? Wouldn't Cole and Elsa and all those people have helped you?"

They would have. Everybody would have. But in those days I just didn't have sense enough to ask. I was used to being responsible for myself—I'd been on my own since I was a teenager. Looking back, I'm glad I didn't seek their help then, because there would be a time when I really needed it and I did ask, and maybe I wouldn't have asked then if I had asked before.

Mabel and I went to work for Jimmy. We'd teamed up with him that second summer in Biarritz. That fall of 1936 he came to me and said, "Bricky, I'm going to open up my own place. Do you mind?" and I said, "No, certainly not." Mabel and I went over to Montparnasse to help him open up, to get the people coming in and all that. Naturally, the place caught on—a lot of those people were just following Bricktop around. Cole and the others just followed me and Mabel to Jimmy's. Mabel and I didn't do this just out of charity—we were getting a per- centage—but it was still hard to make ends meet.

By the late spring of 1937 Jimmy was trying to change the financial arrangement. He was doing a good business, and the idea that he had to pay us a percentage was driving him crazy. He wanted us to work for a salary, but we weren't going to do that, so we split, and Mabel and I were out of work again.

It turned out to be a blessing in disguise for me. That summer I went to Cannes to work. I went back there quite often in those last fretful years before the war hit France.

Back in Paris, we went to work for Madame Fricka and her husband, across the street from where I'd had the big place. They were French- German, from the Alsace region. Their place was more of a restaurant than a club, but they offered good entertainment, and I provided it, working on a percentage basis. Besides Mabel and me, I brought some really fine acts to the Frickas' restaurant.

One of the finest was the great jazz guitarist Django Reinhardt, a French gypsy. Some of the books say I was the first one in Paris to ap- preciate him, but, as I recall, he was already famous when he came to work for me. At least, he was famous for being hard to work with. When I told friends I was going to hire him, they said, "Bricky, you're out of your mind. If he doesn't like the color of your dress, he'll walk out. If he doesn't like the way a client is looking at him, he'll walk out."

As a matter of fact, Django did walk out on me twice. Once he had to go bail out a gypsy gal who'd gotten arrested, and the other time he had a toothache!

He called me *minou* (cat) and when people asked why he worked so well with me and was so temperamental with everyone else, he'd flash a spectacular smile and say, "Because she's a girl and has nice surround- ings. I like the people around her."

Django was a brilliant jazz guitarist, acclaimed by Paul Whiteman, Count Basie, and all the leading musicians who knew his work. What was amazing was that he'd had an automobile accident and the fourth and fifth fingers of his left hand were sort of fused together, so he could only use two fingers and a thumb to play. He was a gypsy who couldn't read or write and who wore tan shoes with his tux, but he was a hit with me. He had a quartet consisting of his brothers and a white French boy, Stéphane Grappelly, and they were the hottest thing in the world.

Even with talent like Django and his group, business at the Frickas' was spotty. We just barely managed to get through the season. Still, I remember 1937 as being the best of the serious Depression years. I had a good time in Cannes and working with the Frickas, and the economy seemed to be looking up. We didn't feel much relief in the club business, but the war talk caused the French government to step up its manufacture of armaments, and that meant more jobs. Also, young men by the thousands were being conscripted into the French army, which at least meant a guaranteed income for them and their families.

That's the way I saw things—from the perspective of the little people. A woman with a grade-school education couldn't be expected to understand the larger implications of what was going on around her. All I knew was that times were hard and that I had to keep looking for a way to pay my rent and buy some food. I must admit, however, that I had a sort of sinking feeling when Mabel decided to leave Paris.

She got a chance to go to America and she took it. The woman who brought her to New York was an Englishwoman named Jo Carstair, the Singer Sewing Machine heiress, who used to race motor cars and motor boats. She offered to bring Mabel to New York, and Mabel took her up on it. In New York, Mabel went to work for Jacobi, who used to be one of the assistant managers at Le Boeuf sur le Toit in Paris. His place in New York was doing very well.

Mabel was very successful at Jacobi's place. Of course, her main drawing card was that she'd just come from Bricktop's.

Mabel left in October 1938. I took over her apartment. I was delighted that she'd had the chance to go to New York, but I missed her. We'd been together for seven years, through good times and bad. She was a good friend—and still is.

Then, about a month after Mabel left, Mama died. I think it was on November 5, 1938. I got a cablegram from Blonzetta. She said she didn't think it was necessary for me to go back for the funeral. "We're going to take Mama to West Virginia," it said, and of course that was where she belonged. I didn't go back for the funeral.

I didn't go to work the night I got the cablegram about Mama's death. Lady Mendl missed me. She arrived at the restaurant, found I wasn't there, and wouldn't go in. She sat out there for about two hours, waiting for me to come to work. Finally, she told her chauffeur to drive away.

Up until Mabel left, even though talk of war was on everyone's lips, public opinion was very much divided. For every person who thought war was just around the corner, there was another who believed that Hitler and Chamberlain would keep "peace in our time." It was all very confusing for me. I didn't have an opinion. I kept my mouth shut and listened and tried to figure out what I should do.

At least, that's what I told myself I was doing, but even after I knew what I should do, which was to get out, I didn't. I realized there was really nowhere for me to go. I'd built my whole career, and lived a sizable part of my life, in France. It had become my home. Returning to America had no appeal for me. I thought of moving to Cannes, where I'd built up a small clientele, but people warned that if war started, Hitler and Mussolini would grab the South of France first.

So I stayed in Paris. I did radio programs for the French government network, singing requests sent in by listeners. I went back to Madame Fricka's for a time. I held on, as did the rest of the people in Paris who would or could not leave.

When Hitler marched into Poland in August 1939, it was almost a relief. We in Paris had lived so long with the fear of war; at least now we knew where we stood. It's hard for people today to understand, but World War II was called the "phony war" for a long time. Until the spring of 1940 and the start of the blitzkrieg across Holland and Belgium, it really wasn't much of a war. Even after the invasion of Poland, France felt safe behind the Maginot Line, and who was I to doubt the experts? Over and over again I heard, "It will all be over before you know it. Hitler's bluffing. France and England are waiting for the right moment to move in and smash the Germans. They will never occupy Paris. It's impossible."

We didn't know what a blitzkrieg was. We didn't know that something like the atomic bomb was on the drawing boards. The scariest thing we could imagine was poison gas. There was talk about possible food shortages and gas rationing, but not in a long-term sense. After all, France was at war, and you had to expect some minor inconveniences. That's how the Parisians felt, and that's how we diehard Americans who were still in Paris felt.

Paris was declared an Open City, but there were blackouts every night to remind us that France was at war. The blackouts did Montmartre in. People didn't go out at night, because they didn't want to get caught in a blackout. Taxis drove along only those streets that were permitted dim lighting. Some places on the Champs-Elysées were able to stay open because they catered to an afternoon and early-evening clientele.

There were civil-defense drills and we were taught what to do in case of an air attack. We were supposed to take refuge in the Métro. I went down once to see what it was all about—I felt I owed that much to the authorities who were so interested in protecting my life—but I got such claustrophobia that I decided I'd rather take my chances above ground in the fresh air. I guess if the city had been sprayed with poison gas, I would have gone down in the Métro, though.

Actually, I did go down in the Métro another time, though not voluntarily. One night the gendarmes came and routed me and everyone else in the building out of our apartments and into the underground. They found me so drunk they had to carry me out; and as a way of getting through a blackout, let me recommend being good and drunk. I didn't feel at all claustrophobic; in fact, I don't remember much of anything about that night.

I had another encounter with the gendarmes. One night I was reading in bed and didn't have my blackout curtains closed tightly enough. They raced up the stairs and gave me a good dressing-down. I deserved it for my carelessness, but I wasn't the only person in Paris who was careless about observing the rules. We all were, because we didn't take it seriously. It is so hard to describe the atmosphere. People like Daisy

Fellowes and Lady Mendl were still giving parties and engaging me to entertain.

Of course there were a lot of people missing from those parties, including many of the Bricktop's crowd. Some had left Paris at the beginning of the hostilities, but they'd acted as if they were just going off on a holiday. They'd leave their keys with the concierge and say to the rest of us, "We'll be back in a few months." Others stayed on a while, and others stayed still longer. Cole Porter didn't want to be routed from the Paris he loved, but eventually even he left.

As it turned out, he might have been better off staying, at least a while longer, because back in America he had that terrible accident. He was horseback riding at the Piping Rock Club, one of those exclusive clubs on Long Island, when the horse he was riding was frightened or something. It fell on top of him and crushed both his legs. That was in 1937, and when I heard about it, I wanted so much to be near him so I could try to cheer him up. I couldn't imagine that fun-loving man confined to a bed, and I laughed when I heard that he was going out to nightclubs on crutches. Those were serious injuries, however, and he went through something like twenty operations on his legs. They were never right again, but he kept on writing, and playing.

By October 1939 the American consulate was warning the rest of us that we'd better start packing. It was a terrible situation, heartbreaking in a lot of cases. The most tragic were those affecting Americans who had married Frenchwomen. There were children to consider. Gene Bullard got caught in this bind. He had a French wife, and he finally had to leave her. It was either that or go to a concentration camp. He later died in New York.

Also sad were those cases involving colored entertainers who had been working in France for twenty years or more. Opal Cooper hadn't been back to the States in that long, and for me it had been nearly sixteen years.

However, the American Consul made no bones about what would happen to us if we stayed. As foreigners, we were subject to internment in a concentration camp. Some entertainers, like Charlie Lewis and Arthur Briggs, decided to take their chances—and they wound up in prison. Opal Cooper decided to go back "home." I didn't know what to do.

After the invasion of Poland, I'd gone to Lady Mendl for advice. She'd suggested that I stay, pointing out that I might eventually be of service. She and the Duchess of Windsor were organizing a soup kitchen for the artists, and I helped out with that. So did the other American entertainers and the English ones. The two foreign colonies had drawn closer together, and when we weren't doing something for the soup kitchens, we played cards, shared food, and counted money pretty carefully. Frankly, though, we were kind of bored.

At any rate, once the consulate and the embassy started sending out their warning bulletins, I knew I had to decide once and for all. One day I looked out from my balcony and saw the Rolls Royce that belonged to Lady Mendl parked across the street. There was a big ballroom over there, and she and the Duchess of Windsor were organizing another one of their free soup kitchens (they called it a one-franc lunch). I crossed the street and entered the bar part of the ballroom, and there I asked for Lady Mendl. In a few minutes the Duchess of Windsor came out.

"Bricky, what are you doing here?" she asked, and I said I wanted to speak to Lady Mendl, wanted to ask her what I should do.

The Duchess said, "Didn't Elsa write to you?" and I said yes, she had. She'd urged me to leave, but reminded me to have the little pill around if I was going to stay. You were supposed to poison yourself rather than let the Germans take you. Some of my friends, like Lady Mendl, carried these "suicide pills," but I didn't.

Then Lady Mendl joined us. The Duchess said to her, "What are we going to do about Bricky?" And Lady Mendl said, "I think she should go home now. It's getting desperate. Cole and the others are in New York. They'll take care of her. She'll be with people who love her."

I was forty-five years old at the time, but I was tired of trying to figure out what to do in a situation where I had no control. I was still Bricktop. If I'd had a club to run, I could have been just as bossy as ever, but I didn't have a club—hadn't had one in too long a time. I put myself into the care of these two women as if I were a small child. In many ways I *was* like a small child—facing an unknown future in an unknown world, the United States.

The Duchess of Windsor and Lady Mendl went down to the offices of the Cunard Line to book my passage to America. According to the story

I heard, the Duchess had a hard time. The man who waited on them was married to a woman who worked for Molyneux, but he didn't know the Duchess by sight. The Duchess told him that Bricktop had to have her own cabin, and she had to have this and she had to have that, and the man brushed her off and didn't pay her any mind. He did pay attention to Lady Mendl, however, because he knew who *she* was, all right. Finally, the Duchess just stopped talking and let Lady Mendl handle the arrangements, and that is an example of what a lady she was. She didn't tell the man who he was talking to. She realized he didn't know who she was. She just stepped back and let Lady Mendl handle things.

They got me a *private cabin.* All kinds of people were trying to book passage, but somehow, by switching people around and just plain canceling reservations, the Cunard people arranged for that private cabin. You'd think that after they'd gone to all that trouble I would have just packed up and left.

But I still didn't want to leave. I hung around for a couple of weeks until Lady Mendl and the Duchess insisted I use that ticket back to America. They said it was a choice of leaving or facing internment. They knew from their high connections that it was only a matter of time before the Germans occupied France. I suppose I experienced more emotions in those weeks than I normally felt in a year. Finally, I realized there was no other possible decision but to go.

My ship was not to leave for a few days, and I spent the time saying goodbye to old friends. One was Eddie Molyneux. Over the years he had become one of my dearest friends, not to mention one of my favorite designers. He wasn't the sort of person who told his friends what to do, but long before I knew it myself, he was quite sure I would leave. Typically, he did something sweet and practical. He made me a "homecoming wardrobe." As he explained, "I want you to look lovely in the United States."

The last night I saw the Paris of Bricktop's, I was with Eddie, and it was just the two of us. He'd sent his car for me, because it was pouring down rain. The car drove through the dimly lit streets at a snail's pace, and I looked out at the city I loved and wondered when I would see it again. At Eddie's I tried to be cheerful and good company, but I was so depressed and worried. On the boat train I met four American musicians who, like me, were among the last entertainers to leave, and we shared our fears about going back to a country we hadn't seen for years and where we would be strangers.

The *Washington* sailed on October 26, 1939. It was one of the last American ships to leave France. I didn't travel in quite the style I had been led to expect. After I got on board and into my cabin, some people arrived who spoke a language I couldn't understand. They had an old lady with them, and they just pushed her into the only available space they saw, and that was my cabin. The whole voyage she just talked gibberish—out of her head. I wasn't much better off. I was so seasick I couldn't even worry about what lay ahead for me. I was convinced I'd be dead by the time the ship docked in New York—and if you've ever had a bad case of seasickness, you'll know exactly what I'm talking about.

"Flaming red hair, a happy freckled face and a pair of beautiful legs and feet": nineteen years old in 1913 and already a veteran Chicago saloon singer

Another picture taken that year. My youth was a plus—it made people feel protective toward me.

1917 in Los Angeles. I signed myself Adah, because it sounded more theatrical. Mama wrote back, "Your name is A-D-A."

1916: Cora Green, Florence Mills, and me—the Panama Trio, dancing and harmonizing our specialty

With Jelly Roll Morton (in bow tie) in 1917. He couldn't decide whether to be a pimp or a piano player. I told him to be both. (FRANK DRIGGS COLLECTION. COURTESY FLOYD LEVIN)

1920 in Vancouver, shortly before "the fight to end all fights"

In 1922, I moved to New York City and began working at Barron's, where gangsters rubbed elbows with high society.

Easter week, 1924, and ready to set off on a new adventure—Paris

Singing at Le Grand Duc, a room so tiny its bar felt crowded with six pairs of elbows leaning on it

BELOW LEFT: *By 1926, I had arrived. Cole and Linda Porter invited me to Venice for the summer and the back of this card says it all: "Sis, I sang and danced for the Crown Prince of Italy yesterday. Ain't I something?"*

BELOW RIGHT: *I married musician Peter Ducongé in 1929. The whole thing never should have happened, and we split a few years later over a girl named Hazel.*

Place Pigalle. By now, I was running Bricktop's, a combination nightclub, mail drop, bank, and neighborhood bar for the most elegant people in Paris. (PHOTOGRAPH BY CARL VAN VECHTEN. COLLECTION OF AMERICAN LITERATURE, THE BEINECKE RARE BOOK AND MANUSCRIPT LIBRARY, YALE UNIVERSITY)

Despite the Depression, business was so good, I opened a bigger club at the old Monico in 1931. The first thing I did was hire an English soprano named Mabel Mercer. (VAN VECHTEN, BEINECKE)

The new Bricktop's

At the Bricktop's bar, with Louis Cole, my piano player

LEFT: *Cole Porter at Bricktop's in 1932. The graffiti is his.*

BELOW: *I always spent the night table-hopping, here with Michael Farmer at the far left—his Bricktop's romance with Gloria Swanson ended in marriage—Ramon Novarro, Mabel Mercer, and Louis Cole.*

Fats Waller (holding bottle) and musicians at Bricktop's (FRANK DRIGGS COLLECTION)

ABOVE: *A country party at my place in Bougival. Fats Waller is sixth from left.*

BELOW: *With Mabel (center, on piano) and Alberta Hunter (right)*

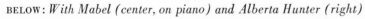

Louis Bromfield was one of my favorite customers—that's him in the center.
His secretary, Jack Hawkins, is with me, and Mabel is at the far right, next to Marjorie
Oelrichs, a famous society beauty and Eddy Duchin's wife.

ABOVE: *A Christmas bash—every year, I invited all
the Negro musicians in Paris to a big party at Bricktop's.*

LEFT: *Me wearing a Molyneux gown. Thanks to
my friends, I was always well-dressed—"the best-kept
woman in Paris," Elsa Schiaparelli said.*

With Burgess Meredith, millionaire Len Hanna, and the Duc de Verduro

ABOVE: *By 1937, the Depression was hurting even me. I'd closed Bricktop's and was presenting entertainment at a restaurant across the street—including Django Reinhardt and Stéphane Grappelly.*

LEFT: *Came the war and I had to flee Europe. This was taken in New York City, where I tried—unsuccessfully —to recapture Bricktop's.*

LEFT: *In 1943, at the age of fifty, I started over again in Mexico City. Cantinflas was one of my favorite people there.*

BELOW: *My return to Paris—the new Bricktop's opened in May, 1950, with, among others, Salvador Dali (far left), Hugh Shannon (far right) and Alexis de Rédé (next to Hugh).*

Barbara Hutton. Her short-lived marriage to Prince Alexis Mdivani in 1933 was cradled in my club.

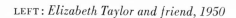

LEFT: *Elizabeth Taylor and friend, 1950*

BELOW: *Duke Ellington and the Peter Sisters, a trio of Negro singers. Duke got his first big New York break in 1922 when I persuaded Barron Wilkins to hire the combo he was playing with, Elmer Snowden's Washingtonians.*

We had royalty, too, here the Princess of Hyderbade and H. H. the Maharene of Cooch Behar.

An outdoor picnic with my musicians

*Performing at Bricktop's,
1950*

The joint is jumpin'.

Making up before a performance, Rome, 1951. Despite flashes of life, Paris wasn't what it had been before the war. I kept hearing that Rome was the place to go—so I went.

With Anna Magnani

With Orson Welles

Pearl Bailey carrying on, 1952

Performing at the casino at Estoril, summer, 1952

BELOW: *New shoes for orphans at a camp near Naples. In 1943, I had converted to Catholicism, and now my charity work began to earn me the nickname "The Holy Hustler."*

Errol Flynn fooling around at a birthday party for his wife, Pat

With Lena Horne and a friend

Playing a mock Carmen with Gimi Beni, a prized member of "Bricktop's Stock Company"

BELOW: *With Edward G. Robinson, one of the sweetest men I knew*

Receiving the blessing of His Holiness Pope John XXIII

BELOW: *Singing at Bricktop's*

The handbill for the 1962 Carnegie Hall benefit. Unfortunately, it had to be canceled at the last minute.

In 1964, I closed my nightclub, but retirement wasn't for me. I came back to the U.S. and started singing again in New York and Chicago. In 1978, Mayor Michael Bilandic of Chicago declared "Bricktop Day" in my honor. The next year, Mayor Kevin White of Boston did the same. That same year, I retired for good—but don't you tempt me!

N E W   Y O R K

COLE PORTER, whose New York apartment was in the Waldorf Towers, knew when I was returning, and so did a few thousand other people, thanks to Lady Mendl. She had cabled Cholly Knickerbocker, the late Maury Paul, who was the society columnist for the New York *Journal*, that I was aboard the *Washington*. The day we docked, Cholly's lead story read: "Lady Mendl has cabled her friends to 'be kind to Bricktop who is coming back to live in the United States after more than sixteen years abroad as the toast of Paris.' "

Cholly's item and, I suspect, some string-pulling by Cole got me one of those famous shipboard receptions from New York's newspapermen. They were wonderful and made me feel right at home, and of course once the ship stopped moving, my seasickness disappeared. One of the first questions they asked me was what I wanted most now that I was back in America, and I answered, "Chitlins."

"Not champagne?" they asked.

"No, I've had plenty of that," I said. "But it's a long time since I ate any chitlins."

The warm, friendly stories in the newspapers the next morning surprised me. I wasn't used to publicity. There had been some in Paris, but I didn't expect any in America.

I went straight to Harlem, to the Teresa Hotel on 125th Street. It had only recently been integrated, although it was right smack in the middle of Harlem. Joe Louis had been the first Negro to check in there, and I became the second. Bill "Bojangles" Robinson, who was dancing at the Cotton Club at the time, made the reservation. New York's Negro newspapers were making a big thing out of the Teresa's new policy, and I became a neighborhood celebrity. People stood outside the hotel waiting for me to come out. I'd never had that happen to me before, and so it didn't occur to me to give them a show. I'd amble out in house shoes and an apron, just as I had in Paris.

What was I doing in house shoes and an apron? Cleaning up. There was a lot of cleaning up to be done at the Teresa, and I wasn't about to wait for the maids to get to it. I'm a little bit like Joan Crawford was when it comes to hotels, though not as obsessive. The newly integrated Teresa was not very impressive. Compared to some of the hotels in Europe that had welcomed me and other Negroes with open arms, it was a fleabag.

Luisa Munn, an old friend, asked why I had chosen the Teresa instead of a hotel like the Algonquin, where Marian Anderson had lived for years. I explained that I had just taken it for granted that I would have to go to Harlem.

The color line was just starting to break down in New York—in hotels, restaurants, and nightclubs that catered to theatrical people. Prejudice and I hadn't met for a long time, and I guess I had subconsciously prepared myself for it before coming home. By going to Harlem, I had reacted like the Negro who had never been away—from habit.

Cole didn't waste any time welcoming me in his own special way. He gave a big party for me the second night I was in New York—and at the Waldorf Towers I walked smack into my first taste of prejudice in the America of 1939. When I asked the receptionist for Cole's apartment, he looked me over as though he'd never seen a Negro woman before.

"Are you expected?" he asked in a pained tone of voice. I told him that I thought I was. "What's your name?" he wanted to know.

"Miss Bricktop," I answered very quietly.

Well, that changed things in a second. He came running out from behind his desk, bowing and scraping as though I'd said, "Mrs. Roosevelt." By the time I got upstairs, I was boiling mad. I told Cole what had happened.

What could he do? Nothing, of course, except to say he was sorry. "Brick, you're going to see more of that. That's why, whenever you thought about coming back, we warned you not to. In Europe you were a queen, sitting on your own very exclusive throne." That didn't make me feel much better, however. I couldn't understand why I had to be a very special Negro to be treated with even common courtesy.

Still, it was wonderful to see Cole again. It hurt me to see that he had trouble getting around, but at least to me he didn't show that it hurt him. He was the same Cole I'd always known and loved—or nearly the same. It did seem to me that some of the gayness had gone out of him, but it hadn't only gone out of him.

Cole's party produced many from the Paris Bricktop's crowd, and so did the affairs that came immediately afterward, but there was a strange feeling. They were like displaced people. These were people who felt more at home in Paris than in New York.

For quite a while after I returned to New York, every time I walked into a room where they were, there was a buzz of excitement. "It's Brick," they'd say, and they'd all flock around, hugging and kissing me. They were my friends and loved me—always had—but in New York I became something more. I became a symbol of their Paris. "When are you going to open up here?" they kept asking. "We need you here. We need something to remind us of Paris."

Opening up in New York was a great idea, and of course it had crossed my mind, but there was a little voice inside me that told me it wouldn't be all that easy. This wasn't Paris, it was New York. I wasn't going to be able to rent a little place, buy a few bottles of champagne, and open up Bricktop's.

I'd seen the New York clubs—the jazz spots on 52nd Street, the big floor-show places like the Latin Quarter and the Copacabana, the tiny

East Side bistros and Greenwich Village spots. They had nothing in common with the intimate clubs of Paris. They didn't attract a Bricktop's crowd. My clients went to the Stork Club, El Morocco, the Colony, and "21." Even if I'd wanted to, and I didn't, I couldn't manage their kind of operation—and I'm not just talking about expenses and size. These were segregated clubs, as Josephine Baker found out when she tried to go to "21" after the war.

It didn't take long for me to figure out where the color line was drawn in New York in 1939, and I wasn't especially looking for it. I never accuse anyone of prejudice until I'm one hundred percent certain, as I was with that newspaperman in Paris who wouldn't use my name in connection with that of Franklin Roosevelt, Jr.; but when it stared you in the face, you had to notice it.

It was especially uncomfortable when I felt it from friends. Not long after I returned to New York, I got in touch with Connie Immerman, whom I hadn't seen since I'd left New York for Paris. By this time Connie's Inn had moved downtown. Connie acted really glad to see me, and he even gave me my own box, but I noticed it was on the segregated side of the club. That annoyed me, and I didn't waste any time giving a piece of my mind to Connie. He fumbled his apologies, and I felt kind of bad about being so rough on him. Connie wasn't in the chips the way he had been. He was only a front for the place. The "boys" had taken over and were just capitalizing on his name.

The last time I saw him was in 1957, when Dorothy Kilgallen's husband, Dick Kollmar, gave a party for me at the Left Bank, a restaurant he owned. A man came over to my table. I looked up and screamed, "Connie!" Then I told everyone within earshot that he had given me my most important break. He was really pleased. "Now Brick," he said, "you come over and tell that to my wife. I've been claiming it for years, but she never believed me."

The last I heard, Connie was working in a restaurant. I didn't try to see him. It would have embarrassed him, and me. Connie belonged on top and wasn't the type to appreciate being patronized, and I think he would have felt patronized if his friends from the old days had visited him and tried to pretend that his position hadn't changed.

I also started feeling uncomfortable when some people who were not my real friends started asking how I felt about being back in America. I remember this one man asking. I answered, "It feels all right. I'm an American. I haven't changed."

Then came the stinger. "But, being away so long, you must find it not quite the same over here, don't you?"

"What do you mean by that?" I shot back. I knew what he meant. He meant how did it feel to meet up with prejudice again.

The man was Jewish. I controlled my temper long enough to say, "I always thought Negroes and Jews needed each other. Maybe you haven't seen what's happening to your people in Europe, but I have." He turned beet red and disappeared.

I had a different reaction when another Jewish man, Irving Berlin, told me practically the same thing, only it really wasn't the same thing. Irving was a gentleman, and not prejudiced.

Soon after I got to New York, he came to the places I was working a couple of times, and he said to me sadly, "Bricky, you just don't belong here." What he meant was that my style was Paris, not New York, and of course he probably also meant that I would encounter prejudice in New York. He wasn't suggesting that as a Negro I'd gotten too big for my britches during those years in Paris, as the other man had.

No matter who told me that I didn't belong in America, and why they said it, I didn't buy it. I couldn't. I was back in America, faced with the responsibility I'd met squarely ever since I'd gone out on the road with the Oma Crosby Trio—earning my own living as an entertainer. I didn't control circumstances, and I wasn't going to waste time worrying about them. There were only two ways to go—up or down—and I liked "up" a lot better, but I wasn't afraid of "down" either.

My old friends were a great source of strength, and incredibly kind. I arrived in New York with only the money the Duchess of Windsor and Lady Mendl had given me. Cole Porter helped me out after I arrived, and so did other good friends like Luisa Wanamaker Munn and Leonard Hanna. Other friends, who didn't have money, offered moral support.

Of course I got in touch with Mabel Mercer as soon as I got back to New York. She wasn't working at the time and so couldn't help me out in that way, but it was nice to be able to see and talk with her again. I also got in touch with Jimmy Hughes—Langston Hughes—who'd been that handsome young busboy at the Grand Duc when I'd arrived in Paris and who had taken me into the kitchen and calmed me down after I had broken into tears at the sight of that tiny little nightclub.

Being seen around New York was pretty important then—still is. Otherwise, people think you're dead. Langston wanted to be seen around with me, so that made two of us. We had lots to talk about, but the main thing was, what would I do now that I was in America? Like my other friends, Langston kept assuring me that it was only a matter of time before something came along. I was sure of that, too—sometimes. At other times I wasn't so sure. Doubting myself wasn't in my nature, but you can't make a big change like I had without getting some butterflies in your stomach.

When the chance came to make a deal at a club on East 56th Street— Jimmy Savini's—I jumped at it. I had many doubts, because I didn't know a thing about how New York clubs were run and because I wasn't doing the running; but I told myself it was now or never. I had to dive in, make a few mistakes, and, I hoped, profit from them.

Well, the opening night was thrilling. For an entertainer who was absolutely unknown in New York, it was a wonderful send-off. Everyone was there—all my Paris clients, all the new friends I'd made in New York. The columnists could not have been kinder, and it really pleased me to know that they'd written such nice things about me after, for most of them at least, seeing me for the first time.

I opened a few weeks before Christmas, because it seemed like a good idea to become established at that time and maybe attract the tourists who came to New York for all the pre-Christmas shopping and displays and for the big New Year's Eve celebration. The plan worked at first, but as Christmas neared, my clients headed for warmer climates, like Florida, California, and the Bahamas. Those who didn't leave just before Christmas left just after Christmas.

Without the people who knew me from Paris, I was lost. I had never attracted the "man off the street" audience, and I was mighty sorry about it in New York. Until New York there had never been any reason to cultivate a broad patronage, but there I was at Savini's playing night after night to a handful of customers. Sherman Billingsley, the manager of the Stork Club, dropped in one night to consider me for a small place he wanted to open; but when he saw the near-empty room, he left without even speaking to me, and he was perfectly right.

Then Jimmy and I fell out over my habit of buying drinks for my clients. My bill for that courtesy was about the same size as my percentage, and I had to admit he was right. It was a clash of two different styles of operating. Two or three weeks later I moved to my second New York club job—at the Coq Rouge, run by a man named Frank Bonnocini.

It was a better arrangement. I controlled the liquor and worked in a small room over the main club. Carol Bruce sang downstairs, and that lovely woman went out of her way to make me feel comfortable. Later a girl named Anne Francine replaced Carol and was just as nice.

Frank was a darling. He was the best part of the Coq Rouge. He liked me personally and admired me professionally, and I started to lose my doubts about making it in New York.

The press helped, too. Once again they trooped to my opening night as if I were some great star. Morris Gilbert wrote in the New York *World-Telegram:*

A little club de nuit, cozy and gay. . . . A number of the best people in it, but not an enormous number because there wouldn't be room. . . . South American millionaires among others.

And in the midst of all this none other than Bricktop, the only Bricktop, who at a well-chosen moment will sing "Miss Otis Regrets" in that negligible voice of hers. And then, will add that other song, "Mean to Me," which, if properly pressed, she will repeat in her regrettable French, Voos Ait May-chant avec M'wah.

Her work is badly needed, Bricktop points out, in a world where merriment shows no surplus on any market and where joy has his finger ever at his lips, bidding, So long Baby.

Business was better at the Coq Rouge than at Savini's, and I was beginning to make a living, but it wasn't what it should have been, and I know I stayed longer than I normally would have, because of Frank's understanding. He kept saying, "America isn't ready for you, Bricktop."

He was right. No other Negro performer had a deal like mine. I had a room named after me, was working for a percentage rather than a salary, had a special deal about buying drinks for my clients. In fact, only a handful of Negro performers even performed downtown at that time. In most places Negro clients, if they even got past the ropes, sat at Jim Crow tables—and here I was hostess of my own room in the East Fifties, standing at the door being embraced and kissed by my white clients.

I could feel the resentment. Patrons who didn't know me, who had come because of the press coverage or word-of-mouth advertising, let me know in not so subtle ways that I ought to go back to my fabled Paris clientele, since they were so liberal. And that was *before* they had heard me sing.

When I got out on the floor, I baffled the audience. I wasn't a torch singer, a funny girl, or a blues singer. I wasn't even a singer. New York didn't understand the idea of a hostess-entertainer, or the flavor of Bricktop's in Paris—a club that gave the illusion of being private and the special property of its clientele. With the clientele I had in New York, I couldn't re-create that illusion.

Eventually, Frank had to let me go. We parted warm, good friends. He hated to fire me, and I hated to face the fact that I was no longer in a position to try to run things. I had to be an ordinary working girl again, and I was determined to do it.

I managed to make one more deal where I could sort of run things, though. It was at a place called the Three Deuces, on 52nd Street. It was a big room, and Mabel wasn't working, and it occurred to me that maybe the two of us could re-create Bricktop's. When I asked Mabel if she wanted to work for me there, she said, "Yes, sure," and we teamed up again briefly.

Next door to the Three Deuces, however, was a place called Tony's— very famous at the time—and Mabel had a thing going with the piano player, Cy. She would run back and forth between the Three Deuces and Tony's, and one day she said to me, "Bricky, Cy has to go into the army, and Tony and Cy want to know if you'd mind if I went over to Tony's to work."

I said, "No, go ahead," and Mabel went to work at Tony's. She was there for seven years, and that's where she made her *big* reputation, just sitting and singing. She acquired a gay following—but only the best, like back in Paris at Le Boeuf sur le Toit.

As it turned out, I wasn't at the Three Deuces long, either. One night the manager came to me and said, "I'm sorry, Brick, I'll have to let you go."

Since this was my third time "up" in New York, the strike-out didn't surprise me. I just said, "Okay, I won't be in tomorrow."

"Sorry," said the manager, "you'll have to leave right now."

That was something new, being fired between performances, but the manager explained that it was a special situation. "One of my partners is coming in," he said. "He doesn't like you. He thinks you're stuck up, you think you're something special. He's a nasty fellow, especially when he's drunk. He's bound to start something, and it's best you just leave now."

Well, that should have been rock bottom for me, but it wasn't. There was one more slap in the face in store for me. It came when I was auditioning at yet another place on West 52nd Street. One of the partners came in and asked, "Is your name Bricktop?" When I told him it was, he turned to the manager and said, "She can't work here."

The manager didn't understand that remark any more than I did. "Why not?" he protested.

The partner completely ignored the manager and turned to me. "Ain't you a friend of Nigger Nate Raymond?" he demanded.

"Why, of course," I said. "What's that got to do with it?"

"No friend of Nigger Nate works here," he said, and just walked away.

I never solved that mystery. Nigger Nate was a white man, a friend of gambler Arnold Rothstein. Nate got his name because of his tight, curly hair. I met him in Vancouver, a whole lifetime away from New York during World War II, and our paths had crossed only a few times since then; but my friendship with Nigger Nate had been enough to get me fired yet again.

I hadn't played split weeks or one-night stands since I'd been a kid, but I was getting used to "limited engagements." It reached the point where friends would say, each time I opened, "We'd better catch Bricktop tonight, because who knows if she'll be there tomorrow."

My next "limited engagement" was at still another place on 52nd Street. About two nights after I opened, Frank Sinatra came in with a couple of his pals. There were three Marines in the place, pretty drunk, and they began insulting Frank, calling him "dago" and a "draft dodger." Of course a fight started up, and of course I stepped in to stop it, as I had done for so many years. Frank yelled, "Lady, let me go."

I said, "Come on, Frank, you can't afford this," but he wouldn't listen.

"I can't afford to let these guys insult me," he shot back, and then he and his pals went after the Marines. The next night I was fired.

In 1953 Frank came into my place in Rome with Ava Gardner. She was on location, making *The Barefoot Contessa*, and she had announced her separation from Frank just before she'd left Hollywood. It was New Year's Eve, and Frank had come over from the United States hoping for a reconciliation, I think. They asked me to join them.

Frank said, "It's funny that we never met before."

I told him that we certainly had met, in a way, on a 52nd Street battleground. At that, he turned to Ava. "I've been looking for this woman for years."

He wanted to know what had happened to me as a result of the fight. I told him I'd been fired, but that it would have happened anyway, sooner or later. "New York and I had a hard time making it," I said.

Did we ever! I managed not to resent it too much—that's poisonous —but it was hard for me not to feel depressed and resentful of New York after being fired from all those places. I kept asking myself how I could have been such a success in Europe and be such a bomb in New York, especially when I had friends in New York who had known the Paris Bricktop's.

Eddie Molyneux had often said, "There's nothing that hurts more than disappointing your friends," and that sentence kept coming back to my mind. Here I was disappointing not just my friends, but myself. Not so long before, I'd been at the top. It was a terrible feeling.

It wasn't just an emotional feeling. I was really strapped financially. In Paris, in the pinches—and there were plenty in the Depression years —there were always friends to go to for money. I didn't mind going to them because I did have a business and good reason to believe I'd be able to pay people back. In my own country, however, I didn't have that kind of security. I'd be borrowing with nothing to back it up.

I'd moved from the Hotel Teresa to an apartment on Seventh Avenue.

I'd become good friends with the manager there, and I'll never forget the expression on his face when he stopped me in the lobby and told me that the owners said he'd have to evict me unless I paid up my back rent.

I couldn't believe what was happening to me. Even in the old vaudeville days or on the saloon circuit I'd never had to do what was a way of life for a lot of entertainers—skipping town without paying the hotel bill. There had always been money—not much, maybe, but enough to keep body and soul together. A good friend spared me the embarrassment of eviction in the kindest way. He paid the back rent and said, "Now, if I give you money to pay the rent for one month, how are you going to get on next month?" I told him the truth: "I don't know." "All right," he said, "I'll give you enough for three months. That will buy you some time."

Money is made for what it can do, and certainly for what it can do for other people. To this day, I think one of the greatest things anyone can do with his money is to get a friend off the hook with his rent, because there is nothing more embarrassing than to have your landlord knock on the door and say, "What about the rent?"

My friend bought me time to think positively, to try to figure out what I was doing wrong. I decided that I'd been so desperate that it had been written all over me, and so when I went to my next spot, Cerutti's on Madison Avenue, run by Frank Cerutti, I was calm and composed and determined to make things work out.

Through Jerry Kirkland, who was the assistant manager, I took over the back room. I brought in Billy Haywood and Cliff and Mae Barnes and four Negro singing waiters. To take care of my own clients, I brought enough money with me every night to pay for the drinks, and I personally collected the tabs. This system gave me the freedom to operate as I always had, and prevented possible disputes with the owners. My back room and its fine stable of entertainers gradually caught on, so I stayed at Cerutti's for two years, 1942–1943, except for about two months when the grind got me down, I guess. Also, I was getting a bit tired of the crowd that came to Cerutti's. In Paris there had been clearly defined seasons, and you always closed up and went someplace else at least for August and part of September. You didn't have those nice breaks in tempo in the New York club scene.

217

Of course, I still had to work. One of my oldest friends was Will Vodery, a musical director who had been involved in a lot of the Ziegfeld and Cotton Club shows. He was a smart fellow with good connections in show business and the sporting world. He had a couple of roominghouses and a saloon in Saratoga, in the Negro section of town on Congress Street. That street was lined with saloons, boardinghouses, and whorehouses. Will's places were not whorehouses; they catered to professional gamblers and family men who were out on a short fling. During Saratoga's brief racing season Bill's houses were always packed, and I asked him if I could run one of them.

"You running a boardinghouse, Brick? You must be out of your head!" was his first reaction.

"Why not? My mother ran a roominghouse. It's an honorable profession. And taking care of people is my business."

Then the idea began to intrigue him. "Think of the publicity! Bricktop running a roominghouse during the season! You could charge as much as you wanted."

Anyway, he agreed and we went to Saratoga to get things organized. I decided to take the larger of Bill's houses, a three-story building with eight big, lovely rooms. We agreed that I would run it for a percentage of the profits.

When the season began, I opened up, determined to bring some class to Congress Street. Word got around that I was running one of Bill's places, and I never had an empty room. I don't know if the guests expected me to throw in my nightclub act or not, but they got their money's worth—a clean, well-managed house and two excellent meals a day.

Of course, there were a couple of smart alecks, like the fellow who said he'd pay anything if Brick would serve him his breakfast in his room. I sent up the man who did the heavy cleaning, who was white. Eventually, the joker and I became friends, and now and then I did bring up his breakfast, threatening to charge him double.

At Bill's place I had one of the few knockdown, drag-out fights of my life. I had to beat up a girl in order to get her out of the place. She was a drunken slut with a mouth so foul that even the racing men complained. I also became a madam for one night. The police had decided to crack down on the Congress Street whorehouses, and two prostitutes who had been working in one of them came to me in desperation. One of their best clients was coming to town—an important fellow and a big spender. Could they rent one of my rooms for a night? They assured me the police would never raid my place, and because I felt sorry for the girls, I said okay.

I was nervous all night, though, and it was quite a night. The girls weren't kidding when they said their client was a big spender. I didn't go near the room—the girls did all the serving—but I knew what kind of food and liquor went up there. Everything went off as the girls had said it would, but I was taking an awful chance. If anyone had tipped off the police and they'd raided the place, it would have been written up in all the papers. The charge of running a whorehouse would have been tough to live down. Still, I didn't let the risks of running a boarding-house in Saratoga prevent me from returning there. I ran the same house for two or three seasons, and enjoyed just about every minute of all of them.

Saratoga just about folded up after the August racing season, and it was after the season of 1943 that I converted to Catholicism.

I'd never been a religious person. Mama had been brought up a Catholic, but when she married Tom Smith she became a Baptist or a Methodist or something. We went to Sunday School as kids, and I'd spent most of my life saying things like, "Well, it didn't happen because God didn't want it to." I really didn't think about God very much, though, and I knew next to nothing about organized religion.

I remember one time in Paris, the night before Easter Sunday, Ramon Novarro was in the club. I heard him say, "I can't have a drink after twelve o'clock." I started to say, "Why not?" But Mabel said, "Shhh, Brick, be quiet. He's going to communion." I said, "What's that?" and Mabel said, "Brick, don't be so ignorant."

Mabel was a great Catholic, and she was right—I *was* ignorant. She'd take me into a church with her, and I'd say something like, "Mabel, keep your hands off those statues or they'll put you in jail."

I can trace my interest in Catholicism back to a colored boy who worked for me in Paris before the war. His name was Lawrence Parker, he was from Florida, and he was a boy that *nobody* could get along with —he disagreed with everything and everybody.

219

He left off working for me and went out to China, and on the boat he met a priest who started talking to him. The priest got off the boat before Parker did, but before he left he gave Parker the name of another priest, whom Parker looked up when he got to Hong Kong. That Hong Kong priest converted him.

A few years later I met Parker in New York. He was a changed man. I said, "My goodness, Parker, you've changed so. You used to be so hard to get along with. Now you'd probably agree with everything."

He said, "Maybe it's because I became a Catholic."

I demanded, "What's *that* got to do with it?"

He said, "You'd be surprised."

He started bringing me little pamphlets to read and talking to me about Catholicism. I started listening to Fulton Sheen, who was broadcasting on Sundays then, and I got very interested in Catholicism. I started going to various Catholic churches, and by and by I said to a priest, "Father, how do you become a Catholic?" He said, "Do you really think you want to?" and I said, "Yes I do," and he took me around to the sacristy to talk to me. I had some questions to ask him about different things that I was mixed up about, and he straightened everything out. He sent me a notice about the next instruction lessons, and after the very first lesson I said, "Yeah, this is for me," and that's how it's been for me ever since—beautiful. I was baptized on December 5, 1943.

If you believe that by turning to religion you're going to see the heavens suddenly open and swallow up all your problems, you're turning the wrong way. My becoming a Catholic didn't solve any of my problems—but it did give me the strength to meet them head-on, and the trust that God would give me the ability to solve them.

One of the first things it did was to help me face the fact that New York just wasn't for me. It held too many memories of too many flops. Besides, the time in Saratoga hadn't eased the Cerutti's grind very much for me. My old clients seldom came by, and I felt more like a relic of the Twenties than a seasoned performer with plenty of years left to make all that experience count.

Once I'd decided to leave New York, my next decision was where to go. I'd been hearing quite a lot about Mexico City for a couple of years. People had been telling me how wonderful it was, and that it had a big

American colony of artists and businessmen, and a large group of displaced Europeans who'd managed to escape with their money. This was my kind of audience.

I also found out that most of the Mexican nightclubs were large, barn-like places featuring marimba bands, dance acts, and native singers. There were very few small, intimate clubs where the atmosphere changed every night depending on the clientele. It seemed to me that Mexico City needed a place like Bricktop's, and I liked the idea that I wouldn't have any competition to speak of.

To get to Mexico City, I needed a stake. The way things had been for me in New York, I hadn't been able to save a penny, so when I heard that Doris Duke was in town, I decided to go to her for help. She was an old and very loyal friend—whenever she came to New York, she found out where I was working and dropped by.

I had first met Doris in 1928 or 1929 when she'd been married to Jimmy Cromwell. People weren't called swingers in those days, but if they had been, the word probably would have been invented to describe Jimmy. Doris was just the opposite—a shy, retiring person. She was a tall, slender girl with dark hair and a face that was not pretty but attractive. She loved jazz, and in Paris she was a Bricktop's steady. Sometimes she came with detectives, because, being the richest girl in the world, she was often threatened with kidnapping.

I called Doris's secretary and companion of many years, whose name I can't remember. She was delighted to hear from me, and so was Doris. We made a date for that very afternoon. "Bring along some pals," said Doris, and I knew that meant she'd want to make some music. Doris was an excellent pianist and loved double piano. So I called Garland Wilson and Mae Barnes, and we all trooped over to Doris's Fifth Avenue brownstone. It was a wonderful afternoon; Doris and Garland played, and Mae and I sang.

At one point Doris took me aside and asked me if there was anything special I wanted to talk about. I explained what I hoped to do.

Doris was her usual thoughtful self. "Brick, I know things haven't been easy for you here. Why don't you take it easy for a while? Go to Honolulu and stay at my home."

But I didn't want that. "Doris, that's the last thing I should do. I'd go

221

out of my mind living in Honolulu, being waited on by servants. I need to work." I explained that I only wanted a ticket and enough money to pay the hotel bill for a couple of months until I could land a job. Doris smiled. "Of course, Brick. We'll take care of things."

I didn't waste much time packing up and leaving New York, and I didn't look back. In 1957 Thelma Carpenter, the singer, drove me up and down 52nd Street so I could thumb my nose at all the places from which I'd been fired, but in 1943 I didn't have time to blame New York for the unhappiness of the past few years. I was almost fifty years old and it was time to get on with life. I was going to Mexico City to start over in *my* kind of club business.

MEXICO CITY

THE MOST prominent of the wheeler-dealers in Mexico City's American colony was a strange, tiny little man called Blumey. He was A. C. Blumenthal, a financier who had his fingers in many pies. He was once married to Peggy Fears, a Ziegfeld showgirl. Blumey went to Mexico City in order to dodge Uncle Sam's tax collectors, and he was just one of many rich Americans who had gone to Mexico City for that reason. The others lived quietly and inconspicuously, but Blumey loved the limelight, and his life in exile was just an extension of the one he'd enjoyed in New York, Palm Beach, and Hollywood. He had a stable of tall, beautiful girls who towered over him, and he could be found holding court every day in the Reforma Hotel, where he was the manager.

Blumey expected everyone to bow and scrape to him, but I'd heard about him and I'd made up my mind to avoid him. There was nothing personal about it; I just didn't want to be ordered about. I'd had enough of that in New York. Everybody said I was making a mistake if I thought I could get established in Mexico City without Blumey's help, but I'd decided that if I was going to succeed in Mexico City, the only help I needed would come from above.

I went to St. Anthony instead of Blumey. I went to church a lot once I got to Mexico City, and with all those churches and statues of the Lady of Guadalupe, it was a perfect place for me. I also found a perfect confessor. Father Thomas Fallon had been in Mexico for forty-five years, but he still had an Irish brogue you could cut with a knife. He was so down to earth and real; there were always lines of people waiting to get into the box with him.

I once took a boy who was on the verge of committing suicide to Father Fallon. Tommy knew he needed help and wanted to go, but he was afraid because he was an Episcopalian. I said that didn't matter. We went to the chapel and the old priest was busy, as usual. I saw a chance to talk to him a minute, and I said, "Father, when you have a chance, please come and talk to a friend of mine who's feeling very low. He's Episcopalian." And when he was free, Father boomed, "Now where's that Episcopalian?" It took Father about ten minutes to turn that boy around.

As we left, I asked how he felt being Episcopalian and going to a Catholic priest. He laughed and told me that Father had said, "We're all going to the same Man. You Episcopalians are just taking a longer route."

Then Tommy said, "Brick, come on, let's have a drink. I feel great, just great."

I really enjoyed going to confession with Father Fallon. Maybe I went too often. An awful lot of people with far bigger problems than I had were waiting in line to see him. I remember one time I went into the chapel, and as I started to kneel, Father came up to me. He made the Sign of the Cross on my forehead and said, "Go on, child."

I looked up. "But, Father, don't you want to hear my confession?"

He said, "I know it. You've just been drunk again."

As soon as I arrived in Mexico City, I started looking around at the clubs that would be suitable for me. One that was available and suitable was called the Minuit. An American was the middleman for the deal, and though I wasn't sure where the money was coming from, it seemed open and above board. I saw no reason not to accept the offer. I went right to work, and it didn't take long at all to get the place ready for an opening night. And when I received a telegram requesting that I "reserve a table for the Chinese Ambassador," I felt just great. What a good sign, I thought; in Paris I'd entertained European royalty, and now in Mexico City I would be entertaining Oriental statesmen.

Halfway through the night, the special table I'd had reserved for the Chinese Ambassador was still vacant. Now, I'm not like Mike Todd, who used to have apoplexy whenever he saw an empty seat, but I did care about opening nights, and that one big, empty table stood out like a sore thumb. I was working the floor a little bit later when Ray Goetz came in with a big party—including Blumey and Dolores Del Rio—and headed straight for the Chinese Ambassador's reserved table. I was puzzled for only an instant, then I broke out laughing.

The idea of calling himself the Chinese Ambassador stemmed from the time in Paris when I'd had that little club, the Band Box, which Ray Goetz and Herbie Fields had insisted on opening up every time they were in Paris. My partner had been a Chinese man. One morning the cashier, who kept an eye on things for me, had called to say that the Chinese man had taken all the receipts. I had dashed over, grabbed the cook, and got my money. Afterward everybody had told me I was crazy —no one went into a cook's kitchen in a temper, not with all those knives around. Ray had really gotten a kick out of that, and whenever he wrote to me, he'd say, "Put more starch in the shirts."

After I joined Ray's party, I found out there was no Chinese Ambassador to Mexico.

The Minuit was something new in Mexico City—a private, intimate club—and it was a success from the start. There was plenty of money around, and the Minuit got its share, and naturally that led to problems with my partners.

That's one reason why I've never liked to work with partners, or to work for a percentage. If the club is a success, one partner always thinks it's because of him, not the other. When you have a percentage arrangement, the silent partners start resenting the big slice of the profits they have to pay out to the active partner. That happened at the Minuit. My percentage was a hefty one, and I was eliminated. I left, and took the business with me, and my big-deal silent partners were left with nothing but headaches.

If I'd had the money, I would have opened up my own place and had no other partner but myself, but I didn't. As a result, I had to go into another partnership, and this time my partner couldn't keep silent.

The spot was run by a man named Chavez, and if he had a first name, I don't think I ever heard it. He had been headwaiter at the Reforma, so of course he'd decided that all he had to do was open up his own place and become a millionaire overnight. As so often happened, things didn't work out quite that way, and when I first went into Chavez's place with Charles Joseph, a big coffee man, there weren't more than ten people in the whole club.

Chavez knew that I was free, and it didn't take him long to say, "Brick, why don't you come in here with me?"

I didn't want any part of it, but he kept on. "Brick, I've got so much trouble—here in this place and here in my stomach. I'm sick. I want to take it easy. You run the place for me."

Then Charles stepped in. "Why not, Brick?" he said. "It looks like a good place for you. It's the right size."

I had to agree with that, but the thought of having Chavez on my back was not what I'd come to Mexico City for. Against my better judgment, I started talking a deal with Chavez.

When it came down to making it formal, I said for the twenty-fifth time, "Now, Chavez, you let me run the place myself. You go home and rest." However, we'd already clashed—over an entertainer named Reva Reyes, who had worked with him at the Reforma. She was a big favorite in Mexico City, and I knew I needed a Spanish-speaking entertainer to help me out. Reva drank a lot and really got down to business after hours, but I figured I'd been running saloons long enough to know how to handle Reva. Besides, when she wasn't drunk, she was a pleasure to be around. But Chavez complained that Reva had talked about his mother.

That ridiculous Spanish male pride! I said, "Does Reva *know* your mother?" Chavez said she didn't. "Well then, forget it," I said. I just had a feeling, however, that Chavez wouldn't be able to stay away.

I opened up the club with Reva, and she turned out just as I had expected. She was a big help, and right away business started to shape up. For the first time since Paris I began to see and feel some of the quality of the old Bricktop's. I'd brought along Sam Harris, too. He was a Negro boy, a florist by trade, who had made the Minuit a garden every night. At Chavez's place he not only did the flower-arranging, he also did the ordering and the bookkeeping.

After Chavez's started to be successful, I really began to settle down in Mexico City. It wasn't Paris. I didn't feel like the great Bricktop; I was just making a living. I was finding rewards in just living, however, that I had never known before. My religion was making life happy for me again.

Every day I found myself drawn to it. I like the mystery of the Catholic Church, the insistence on blind faith in God. I found richness in the solitude of going to church, and the stresses of everyday life just didn't seem as important anymore. To this day, however, I can't quite figure out what led me to my vow of celibacy.

It was August 14, 1945, my fifty-first birthday. I was in church. Without even thinking about it, I looked up at a statue of Our Blessed Mother and said, "From this day until I'm divorced and remarried, I'm never going to sleep with anyone again."

I wasn't even out of the church before I was saying to myself, "Where in the world did that come from? I'm a Leo. I'm supposed to be a hot pepper." But I kept my vow. It wasn't easy. Some good-looking fellow would walk into my life and show an interest in me, and I'd go running to church. "Take him away," I'd pray to the Blessed Mother, and pretty soon away he'd go. He'd do something I didn't like, and I'd be able to just turn off.

When I made that vow, I was just in my fifties, and that's a dangerous age for a woman. Still, I realize now that that vow fulfilled a resolution I'd made long before I ever became a Catholic: "Lord, never let me be a foolish old woman."

There's an old saying: "Stand behind the bar and you'll see just about everything in life." I'd found that to be true, and one of the things I'd seen that I didn't like at all was foolish women—women who let men make them cry, women who would do anything in return for the feeling of being loved. Ever since I'd heard my own mama cry over a man, I'd determined not to let the same thing happen to me, and so any time I thought I was going to get the worst of it, I ran (except in the case of Walter—and I admit it). Maybe I missed out on a lot of things. I don't know—but I do know that whenever I looked out across that sea of faces at Bricktop's and saw rich women with their paid gigolos, I didn't feel that I was missing anything.

If I didn't like seeing foolish women, I especially didn't like seeing foolish *old* women. I never wanted to end up like one—frustrated, trying to support the pretense of youth, longing for sex that common sense says is ridiculous. No matter what the circumstances, the bottom line was always the same. I remember one old gal who informed me that a young Argentinian was so crazy about her that he threatened to kill her if he ever found her with someone else. "Sure," I said, "he doesn't want anyone to lay his hands on all your money." She bit her lip and held back the tears, because she knew I was telling the truth.

There was another woman, very well liked and popular in Europe, who ended up falling in love with a gangster who was ten or fifteen years younger than she was. He went for broke and, like many rich people, she happened to be short of cash at the time. She went to a friend, one of the biggest publishers in the United States, and begged for money. The publisher was horrified. He called his secretary and asked that the woman be escorted out of the office.

I wondered then—and still do—if these women ever look at themselves in the mirror before they put their faces on. Do they ever think about how they look in the morning to those kids who share their beds? That's the test.

But a woman is still a woman. Those feelings and desires for sex and love don't just go out the window when you turn fifty. It's just that there aren't many men around who are their age and who want to give them love. When she has to start paying for it, that's when she ought to start looking for a way to put dignity back into her life—whether it's through religion, reading, social work, or just old-fashioned cold showers. In my church I found the strength to keep my dignity.

I often thanked God for the sense of serenity my religion had given me during my years in Mexico City, because those Mexicans were some hot-blooded people. For that matter, so were a lot of the foreigners—maybe it rubbed off.

A couple of incidents come to mind. One night a Mexican general got drunk and abusive and decided to make me his target. "Why don't you speak Spanish?" he growled.

"Why don't *you?*" I flipped back. "You don't speak Spanish, you speak Mexican." I admit that wasn't the smartest thing to say.

The general made a sudden move, and I thought he was reaching for a gun. So did a little man at the bar. Instantly, he was at the general's table. "Don't you abuse Madame Bricktop. She is good to the Mexicans." I don't know why, but that stopped the general and he left. I thought the little Mexican would be killed for sure.

The following night the general was back, very sober and sincere. "Miss Bricktop, I'm not making any excuse for my behavior. I have found out about your work among the poor." I was doing charity work, as I had in Europe. "I'm sorry I tried to abuse you." The general invited me to have a drink and I accepted and we eventually became good friends.

One of my most hot-blooded clients was Virginia Hill. She was also one of the most loyal. Virginia was one of the more spectacular celebrities around Mexico City, the friend of mobster Bugsy Siegel and a number of other underworld figures. She liked me and my place so much that it seemed some weeks she never went home. Virginia didn't spend money, she threw it away. There was a table she claimed as her own, on a tiny balcony about ten steps from the bar. It could seat eight or ten people. I was at it one evening with Sam, Reva, and Eddie Matthews of *Porgy and Bess*, who was enjoying a great success singing nightclub dates in Mexico. Virginia came in with an American flyer and headed right for us.

There was a Mexican fellow downstairs, the black sheep of a prominent family who had gotten lost somewhere between drink and dope. He staggered up the steps and sat down at the table, too.

Well, Virginia was known to use pretty rough language, and she could do it in Spanish or English. What she said in Spanish to this fellow can be roughly translated as, "What the hell are you doing at my table?"

"I just thought I'd join the party," he said.

Virginia yelled at him to get away, and that was the cue for the flyer to get up and start after the Mexican. Before you could bat an eye, the Mexican had a gun in his hand. "Sit down before I blow you down," he warned.

Reva literally peed in her panties. Eddie started to jump away, but had second thoughts. As for me, my after-effects metabolism was in play, so I just sat there. The flyer had some sense, so he sat down, but Virginia kept yelling, calling the Mexican every foul name in the world. *Finally*, the Mexican backed down. "You're a woman," he said. "I can't argue with you." He went back to his own table.

Only then did we realize that the American flyer had slipped away at some point. We hadn't even noticed, we were so worried about the Mexican and his gun.

About half an hour later, in walked the flyer with two Mexican pilots in uniform. I don't know what he thought he was doing. As soon as they recognized the playboy, they started begging his pardon and backed themselves out the door, but Virginia got upset again and started screaming dirty words at all of them.

Eventually, everything went back to normal. Except for Virginia's screaming and Reva's little accident, no one in the club got very excited. The waiters went right on serving drinks and the pianist never missed a note. It was nothing strange for Mexicans to pull out their guns and shoot up a place.

Except for the fact that she had the foulest mouth I'd ever encountered, I really liked Virginia. I went to her house quite often. She always had a crowd there, and when they asked me, I sang. I was a far cry from the Bricktop who wouldn't go to a party and sing unless I was well paid. I still went to parties, though, mostly because it was good business to do so. Virginia was a good spender, and I liked her.

I never mentioned being paid. She was the one who brought it up. One night she said, "Look, Brick, you need some new clothes. I'm tired of seeing you in the same outfits. I know you usually get paid for entertaining privately, but I was too embarrassed to ask how much."

I interrupted her. "If you ever invite me to perform privately, I won't be embarrassed to tell you the fee."

Of course she said something foul in response, but she was smiling. "Okay, then, let's square things this way. You go to Henri Chationne, get some clothes, and charge them to me." I couldn't object to that.

Chationne, a couturier from Paris, was the rage of Mexico City at the time. I had a great time picking out designs. It reminded me of the old days in Paris when I could walk into Molyneux or Patou and just pick out what I wanted. When Virginia saw the bill, she exclaimed, "Bricktop's clothes cost more than mine!" But she paid it.

A few years later Virginia was the star of Senator Estes Kefauver's televised hearings on organized crime. She gave such wonderful dumb-blonde answers. Her testimony about how she used to find rolls of hundred-dollar bills in her pocketbook and didn't have any idea where they came from broke up even the stern-faced Senator Kefauver. She didn't give the committee any ammunition at all, and it took a smart woman to get out of that mess by playing the dumb blonde perfectly.

I had a good time at Chavez's, but there were problems. The worst was Chavez. At first he made a half-hearted attempt to stay away, but he just couldn't do it, and he just couldn't let up on Reva. I finally had to let her go. She met a wealthy American and married him, I think, and was killed in a car accident a few years later. She was one of the finest people I ever knew, and I resented Chavez for making me fire her. Other than that, we generally got along—until I decided I needed a vacation.

My spirit was fine, but my body wasn't. There was nothing seriously wrong—just fatigue. I was tired of counting bottles, greeting a stream of faces night after night, coping with the usual problems of operating a club. I wasn't going to invite another breakdown, so I decided to take a vacation.

Chavez didn't like the idea at all, but I didn't realize what would happen when I overrode his objections. Actually, I had an idea what would happen; I just didn't realize how strongly it would affect him. What happened was that people came into the club and asked, "Where's Brick?" Hearing that I was on vacation, they left. That hurt Chavez deeply, and I was barely back from my holiday when he announced he wanted to take the place back and run it himself.

By now I was well established in Mexico City. I could have moved to any number of places—but I liked Chavez. He had been a good partner —a little difficult at times, but who wasn't? He was a sick man and belonged at home. We had a good thing going for us. Why break it up?

Chavez wouldn't budge, though. He was a proud, typically Latin man, and so he didn't know how to back down gracefully from a decision. He was all confused by his pride, because he was proud that I had made a success of the place, and too proud to admit that he was jealous. I made quite a few attempts to talk him out of it, but when I realized I couldn't, I bowed out.

I set up at another location almost immediately. It was a chic restaurant across the street from the Reforma, run by a Mexican and patronized by Germans, most of whom were legitimate refugees. The crowd from Chavez's followed me there.

The Spanish are like the English. Once they like you, they like you, and they like you best if you don't try to be something you're not. I was the only singer who never tried to sing in Spanish, and that was the way the Mexicans wanted it.

I loved the country and adored the people. Some Latin men could have such great pride that it was infuriating, but they weren't all like that. One of the kindest, most generous men I ever met was Mexican, a thin wisp of a man with a pencil-thin mustache whose real name was Mario Moreno. He is better known as the celebrated Cantinflas. He is idolized in Latin America, and English-speaking audiences can be grateful to Mike Todd for introducing him to us in *Around the World in 80 Days*.

The side of Cantinflas I knew had nothing to do with his artistry, but with his humanity. If ever I have met a saint on earth, it's Cantinflas. I used to go out of my way to see him, because just being around him made me feel good. He is a millionaire many times over, and when I was in Mexico City he had a huge, luxurious office that handled his business affairs. He was rarely there in the daytime, but at night, after his employees and partners had gone home, he would go there and sit in his office and receive people who came from all over Mexico to ask for his help. He would listen to every request, and then he would do his best to help. He'd get someone out of jail, pay the rent for a newly married couple, pick up the grocery bill for an abandoned wife and children, arrange for the funeral of a derelict.

I told him once, "Mario, you are an angel." He answered simply, "No, Brick, darling. Only a few years ago I was hungry, too, and I haven't forgotten it."

He'd been a roustabout with a circus. When the star comedian had fallen sick, he had been pushed into the ring—and he'd become an instant star. From there he'd gone into the movies and on to incredible success.

Outside his home there was a little chapel and a statue of our Lady of Guadalupe. Groups of Indians would sit there day and night, waiting for him. When he arrived home, he always emptied his pockets. He was a man with a lovely heart.

Everything was going fine for me until it occurred to me that I'd been in Mexico for about five years and it was time to look into my working papers.

Actually, it wasn't even my idea to find out about them. I was used to the way things had been done in France before the war, where my papers had always been automatically renewed with little red tape. I foolishly took it for granted that things were handled the same way all over the world.

The first papers I took out in Mexico were good for five years, I thought, but one day Sam Harris asked me about them, and I really wasn't sure. He suggested that I check into it. In Mexico, alien affairs are handled by the police. They informed me that my papers had been invalid for the last two years; they had been canceled by one of the Mexicans involved in the financing of the Minuit.

The next time the man came into the club, with his wife and some friends, I walked over to his table and told him what I thought of him and the shabby treatment I was getting. He didn't say a word, just suggested that I come to his office to talk things over.

I refused to go. Sam Harris was worried. He reminded me that a man with his influence could have me put out of the country.

I knew what the Mexican wanted, however. He wanted me to apologize for dressing him down in front of his friends. I told Sam, "I'll die first."

Sam kept after me, however, and finally I went with him to the man's office. There he sat, with some of his friends, and, as I'd expected, he said, "I want you to say you're sorry for the things you said the other night in front of my friends."

Sam nudged me. "Say you're sorry, Brick."

The man continued, "If you don't, I'll see that you're put on the first plane for Texas." So I said I was sorry, although it killed me to do it, and I thought the matter was ended.

Sam wasn't so sure, though, and neither was the owner of the new club where I was working. He knew the Minister of the Interior, and he suggested I talk to him. The Minister of the Interior said that the wisest course would be to leave the country, obtain a new permit, and then return. That seemed like an awful lot of bother.

I didn't know what to do. I asked the opinions of lots of people, and the general consensus was that the Minister was an honest politician and probably knew best. It was July 1949. I had been in Mexico about six years. Since I had sublet my apartment in New York, I thought it was a good time to go there and close it up.

Since I expected to be back in Mexico City within a few weeks, I left some clothes, some precious photographs, and a little jewelry behind. But ten years would pass before I visited Mexico City again. God had other plans for me.

R E T U R N   T O   P A R I S

BECAUSE I LEFT Mexico so abruptly, there were wild rumors that I had been kicked out of the country. How they started or who started them, I don't know. You don't try to track down things like that—it's best to allow them to die naturally. Anyway, I thought I'd be back in Mexico soon, which would put an end to the rumors. Almost as soon as I got to New York, I put in for the official papers that would allow me to re-enter Mexico.

I had mixed feelings about returning to New York. It brought back some painful memories, so it wasn't hard to give up the apartment and attend to the other things necessary to "close up shop" there. I also had a lot of old friends in New York, though, and it was nice to see and talk with them again.

The war was over by now, and everyone was talking excitedly about getting back to Europe. "Why don't you go back to Paris and reopen

235

Bricktop's?" they urged. I'd say that I was happy in Mexico City, but I did start thinking about the Paris idea. Meanwhile, my application for a Mexican visa had become fouled up in red tape, which gave me extra time to think about returning to Paris.

While I waited for the visa to come through, my friends saw to it that I didn't sit around with time on my hands. I visited around, went to parties, took in the clubs, and generally found out what was going on in the New York entertainment world. One night two fellows decided to take me to hear Hugh Shannon, who had his own room at a club on 55th Street. He was a newcomer, but word had got around quickly among those who knew saloon singing that he could really sing Negro blues, even though he was white.

Still, I wasn't prepared for this beautiful blond boy, spotlighted in a darkened room, singing the blues. And I certainly wasn't expecting to hear him launch into "Ballin' the Jack."

"Hey," I cried, "that's my song!" Hugh stopped cold, then recovered and continued the song, but he kept looking over in my direction. After his set was over, one of the fellows I was with called him to our table. "Tell him who you are," my friend said.

"I'm Bricktop," I announced, and Hugh got all flustered. He'd been reading about me—in the writings of Scott Fitzgerald, Hemingway, Evelyn Waugh—since he'd been seventeen. Now, here I was in the flesh.

I was curious about this white boy and his authentic way of singing the blues. "Are you sure of yourself?" I wanted to know.

"I'm one-quarter Sioux Indian," he announced. Although that didn't seem to me to have much to do with anything, I liked him. Before the night was over, I'd gotten up there with him and sung several songs, including a duet with him on "Ballin' the Jack."

We became good friends, and we had a lot of talks over the next couple of weeks. He wanted to hear all about the Paris years, and I could see he was anxious to go to Paris. Of course, the more I told him about that golden time, the more homesick for Paris I became. We started talking about going there together and opening up a new Bricktop's, and suddenly it all seemed possible.

I frankly don't remember if the mess with my Mexican papers got straightened out or not. If it did, I was already bent on going to Paris.

However, it seemed like everyone else had the same idea. We couldn't get on a ship to France, at least not at a passage we could afford, so we had to take a roundabout route. We went by freighter to Genoa, and I had the worst case of seasickness I've ever had in my life. When we finally docked, all I could think about was getting to a church to give thanks that I was still alive. Since I was in Italy, I also talked Hugh into going to Rome for a couple of days. It was my first visit to the Eternal City since becoming a Catholic, and I wanted to go to the Vatican.

From there we went to Capri. Franklin Hughes, the designer, had invited me to visit him at his villa there, and since it was July 1949—and July was no time to open up anything in Paris—Capri seemed a logical place for Hugh and me to start out. It was a great jumping-off point. I got us booked into a local club, and Hugh was just a sensation. In fact, we fooled around with the idea of opening a club on the island, but those first post-war years were complicated times, full of red tape and self-important bureaucrats. For all its beauty, Capri didn't seem inviting enough to warrant all the headaches involved. Besides, where we really wanted to be was Paris. After a few weeks in Capri, that's where I headed. Hugh went on to the Riviera to make some money while I set about arranging the reopening of Bricktop's.

In Paris I was met at the train station by Georgina, a Belgian girl who was married to Arthur Briggs, my ex-neighbor. I was really excited—I was back in Paris at last, and everything about it looked wonderful to me. Georgina sensed how I felt, and right away she began preparing me for a Paris that was far different from the one I had known. "Bricky, get ready for a big change," she said. "You won't find Paris like it used to be."

I laughed, "It couldn't have changed that much!"

Very quietly she said, "You'll see," as though she was afraid of stepping on my heart.

All too soon I began to see what she meant. Montmartre looked like a wreck. It hadn't looked all that great by daylight even in the Twenties, but now it wasn't just shabby, it was almost slummy. The hotel I went to, which I remembered from the old days, wasn't the same. The atmosphere just wasn't the same. At night the atmosphere didn't get much better. The places on the Rue Pigalle and Rue Fontaine closed up either at midnight or at one a.m. That was sad. In my day, things were just getting started at that time.

There were other sad things about post-war Paris. There was a lot of resentment toward Americans—YANKEE GO HOME signs all over the place. At the same time, the Parisians had started picking up some distinctly American attitudes toward Negroes.

It started with the American soldiers, I'm told. I never saw them in Paris. When I was there, World War I was over and World War II hadn't reached Paris. People who stayed there through World War II, though, told me that the minute the American soldiers came to France, you could just feel the prejudice in the streets. The white American soldier brought it. After the war more and more Americans—average Americans, not the quality of Cole and his crowd—started coming, and they made it even worse.

I remember hearing a French prostitute call somebody a nigger. I walked over to her and said, "Where in the world did you get that from?" She pointed to a white musician. "He told me. He told me in U.S. you don't treat them the same. *You* know, Bricktop."

I said, "Don't you ever . . ." I should have knocked her down, because she became one of the biggest nigger-haters I've ever known. And all this because of a white American. Big Brother to Europe?

The French authorities closed up a place because it refused to serve an African prince. He'd been going there for years and never had any trouble, but American tourists started coming, and they complained, and he was told he would no longer be served. He took his case to court, and the court ordered the place closed. It stayed closed for ten or fifteen years.

Things were changing under the influence of all those prejudiced Americans who started coming to Paris after the war. Art Buchwald was with the Paris Bureau of the *New York Herald Tribune* when I went back. A newspaperwoman friend, a Negro woman, was coming over from America, and he went to one of the small hotels off the Champs-Elysées to reserve a room for her. It was just a middle-class place, not one of the best. He made the reservation and left. A few days before she was to arrive, he went back to the hotel to make sure everything was arranged. He said to the woman at the desk, "You'll be able to recognize this lady. She's Negro."

Suddenly, everything changed. The woman went away and came back and said there'd been a mistake and all that. Well, Art, who's one of the nicest and most unprejudiced men in the world, wasn't going to stand for that. He had that woman brought to court.

In court she said she had many white American guests, and the first thing they always asked was if any Negroes lived there. That was the first time a French judge said a proprietor had the right to discriminate because of color, and I found it incredible. There were black judges in France, Negroes in the highest positions—and all those Martiniquans who were so high-class they didn't even speak to me!

It made me sad to see all that happening in Paris, the city I loved so much, but I wasn't going to let it keep me from opening up Bricktop's again.

The second night after I arrived, I started going around to talk to the club owners and managers. I wanted to know what the nightclub scene was like in Paris now. There were plenty of new faces, but quite a few old ones, too. I recognized some street girls at the Sans Souci. They recognized me, too, and we were all glad to see someone from the old days.

I found that there were some late places to go to, and one early morning I went to one. Edith Piaf was there. By then she was *the* Piaf, and she was someone I wanted to meet. I didn't usually make myself known to people or speak to anyone just because he or she was famous, and I still don't, but I went over to her table and said, "Miss Piaf, I want to say how happy I am to know you and how great an artist I think you are." She thanked me. Then I said, "I am Bricktop."

"Bricktop!" she cried. "*La* great Bricktop?" She turned to the man beside her. "I used to sing out in the streets in front of her door."

I said, "Well, you're not singing out there anymore," and she said, "No, thank God." She was a sweet lady, but she was knocked down and dragged out. They made a son-of-a-bitch out of her.

Word got around that I was back in Paris, and when Elsa Schiaparelli heard the news, she got in touch with me and said she wanted to give me a cocktail party. It was a wonderful party. I hadn't seen friends like Arturo Lopez and Donald Bloomingdale for over ten years, but it seemed as if those years had never happened. For them, as for the people in New York, I was a symbol of a time they remembered with joy and wanted to recapture. At that party we were able to recapture some of that feeling.

"When are you going to open up?" they asked.

I said, "With what? I don't have any money."

"Leave it to me," said Schiapi, and in no time at all she and Arturo and Donald and a couple others had got together and put up a stake for me.

In the nightclub business, that could only be called a miracle. No one, at least no one I've ever heard of, came back to town after a war to discover everything at her fingertips—money, word-of-mouth publicity, and an audience reserving tables for the opening night of a club that didn't even have an address yet. Schiapi joked, "Bricky, you're the best-kept woman in Paris. Arturo and Donald see to your bills before they see that their wives' bills are paid!"

It would have taken more than a miracle to stop the red tape, however. First came the problem of my licenses to run the club. Originally, they had been in my maiden name, but after Peter and I had married he'd had to appear before the proper commission and grant his permission for new licenses to be issued in the name of Mrs. Ada Smith Ducongé. I remember that he was delighted about it: "You've finally had to get someone's permission to do something," he teased. Under French law, a wife could not own property in her own name without the consent of her husband—and it hasn't been all that long since that outdated law was finally changed.

Naturally, I wanted the licenses renewed in my name only, but I was told I couldn't do that. Okay, I said, I'd like them renewed in my married name—I was still technically married to Peter. I was told I couldn't do that either. Then I was told that I would have to start fresh.

"Not me," I insisted. "I was in business in Paris for sixteen years, paying more taxes than any other nightclub my size in the city." I added, "And more than some of the big ones, too," because I knew all about the graft and the political favors some of the big club owners had been in on.

The bureaucrat looked at me coldly. "Then why did you run away?"

I nearly exploded. "Run away? Why, that's crazy. I would have been an enemy alien. I would have been locked up in a concentration camp."

240

"Why did you wait so long to come back?" he wanted to know.

"Because I didn't have the money," I said between my teeth. I couldn't believe all this. I was baffled and infuriated by the man's attitude. I had done my share of dealing with French officials, and for every sour one I'd found a dozen who were delightful—but none had ever been as rude and contemptuous as this man.

Next he wanted to know why I hadn't just gotten the money from all my fabled millionaire clients. I tried to keep calm. "They didn't bring me into the world. *I'm* responsible for me, not them."

He then told me I had to get a "good conduct" certificate from the American embassy certifying that I had never been in trouble in any part of the world. That was pretty easy to get, but when I brought it to the police, they told me it would take about a year to get all the necessary licenses.

By then I had found a place on the Rue Fontaine. "But I'm ready to open now," I protested. The official shrugged his shoulders. I realized I wasn't going to get anywhere with him.

Meanwhile, I'd been trying to line up musicians—and I'd run into more bureaucratic red tape with the entertainers' union. I was told that France had enough competent jazz musicians now and could do without Americans. Only foreign entertainers with "unique" talents were granted permission to perform. It took me a few minutes to realize that they weren't just talking about the musicians I wanted to line up, they were also talking about me. If I wanted to entertain as well as manage, I had to be in the union.

"What is unique about you?" they asked.

"Plenty," I shot back, and I started in on how I'd run a successful nightclub for years, employed hundreds of people, contributed something unique to Montmartre. They weren't very impressed.

Finally, we worked out a compromise. I was given a provisional work permit that enabled me to perform while the union considered my application for permanent papers. However, the problem of all the necessary licenses for the club itself remained.

I don't know how many times I was interrogated by the police. They wanted to know how often I'd been out of France, where I'd gone and with whom. Had I been to Biarritz? Could I recall the dates? Since they'd told me they had a dossier on me, I finally asked why they didn't just consult it. "We just want to refresh our memory," was the reply.

When I'd left France, I'd carried a white paper stating that I'd never been involved in any scandal, nor had my club. I told them about it and said there must be some record of it. They weren't in any hurry to search for it.

Most of the time I was saddled with this one rude, contemptuous, impossible official. I kept thinking that if only I could talk to somebody else I wouldn't have so many problems, but I was afraid that if I asked to speak to anybody else this fellow would come down on me even harder.

Then one day I noticed another man. He was at a nearby desk, and he seemed to be doing more listening than working. My inquisitor chose this day to ask me about money. "How much do you have?"

I answered that I had a million and a half francs.

"But you didn't have that much when you arrived in France."

"That's right. I had about fifty dollars. I got the rest from my friends after I got over here."

"What friends?"

"Madame Schiaparelli, Monsieur Lopez, Monsieur Bloomingdale. The money is to be used to reopen Bricktop's. Other friends have promised more money."

He wanted the addresses of my friends so he could investigate my statement.

At that point the man at the other desk got up and came over. He held a piece of paper in front of my interrogator. I have no idea what was written on it. As he held the paper in front of the man's nose, he said, "You have this woman's record. Everything shows that it is a clean one."

I took the opportunity to use the only piece of ammunition I had. Years before, when the Baron had tried to muscle in on my business, the chief investigator had helped out. I hadn't dealt with him personally —I'd let my headwaiter handle that—but I had taken down his name in my little address book. I fumbled in my purse for the address book and held it out to the inspector. "Do you know this man?" I asked.

"Of course. Why didn't you say you knew him?"

"I don't go around saying I know chief inspectors," I said. "Besides, I wasn't the one who dealt with him. My headwaiter did."

"Who was your headwaiter?"

"Jimmy of Jimmy's. He's pretty famous now, but he started out with me as a busboy."

Suddenly, there was a big change in the atmosphere. We got to talking and it turned out that we had mutual friends, and pretty soon we were acting like kissin' cousins. I didn't have any more trouble with the police about licenses after that.

Bricktop's came back to Paris in May 1950. The opening was sensational—so jammed that people were sitting on the floor. Arturo Lopez bought some lovely gowns for me. Schiaparelli designed them and did her usual brilliant job. Remembering how I had worked with feather boas before, she created a series of them that I changed throughout the evening. That was the beginning of the revival of the feather boa.

It was a wonderful, wonderful evening. I sang the old songs, fractured French, and even wrote special lyrics to "Thanks for the Memory":

> Thanks for the memories, of Paris in the spring,
> The Cole Porter songs we'd sing,
> Of the old Grand Duc and onion soup
> And other priceless things.
> I thank you so much.
>
> Thanks for the memories, of Molyneux gowns
> And sweet perfume,
> The Champs-Elysées in the afternoon.
> I thank you so much.

Janet Flanner, Paris correspondent for *The New Yorker* wrote:

In the May 1925 number of *Vogue* appeared the words: "Bricktop is a pale, unspoiled beauty. She sings and dances like a star. She is young and new to Paris." With pleasure, this correspondent can announce that Bricktop, still unspoiled in 1950, is back again in Paris, in a new red, gold, and white damask club of her own, on the Rue Fontaine. Her recent opening night was an extraordinary jam of people who were pale beauties in Bricktop's circle twenty-five years ago. In her old top-hat, cakewalking period, she was the greatest American professional personality in Montmartre's night life. In those days, as dawn came, there could often be seen Mme. Bricktop herself, the Lancashire singer, Mabel Mercer, and the Prince of Wales deep in mutually respectful conversation.

Art Buchwald wrote in the Paris edition of the *New York Herald Tribune:*

A bit of old Montmartre came to life Tuesday evening when Bricktop, one of Paris's most famous singer-hostesses, opened a new club at 26 Rue Fontaine. A slew of celebrities turned out to welcome Brick back to her old hunting grounds, and the tiny room was jammed with furs, diamonds, and gold swizzlesticks. From our vantage point we could see Elsa Schiaparelli, Baron de Rédé, the eleventh Duke of Argyll—heir to a Spanish galleon fortune of ducats—the Duke of Verdura, Marcel Achard, Salvador Dali, Simone Simon, Jean Sablon and others of the elegant international set.

Since the dance floor was filled with tables, there was nothing the well-dressed crowd could do except ogle each other and scream. When Hugh Shannon, Bricktop's singing, piano-playing attraction, started to perform, the ogling stopped, though the screaming continued.

... When Bricktop took over the singing, the room quieted down. She thanked everyone for the memories and sang several sentimental songs. While eyes remained dry, Brick received a warm reception.

That's how it went as the night wore on. We were all so happy and grateful to be together again. I sang over and over, and Hugh was a big hit, as I knew he would be.

Like Mabel, Hugh always said he learned how to run a successful saloon from me, but I have to say in turn that they were both wonderful people to work with. Like Mabel, Hugh was very well-bred, and he had a nice way of putting people at their ease. I've seen the shyest of shy people walk over to his piano and timidly make a song request. "Hugo's the name," he'd say, grinning from ear to ear, and the person's shyness would just vanish. His knowledge of tunes, old and new, was amazing, but he knew how to decline a request for a poor song gracefully. He was always in tune with the audience and knew when to shift tempo to vary the ambience of the performance.

While we were getting the club ready to open, Hugh kept asking why I'd wanted to put in two pianos. The night after the opening he found out. I said, "Hugo, you take that second piano you've been worrying about, roll it around from table to table, and just play any song they want to hear." I sent the orchestra home, went upstairs—my apartment was over the club—and left him alone to cater to the customers.

Porfirio Rubirosa, the rich, handsome diplomat from the Dominican Republic, adored Hugh's singing. Sometimes at ten o'clock in the morning he'd still be there on the floor, his head resting against the leg of the piano, listening to Hugh's songs—and of course Hugh must have been playing and singing continuously since the previous evening.

I can still see the Duke of Windsor sitting on the floor, enjoying his requested "When the Red, Red Robin Comes Bob-Bob-Bobbing Along," and remember Hugh's consternation at having to learn "If I Knew You Were Comin', I'd Have Baked a Cake" because Elsa Schiaparelli liked it. He knew enough not to decline a request from Elsa Schiaparelli.

We tried very hard to bring back the golden years. When the Duke and Duchess of Windsor took a new home in Paris, a great big party was held to celebrate the event. Elsa Schiaparelli told one of the Duke's secretaries that the Duke and Duchess might enjoy having Bricktop entertain, so I was invited, and I took Hugh along to play for me. When I was through performing, the Duchess said, "I'm afraid a lot of the young people here don't know the songs you've been singing."

The Duke smiled. "But I knew them and that's why Brick sang them."

Hugh and I were about to leave when I heard some commotion behind me. I turned around and there was the Duke. "Brick, where were you born?" he asked.

I answered, "Alderson, West Virginia, right by White Sulphur Springs."

He smiled broadly. "That's what I told the Duchess," he exclaimed. "You know, we go to the Springs every year to play golf, and I told her that Brick was born somewhere around here."

245

We were fooling ourselves, trying to re-create the old Paris days. It was like putting Humpty Dumpty together again. Oh, there were some nights, like the opening of Bricktop's, when the place was jammed with people who knew one another. There weren't enough of those nights to keep Bricktop's alive, though. When the season ended on the last of June, I was relieved.

My nerves were raw. As if the problems of opening up had not been enough, managing Bricktop's had become a five-aspirin headache. The waiters were insolent, the musicians troublesome. New York and Mexico City hadn't improved my French, but, like anyone else who has lived abroad, I understood much more than I spoke, so my employees didn't put much over on me. I had to watch them every minute. Still, my friends kept telling me not to give up—things would be better in the fall. They urged me to go to Biarritz for the summer.

Hugh Shannon didn't go to Biarritz with me. He went to the Virgin Islands. He had met and fallen in love with a girl named Betty, and after I closed up they went to the Virgin Islands to get married. He did not return to work for me in Paris, but he did work for me a couple of times in Rome, and when I returned to New York, that's when we really got together.

In Biarritz, I couldn't get any of the places I really wanted and had to settle for second best. I made a deal with a woman who had quite a reputation in town, except that I didn't know about it. There was a typical Bricktop's opening, with everyone there, including Porfirio Rubirosa, one of the big, big spenders of all time. He liked to say, "Some men save money, but I like to spend it."

At the time, he had just separated from Danielle Darrieux, but he didn't lack for female company. Women adored him. He was a great dancer and very, very handsome. He didn't look exactly white or exactly Negro, and people always wondered what he was. A fresh fellow once asked him in the club. Rubi looked at him and said, "What do you think?" He was Negro, and he never denied it.

Rubi gave a big party at Bricktop's and the place was packed. I had only been open four nights, though, when I got wind that the woman with whom I'd made the deal for the club was about to take over the place herself. That was the way she operated. As soon as a tenant made good at her club, she found some excuse to get the tenant out and put herself in charge.

My liquor and silver were in the place, so early one morning I ran a couple of trucks over to the club, with my waiters aboard. We took out everything that belonged to Bricktop's, and I was stuck with liquor and silver and no club. I stayed on in Biarritz, entertaining at parties, including one at Betty Dodge's villa, and tried to get enthusiastic about returning to Paris in the fall.

I never did get up much enthusiasm, but I reopened. The *Herald Tribune* carried another nice article:

That elegant boîte bordering on Pigalle, Bricktop's, opened up again for the winter the other night after a two-month siesta. . . . A woman who places value on friendship and has devoted most of her life to entertaining Europe's most elegant crowd was busy welcoming old friends. One night at Bricktop's is much like any other—all good. In a few words, it's champagne from way back, songs by Brick, music by Charlie Lewis's band, an impromptu Charleston lesson. Brick, who can't sing, puts over a song better than most of those who can.

In spite of the nice publicity, however, the fall of 1950 was like spring all over again. There just weren't enough of the old crowd around to support Bricktop's, and by November I was very worried. December is a treacherous month in the nightclub business, and I was convinced I couldn't survive it.

In Rome the previous year I had looked up Gino, an old headwaiter of mine. After the war he had settled in Rome and fallen in love with it. He told me I should open up there, explaining, "There's nothing like Bricktop's here. If you opened, you would have a tremendous success."

Although I loved Rome, too, and knew it had nothing in the way of a smart, intimate club, I couldn't see it. Maybe it was just that I was blind to anyplace but Paris, but I couldn't see a Bricktop's amid the big vaudeville establishments like the Jiki Club and the coffee bars that lined the sidewalks. In addition, the aristocrats in Rome traveled with the seasons, and entertained at home during the winter months they spent in Rome.

During the next year I started hearing more and more about Rome as a place to go. Tourists were cutting their Paris stays short in order to spend more time in Rome. Who could blame them? Those YANKEE GO HOME signs they saw all over Paris sure didn't spell out WELCOME. Italians were less bitter about the war than the French, and Americans felt more comfortable among them. Then, too, the movie *Quo Vadis* had spotlighted Rome as an ideal city for movie production, and brought more actors, directors and producers. A substantial American colony was beginning to make itself felt in Rome. I didn't want to leave my beloved Paris, but I was getting pretty discouraged there. I decided to look at the possibilities in Rome.

I hopped on a plane and didn't tell anyone where I was going or why. I'd let Gino know I was coming, and he was way ahead of me. He had already scouted locations and had a list ready for me. The room that impressed me most was downstairs in the Ambassador Hotel, directly across from the American embassy on the Via Veneto. The Via Veneto was already the Main Street of the foreign colony, the center of tourist traffic. Its biggest attraction was Doney's, a huge sidewalk café next to the Excelsior Hotel. Victor's, a popular bar, was also on the street, and the Jiki Club was located farther down the hill near the Piazza Barberini.

I met the manager of the Ambassador Hotel and we talked terms. When he asked for references, I mentioned the Contessa Pecci Blunt. She'd had two or three Popes in her family. He left the room. A few minutes later he came back and said, "Madame Bricktop, everything is arranged." I later found out that he had called the Contessa and that she had assured him I would have her full support in opening Bricktop's in Rome.

I flew back to Paris, called all the waiters and the cook together, and said, "I'm leaving." They pleaded, "No, Madame, you can't. Christmas is coming."

I felt sorry for them—finding work at that time of year would be difficult—but as a businesswoman I had to face facts. I might have had the strength to ride out the season if I'd had some support from my employees, but the waiters who cried when I closed them out had done very little to help me. A week or so later, when I was all packed up, I just took the key and threw it out into the middle of the street. "There's your nightclub," I said.

Leaving Paris wasn't easy for me, emotionally. It still held my fondest memories, and I wasn't about to forget how much I owed to that city. Maybe I would go back—after the French, who'd just done an about-face on Americans, did another about-face and started making us feel welcome.

I had one real regret about leaving Paris at that time. I'd had a falling out with Elsa Schiaparelli, and though I'd tried, I hadn't been able to patch things up. I'm vague about exactly what happened. One night she came to the club with some other people; she had been drinking quite a bit, and I think when they were given the bill, they wanted to sign it instead of pay it. The waiter came over and told me, and I went over and said, "No, I'd like for you to pay the bill." Elsa was like anyone else—after she'd had a few drinks, she might have become just a little bit impossible. I used to be pretty hot-headed and very impulsive in speech. I should never have had any words with Schiapi, because she surely was good to me.

However, I couldn't dwell on regrets. It was Christmas 1950. I was fifty-six years old and making another new start.

THE HOLY HUSTLER

THE ROOM at the Ambassador Hotel was bigger than I wanted, but it represented the changing times. I had to keep up with them. The days of Le Grand Duc with its tiny bar were over, as were the nights when we had survived by selling just five bottles of champagne.

There were other changes in the nightclub business after the war. Many of the millionaires that the giant broom called the Depression had swept out never drifted back in. The same was true of the European nobility. There were still plenty of counts and marquis and marquises and princesses around, but they didn't have as much money as they used to, or they preferred to socialize at home. Of course, all the ones who used to come to the old Bricktop's in Paris were getting old themselves. Their sons and daughters were more casual about how they behaved and with whom they hung around.

I had to relax my dress standards. If I'd insisted that my clients wear evening gowns and dress suits, I would have had to close up before I even opened. Gone were the days when most movie stars couldn't even get past the ropes at Bricktop's. After the war they became the new royalty. I had to attract them if I wanted to stay in business. What's more, I also had to attract the man-off-the-street trade, which was unheard of in the golden Paris days. I was a businesswoman, however, and running a club was the only business I knew, so I was willing for Bricktop's to go with the times.

There were a few things I refused to change. I still didn't want any hustlers, so I wouldn't let unescorted women into the club, though the hustlers were always trying to get around that. They'd get men to escort them in and then leave. I had to keep a constant eye out for that kind of trick. One night I spied two women alone and I went over to them and said I didn't serve unescorted women. They explained that the men who had brought them in were coming back. Since my Italian wasn't very good, I had my headwaiter, Angelo, explain that I knew that old gimmick. They left, and returned with a policeman. The officer said, "You put these women out. They are Italians. One is the wife of a commendatore."

Angelo laughed. "Is she? Since when is the wife of a commendatore out alone at one o'clock in the morning? No Italian lady is out alone at this hour."

The officer told the girls it would be a good idea if they left.

When Polly Adler, probably the most famous madam of her time, arrived in Rome with a letter of introduction to me, I relaxed my own rule. I asked one of the entertainers to be her escort while she was in Bricktop's.

She wanted to visit the whorehouses. Most of them had been closed for a couple of years, but there were still a few in operation. I got in touch with Reynolds Packard, the Rome correspondent for the New York *Daily News*, and he agreed to show her around. They didn't get very far, though. At the very first place, when Pack introduced Polly to her opposite number, the Italian madam screamed, "Get away from here! Here we are always in trouble with the police, and you show up with the most famous landlady in the world!" Word got around, and

Polly found she wasn't welcome at any of the houses that had managed to stay in operation.

A few weeks later I happened to be in Madrid and so was Polly. Some friends and I took her to dinner at a very chic restaurant. There were some men from the American embassy at an adjoining table, and they were horrified. One of them took me aside and said, "Brick, you can't afford to be seen out with Polly Adler." I let him have it: "I can afford to do anything I want. Polly's no bum. She just ran a whorehouse all her life, and it was one of the best."

Another rule I tried to stick to was to forbid photographers in the place unless a client specifically requested one. It was hard, though, with all those papparazzi. They would clutter the entrance, offer me bribes, do anything they could to get in. I always refused the bribes, but I had some waiters who couldn't resist. It was a constant battle, and sometimes it really frazzled my nerves. I could only imagine what it was like for those famous people that the papparazzi trailed like a pack of hungry dogs. Princess Margaret couldn't even go to the bathroom without having her picture snapped. The heaviest bribe offers I ever got came when Elizabeth Taylor was in town. They managed to get a picture of Ava Gardner and Tony Franciosa in my place once, and after that I seriously considered hiring a bouncer, though I never did.

I think the reason why the papparazzi flourished in Rome was that the Italians really did want to see and be seen—and so did plenty of foreigners. The Via Veneto was just beginning to become one of those places for public gawking and public display, so not everyone who went there wanted to show off. Nowadays anyone who talks privacy but goes to the Via Veneto is clearly protesting too much. The same is true of the woman who goes to Rome and complains about being pinched on the behind. Italy is one of those Latin countries a woman should visit to find out how attractive she is. When you're not whistled at, that's the time to worry. Latin men don't put the same emphasis on youth as Americans do. Away from America, a woman is a woman as long as she can walk. I think the sexiest women I've seen have been ugly ones. Beautiful women are so busy taking care of their looks that they forget to be natural. A natural woman, if she's a real woman, is a sexy woman—like Anna Magnani. Any man would go out of his mind to get next to a woman like that.

In spite of their protests, women like the attention that they get from Italian men. I remember seeing one of the most beautiful women in the world break into tears at the thought of going home. She'd been in Rome for a movie and was returning to Hollywood and a fat contract. I wanted to know what she was crying about. "Oh, Brick," she said, "how I'm going to miss those whistles!" Later on, after the Via Veneto turned into the Italian version of Hollywood Boulevard, I'd hear the American women complaining about the Italian men and I'd remember the refreshing honesty of this woman. If the bottom-pinching bothered them so much, why were they on the Via Veneto in the first place?

The first Rome Bricktop's opened in early 1951, with Charlie Lewis's band and so many clients that the big room was overflowing. The clientele read like a *Who's Who* of Italian society, and on top of that were a lot of people from the American embassy and the ambassadors from Mexico and Chile. Looking back, however, I remember that night most fondly because Anna Magnani was there.

At the time, she was Italy's top film star. I knew who she was, but didn't pay that much attention on opening night. It was during the nights after the opening that I got to know her and discovered to my surprise and delight that she was a real sport and a night owl who would prowl around Rome's night spots until the small hours of the morning. She came night after night, bringing large parties and obviously interested in helping me. I was very grateful.

I loved Anna most when she sat at her favorite table, holding court and having her hand kissed by Italy's nobility. She would wink at me as if to say, "What phonies! If I weren't Anna Magnani, these people wouldn't come near me."

A lot of newspapers covered the opening night of Bricktop's. The *Rome American* raved, "Bricktop's opening last night at the ABC Room of the Hotel Ambassador was in the old tradition—a setting jampacked with celebrities, and Bricktop herself the same warm and wonderful personality that has made her famous throughout the world." For a few months Bricktop's lived up to that description, but after a while business dropped off. Anna Magnani remained loyal, but it took more than Anna and her parties to fill that big room every night. It is the nature of Italians to come not to be entertained but to see and be seen, and after a time they get bored. I didn't like seeing all those empty tables, but there wasn't much I could, or was willing to, do about it. I might have picked up some business from those Cook's and American Express "night tours of the city," but that meant planning a regular schedule of performances, which didn't belong in Bricktop's.

I held on, though. I stayed at the Ambassador about a year and a half, which is longer than I should have. By the time I closed up, I was pretty depressed about my chances of success in Rome. I decided to take a vacation. It was the summer of 1952, and the Duchessa du Bagnole had offered me her villa in Capri. I was on a novena, and that seemed like the perfect place, so I took her up on her offer.

I hadn't been there long when the first secretary to King Farouk called. Actually, Farouk was no longer king; he'd just abdicated, but everyone still called him king. The secretary's name was Amin, and his father had been secretary to Farouk's father. When Amin said, "Brick, come on down and see the King," I said, "Which king?"

"*My* king, Farouk," he said.

I protested, "But I'm not drinking. I'm on a novena."

Amin said, "We're not drinking either, but we're with everybody here at the hotel. They're all talking about you, and my king wants to meet the woman who makes everyone scream when she walks through the door."

I put my clothes on and went over to the hotel, and there was Ella Logan, the Scottish singer; her husband, Freddie Finklehoffe (he wrote the play *Brother Rat* and several famous screenplays); and the whole gang who used to go to Capri every summer. When I walked into the room, sure enough, they all started screaming "Brick! Bricky!"

Amin took me over and introduced me to the King, and we just fell in love with each other. He was in his early thirties, just a boy really, but he had the greatest sense of humor. I wound up asking him to the dinner party I was having the next night. He said he couldn't come to dinner, but if I'd send someone to meet him in the piazza, he'd come after dinner. I arranged for Sidney Gordon, a white boy who now lives in Palm Springs, to meet the King and bring him to the party.

By the next day all the Italian nobility in Capri seemed to have found out that King Farouk was coming to my party. They'd all invited him to parties and he had declined, so *they* wanted to come to my party. I turned them down. "I'm not going to have the man on exhibition," I said. However, they crashed the party anyway, and when the King arrived with Sid, he saw all those gate-crashers and didn't want to come in. When I met him at the foot of the walk, he said, "Bricky, do you mind if I just go and sit on the porch?"

He went to the veranda and sat down, and continued to sit while all those Italians walked around grinning and carrying on. He was very polite with everyone, but he just sat and sat, and finally he outsat them. Most of them went home, and then he said, "Now I'll come inside."

Ella and I were trading songs. Ella saw him and said, "Your Majesty, I'm going to sing you a special song," and she launched into "Go Down, Moses," which I thought was kind of nasty. Farouk just squatted on the floor with his legs underneath him, and when she got through, he said, "Ella, I think you're singing about ol' man Moses. He's dead."

Ella's husband, Freddie, said to her, "Well, that oughtta teach you to stay in your place."

In spite of that incident, Farouk and I had a great time just talking, and when I went back to Rome for the winter season, he was in my place every night. He loved the slot machine I had by the door as you came in. He was always at it. One night a man came up behind him and slapped him on the back. Farouk swung around and hit him, and it was no light tap. Farouk was a great big boy. The man went back to his table right away quick, with me on his heels. I wanted to know why he'd hit the King. He explained that he just wanted to go back to America and tell everybody that he'd slapped a king on the back. He was looking pretty sheepish and wanted to apologize. I said, "Wait a minute," and went over to tell Farouk that the man wanted to apologize. He said, "I don't want an apology. He should apologize to *you*. This is your place; why should he cause a disturbance in here?"

That was Farouk. He liked and respected me. He was dividing his time mostly between Rome and Switzerland, where he'd taken his children for their safety. Every time he came to Rome from Switzerland, he had some small gift for me, like a bottle of perfume. Once he brought me some little cigars with red plastic tips. I said, "But I don't smoke, Majesty."

It was true. The first cigarette I had ever smoked was in Paris, and that was because *everybody* in Europe smoked. People would say, "Have a cigarette," and when I declined they'd say, "You don't smoke?!" It was like saying you didn't breathe. I got so I could take a cigarette or leave it, but I still wasn't a smoker. King Farouk said, "I know you don't smoke, Bricky. Just do it for publicity." So I tried it. I started carrying around those little cigars, puffin' and blowin' and carryin' on, and, sure enough, the reporters started writing, "Bricktop drinks Rémy Martin and smokes little cigars that King Farouk brings her."

He used to tell me everything. He told me how he'd smuggled out money and jewels before he'd abdicated, knowing that he would be forced to leave the country after he stepped down. He told me he'd smuggled out a ring with a huge gem in it—an emerald or a ruby—by means of a handshake. As he was shaking hands with all the top government officials, saying goodbye, he'd put the ring in the hand of an official who was sympathetic to him, and that man had made sure Farouk got the ring after he'd left Egypt. Of course, everybody knew he had the ring, although no one knew how he'd gotten it, and Harry Winston, the big jeweler in New York, wanted that gem more than anything. Harry Winston sent representatives to talk to Farouk, but he wouldn't see them, because he wasn't interested in selling it. Then a representative came to me, to see if they could get to him that way. He came to my place when Farouk was there. I listened to him and said I'd ask the King if he wanted to talk to the man. I went over to Farouk, but before I could open my mouth, he said, "Go back and tell him no, Bricky."

I said, "Tell him no what?"

"I know he sent you to talk to me about that gem."

I don't know how he knew it, but he did. Harry Winston never got that gem from Farouk, and he had a way of getting those famous jewels, like the Star of India. However, Farouk was brought up smart—he was ruling Egypt when he was twelve years old.

He had great dignity. People would rush over to grab his hand, but he would just keep it right down at his side and look at them as if to say, "What? What is it?" Of course they would back off. We finally had a falling out over Amin. Farouk fired Amin, and he didn't want me to have anything to do with his former secretary. I told him, "Majesty, I didn't even allow my mother to choose my friends for me." He stopped coming to the club and I never saw him again.

* * *

After I left Capri, I went on to Madrid for a while and then to Estoril, which was the Portuguese equivalent of Palm Beach. It was just outside of Lisbon—you could take the tramway down there—and there was a casino and lots of rich people. The next village was Cascais, and people called it King City because so many past kings lived there—King Carol of Rumania, Umberto of Italy. It was Umberto who invited me to Estoril. I was at my hotel in Madrid when I got the call. Umberto was having a party and wanted me to come and entertain.

I'd first met Umberto when he was the Crown Prince of Italy. I'd been with Cole in Venice in 1926, and he'd had me entertain at a surprise party for His Highness. Here it was twenty-six years later. He'd only reigned for a short time, a little over a month, and his official title now was Count of Sarre, but in Europe, once a king, always a king. When he saw me, he jumped up and came running over and grabbed me, and of course when he did that, everybody else had to stand up because the King was on his feet.

After that kind of welcome I decided that Estoril might be a nice place to work, so I inquired about working at the casino. There were still a lot of restrictions on foreign entertainers working in Europe, and I had to go out of the country to apply for permission to work at the casino. It didn't take long, and I was back in a matter of days.

The night I opened at the casino, people carried on so—they were hanging from the rafters—but that worked against me. I didn't use a microphone, and I went from table to table as I generally did, and the people couldn't hear me. I was not a success, and I knew it. Three or four nights later I was talking to Umberto, and he said to me, "Bricky, you're not taking charge. You're not taking care of things."

"Now what?" I sighed.

Umberto said, "A great friend of yours is here and you haven't even said hello to him yet."

It turned out he was talking about King Carol of Rumania, and he was right—I should have noticed that he was there. He'd been a great client in Paris. I went straight over to Carol. "Your Majesty, please excuse me," I apologized.

He said, "Yeah, I know. You're so busy with that spaghetti over there you don't have time for anyone else." He had a twinkle in his eye when he said it, though. He was with his mistress, Magda Lupescu—she was a commoner and he had lost the throne because of her. He said, "Sing my song," and for the life of me I couldn't remember what it was. Lupescu was behind him, mouthing the words of the title, and I finally managed to read her lips. I said, "Oh, 'All Alone'!" and he was happy. I went and got the piano player and rehearsed a couple minutes, and then I sang it for him.

Everybody was talking about how those two kings were vying with each other for my attention, and that's how the saying started that I wasn't happy unless I had three or four kings in my place. However, that was the only time I was in the same place even with two.

At the end of the summer I returned to Rome and faced the fact that I had no Bricktop's. I had to open up somewhere, and I finally found a room behind a florist's shop on the Via Veneto. It's typical of the fickle nightclub business that I had more success there than at the Ambassador. Unfortunately, I didn't stay there long. The building was owned by some priests, and they objected to the music in the small hours of the morning. They didn't make me close the club, but they did stop the music, and what was Bricktop's without music? I stayed at the florist-shop location only a few months and soon found myself looking for another home for Bricktop's.

I put Gino and other friends on the search. One was the singer Dewey Martin. Another, who became a very special friend, was Jody Desmond. She was a white girl, quite young, and I don't remember now why she was in Rome. She had something to do with the picture business. She was one of what I used to call the "out-real people"—the people who didn't really belong, but who sort of hung around on the fringes. Jody was very popular, and she and I became quite close. It was she who found the cellar location on the Via Veneto that most people remember as the Rome Bricktop's.

I was never crazy about the place. The décor was more that of a restaurant than a nightclub. It was very chic, but it didn't have that intimacy. A lot of my clients confessed that they didn't like it either, but eventually we changed it around. I didn't have the money to redecorate, but we sort of rearranged things—a chair here, a table there—and finally we got it to look better. Before we opened, I went to Paris to look around for musicians, especially a pianist for me. Hugh Shannon had gone off to play gigs in other parts of Europe. His favorite city was Paris. He wasn't disillusioned with it the way I was. I didn't expect him to stay with me indefinitely, and I let him know that he was always welcome at Bricktop's.

In Paris I was at the Mars Club, a little spot off the Champs-Elysées, talking to the owner, when my ears perked up at the sounds being made by the young American piano player. I asked the owner who he was. "That's Ralph," he said. I went over to the piano, introduced myself, and asked if he was interested in coming to Rome and working with me. The young man jumped at the idea, but said he couldn't make the opening. He was traveling with Woody Herman's band. He'd be there a day or so later. "Okay," I said. "Now, this is the deal. I pay seven thousand lire a night. That's double what Italian musicians get. You get two drinks on the house every night. You know the songs I do. Just play them. Be there. Don't come to work drunk."

The night Ralph showed up in Rome, I had a cold and was trying to get out of working. It wasn't easy, because Dewey Martin and Jody Desmond were there and wanted "It's the Wrong Time." "Go on, Brick," Jody pressed. "Talk it if you can't sing the notes." I told Ralph to go out and start playing. As soon as he hit those chords, I got up and sang and forgot all about my cold. He was wonderful, the only pianist I ever really followed. A few nights later, as I was going into the club, a man and a woman passed me on their way out. The woman seemed to know me. "It's nice to find you in Rome, Brick," she said. "We'll be back."

They did come back, and I joined them at their table, but I still didn't know who they were. When I got up to work, Ralph told me they were Dorothy Kilgallen and her husband. After the set I rejoined them. "Why didn't you tell me who you were?"

Dorothy laughed, "I don't like going around advertising myself. By the way, you've got a great pianist there."

"Yes, he *is* good, isn't he?" I said.

Dorothy looked at me as if I'd said something insulting. "Good!" she cried. "How can you say that Ralph Burns is just 'good'?"

Now it was my turn to be shocked. Ralph Burns was one of the great-

259

est musical arrangers who'd ever lived—and he'd probably never worked for seven thousand lire, even when he was starting out! I went to the piano. "Young man, when you wind up that set, you meet me outside." When he got there, I said. "Why didn't you tell me who you were? I wouldn't have dared ask you to work for eleven dollars a night."

"Aw, forget it, Brick," he said. "I would have been in here every night anyway. You can't go back to America and say you haven't seen Bricktop. This way I'm getting paid to enjoy myself."

Ralph stayed on for several weeks, until I made the mistake of trying to do something special for him. I invited him and Danny Ballentine to Capri. We stayed for a weekend and Ralph fell in love with the place. A few weeks later, his time in Europe nearly over, Ralph left to spend the last days of it in Capri. However, that wasn't the last I saw of my charming and brilliant "cut-rate" pianist. Whenever I worked in New York on television, there was Ralph at the piano, working for scale. When other musicians asked why, Ralph answered, "Bricktop has something no other singer has. I can't explain it. I just get a kick out of working with her."

Even with Ralph Burns at the piano, Bricktop's had a slow start in that cellar a few steps down from the Via Veneto. Don't ask me why. If I had the answer, I'd be a millionaire. A place can have the ropes up in one location for twenty years, move across the street, and fold right up. The new Bricktop's, in full view, didn't do half the business the old one had, even though the old one had been hidden behind a florist shop. I knew Rome was for me by then, however, and I determined to sit it out. Actually, the really lean times only lasted about two months. At first my old friends just dribbled in, but their numbers grew. I got the embassy crowd. The place caught on with the movie people, and it became a second home to the local and visiting American and English newspaper reporters.

One of the American reporters who visited Bricktop's with his wife every time they were in Rome was Bob Considine. I adored both of them and respected Bob's work enormously. In 1952 I read an article he had written about two of the many boys' camps that were operating throughout Italy for kids orphaned during the war. His story pointed out the contrasts between the two camps, which were located quite close to one another. One, maintained by priests, was barely able to survive. The other, operated by Communists, had just about everything it needed —tools and equipment to teach the children trades, recreational facilities, good living conditions, and meat three times a week. I wondered if I couldn't help the priests' camp.

Business at the new Bricktop's was beginning to pick up at the time— not so much that I could do a lot myself, but attracting enough well-heeled clients so that I decided maybe I could get them to help. I started putting cards on the tables that had little inscriptions like "The only thing a dead man holds in his hands are the things he gave away." That was a strong statement, and I chose it deliberately. After three or four whiskeys, anyone—even the Devil—would react to that. I started collecting and pretty soon I had three hundred and fifty thousand lire. I went to the camp, which was near Naples, and presented the money to the fathers, then I went back to Rome to raise more money. I stayed with the project for two or three years, collecting money and tons of clothes. Along with the money orders I sent lists of the people who had made the donations. Clients said, "Please, Brick, don't give them our names. Now we're on all the begging-letter lists in both America and Italy." People started calling me the "Holy Hustler."

Actually, I've always preferred helping out individuals, especially children, or families with children. It means more to me than just contributing to some big fund—you don't know exactly where the money is going or whom it is helping. Back in Paris before the war, a club had so many taxes to pay that today I can't even remember what they were for, except one. It was the *taxe pour les pauvres*, about three percent. A man came around to collect, and, like other tax men, he wasn't very strict. You said how much your business had made and they took your word for it. At Christmas time, it must have been around 1932, I asked the *taxe pour les pauvres* collector if he really knew anything about the situation among the poor, or was he only a bookkeeper? "No one has ever asked me that before," he said in surprise. "They take it for granted I am only a collector, but my work brings me into direct contact with poor people." I asked him to find a family I could help, and he told me about one with nine children. Peter and I went to the home while the parents were at work. We didn't tell the children who we were, but took the oldest child to a neighborhood store, bought bags and bags of food, and left an order for Christmas. Just before Christmas we bought a ton of toys and sent them. The parents never found out who we were, and that, I know, was one of the finest Christmases of my life.

Until that time I'd never really thought about charitable works outside my own circle. I'd participated in that charity ball in Venice back in the summer of 1926, but I'd been paid for that. I'd never considered that helping out my friends in show business was charity, anyway. I had always taken it for granted that it was the thing to do; I felt an instinctive need to help people. I brought over the wives and children of the musicians and then took care of them when they got to Paris—things like that. Even before I had any money to speak of, I was known as a soft touch—either that or a sucker. I still laugh over one pitch. It was the late Twenties or early Thirties, when things were going great, and one night the doorman told me there was a man outside the club who desperately needed to see me. I went outside and there was an American white man who looked pretty comfortable in good, if not expensive, clothes. He told me he was stranded and needed money. "But why come to me?" I asked. The fellow explained that he'd been telling his tale of woe at Harry's Bar and one of those sporty, rich Americans who hung out there had told him, "Go over to Brick's. She'll help you out." I don't remember how much the man needed, but he got it. "I know those boys down at Harry's Bar," I said, "and they're going to hear from me. But if they said I'll help you, then I've got to do it." That's how I explained it to him and to myself.

After I converted to Catholicism, I became more aware of how necessary it was for those who had to help those who hadn't, and in Rome I became deeply involved in charity work. Besides Boys' Town, I took care of some girls in Rome—unwed mothers. I had a box in the club, and if a customer had three drinks, the money for the third drink went into the box to buy milk for the babies. I also helped individuals, even in the lean times, through the kindness of other people. People were very generous—I'd get bundles of clothes and food. Most people are charitable. They just have to be reminded. The world goes so fast that people tend to forget the man next door who might be hurting a little.

I got stung a few times. Once when I was visiting Naples, I fell for a ragged, dirty little boy. I took him into a store and got him dolled up in a new suit with all the trimmings. The owner of the store warned me I was making a mistake: "Madame, you're being very foolish. That boy's mother will be in here tomorrow selling these things right back to me." How right he was! After I returned a few weeks later from Capri, there was my little fellow, back on his old beat, begging from the tourists and waiting for another pigeon like me. However, one sour apple doesn't ruin the barrel when it comes to human beings, especially children.

It was through my charity work that I got to know Bishop Fulton J. Sheen a few years later. A man came into Bricktop's one night and said, "Brick, how would you like to meet Bishop Sheen?" Of course I wanted to. I was supposed to go to his hotel the next day to meet him, but, of course, being Bricktop, I didn't get there. My heart was giving me trouble at the time and some nights I didn't even make it to Bricktop's.

Well, the man went to the club looking for me, and they called me from there. When he told me the Bishop had waited half an hour for me, I really felt bad. I wanted to know what I could do to make up for it, and the man said I should call the Bishop. I called him and apologized. "Do you think you'll be able to see me before you leave?" I asked. He told me to come the next day *and to be on time*. Well, the next day I was so early I walked up and down in front of his hotel for an hour! It was a beautiful meeting, and I'll never forget it.

I met him again in Rome a couple of years later. I was broke at the time, and I told him I needed some money. He went and got a checkbook. "What do you need? Five hundred dollars, five thousand, what?" I said five hundred would be fine, so he gave me the five hundred. Some years after that, after my sister had died and I was in New York, I called his office and made an appointment to see him. I wanted to give him back the money. The Bishop said to his secretary, "Edith, how long have you been working for me?" She answered something like twenty-five years. He said, "Have you ever seen anyone do this?" She laughed. "No, they all take money, but they never bring it back."

Bishop Sheen wasn't the only cleric from whom I ever borrowed money. I used to borrow money regularly from an Irish priest in Rome. January and February were bad months for the nightclub business in the city, but, bad or not, you still had to pay your taxes at the end of

March. I usually borrowed money for the taxes from this priest. He knew I'd pay it back at the end of a good season, when I had more money than I wanted the tax collectors to know about. He used to help me "launder" the money. He had an in with the Vatican Bank, and he'd get my lire exchanged into dollars there, and then he'd arrange a transfer of those dollars to my account at Chase Manhattan Bank in New York, and I wouldn't have to pay taxes on it. If it sounds strange that a priest would do such a thing, it really wasn't—not in Italy. As he used to say, "With the Italians, you have no conscience." Anyway, he knew I'd wind up giving it to charity in one way or another.

HOLLYWOOD - ON - THE - TIBER

By THE TIME I opened up in that cellar on the Via Veneto, not just Bricktop's but Bricktop herself had become something of an institution —not a venerable one, but a comfortable one. I was kidded more in Rome than I ever was in Paris, and I don't know if that was because my clients were more casual, or because I was, or if it was a little bit of both.

There were no pretensions to the chic and elegance of the pre-war days. Clients no longer dressed, and I didn't either, although gentlemen were expected to wear neckties. Prices were reasonable—a dollar fifty a drink, the same as in most of the first-class bars in Rome that didn't offer entertainment. The majority of my liquor sales were by the drink, not by the bottle as in the pre-war days, and it was hard to believe that I'd once caused a stir by selling whiskey at the tables. Things started late, around eleven o'clock, as they had in the pre-war days, but for a different reason. Late hours were more suited to the season, which in Rome was summertime. The siesta hours are longer in the hot months, and dinner came later.

As I've said, there was no regular schedule of entertainment. I always had a band or a piano player. Sometimes I had a singer, sometimes not. I got up and sang whenever a client requested it and I felt like it. I didn't try to keep up with the new songs. My Rome clients liked to kid me, saying, "Brick is the only entertainer in the world who's made a career of singing seventeen songs," but it was the audience that cut my numbers down to seventeen or however many there were. They wanted the standards, the songs associated with me, and that's what I did night after night. I didn't mind, because those songs meant something to me, too. Even so, a performer wants to try something new once in a while, and I managed to sneak a few new songs in. When I first sang "September Song" and "Moon River," they went over great with the tourists, but some of the old clients just wouldn't accept them. I stuck with them long enough so that eventually the new people assumed they had been part of the original seventeen.

My repertoire included several Cole Porter songs, of course. When I first heard Cole's "It's All Right with Me," Ted Streeter was playing it in a club in Capri. I spoke to him about the tempo—I didn't think Cole had meant it to be played like that. Ted shrugged his shoulders. "That's how they're doing it in *Can-Can.*" I pulled down the tempo, sang it slow, and Frank Sinatra later recorded it that way. It's one of my favorites, and I must have sung that one ten times a night from the day I learned it. And of course there was "Miss Otis Regrets," my signature song. Peter O'Toole wanted me to do it forty times a night.

Gershwin's "Embraceable You" was always John Steinbeck's favorite. He once wrote, "When Brick sings 'Embraceable You,' she takes twenty years off a man's life." In the early years I enjoyed "Ace in the Hole," "Melancholy Baby," "The Man I Love," "Blue Room," and "Blue Skies." A Johnny Mercer-Harold Arlen song that I especially like is "One for My Baby," and then there is Irving Berlin's "How Deep Is the Ocean?" "How Deep Is the Ocean?" has such beautiful sentiments in it; I often wished they could have happened in my life. I didn't know Johnny Mercer was in the club one night when I sang "One for My

Baby." He told me it was a man's song, something I hadn't thought about, but he liked the way I did it, and that was the main thing.

Noel Coward's "I'll See You Again" wouldn't seem my kind of song, but it was, for a long time. So were "September in the Rain" and "Darktown Strutters' Ball." A couple of old, old favorites were "I'm a Little Blackbird" and "St. Louis Woman." "Silver Rose" was a favorite of the Prince of Wales. King Umberto of Italy always requested "Poor Papa."

By the time I opened in the cellar place, most of the clients who asked me to sing my songs were too young to remember them, but that didn't prevent Bricktop's from being successful. After a slow start the place gradually caught on. As I've said, I got the embassy people—and not just the grownups but their sons and daughters, too. The parents knew that there were no hustlers at Bricktop's—and no dope sellers that I knew of. It was a clean, safe place, and the embassy people recommended it to tourists. Thanks to that kind of word-of-mouth publicity, I started getting the man-off-the-street crowd. After battling all day with the Italian language, English and American tourists were relieved to come to a place where they could relax and speak English and enjoy a scotch-and-soda with the right-size ice cubes. Sometimes there were sentimental visitors from the Paris days. We would have reunion nights. There weren't very many of those, though. Most of the big names who came to Bricktop's in Rome were from the new celebrity set of Hollywood.

By the mid-Fifties, Rome had become a mecca for Hollywood people. American productions, co-productions, all sorts of productions came to what they started calling Hollywood-on-the-Tiber. And if Rome was Hollywood-on-the-Tiber, then the Via Veneto was "The Beach," as Sam Steinman of the *Hollywood Reporter* dubbed it. Bricktop's saw most of the stars: Esther Williams, Orson Welles, Humphrey Bogart, Stanley Baker, Roddy McDowall, Anthony Quinn, Laurence Harvey, Peter O'Toole, Shirley Booth, and many, many more. Very few of them made an impression on me, however. One reason was that I was so much older than most of them. In the Paris years I had been the same age as or younger than, many of my clients.

However, meeting Bette Davis was special. When she came into

Bricktop's, I was busy at the bar and didn't notice; then a man came over to me and asked if I'd like to meet her, and I said I'd love to. He took me by the hand and led me over to the table, and before we even got there, she was on her feet, leaning forward with her hand out. We didn't have a long conversation, but it was memorable for me because I admired her so much. She had an air about her that said, "I don't need to worry about who I am. I know." When she was getting on and nobody was offering her any good parts, she put an ad in the trade papers: "Good actress wants a job." Nobody but Bette Davis would have done that. She was one of the few actresses whose movies I went out of my way to see.

One of the few actors I just couldn't miss seeing was Edward G. Robinson. I'd had a crush on him since the Paris years, and so I was really excited when he showed up right outside my door in Rome. The picture was *Two Weeks in Another Town*, and they were shooting some scenes on the Via Veneto. I said to a fellow who was doing publicity for the picture, "If Edward G. Robinson gets a break, I want to speak to him." The fellow came and got me when there was a lull, and I went upstairs to the street.

"Excuse me, Mr. Robinson," I said. "I'd like to say hello. You don't remember, but I met you in Paris."

He said, "Paris? Paris? Wait a minute—you're Bricktop!" We talked for a while, and then I said, "I'm going to ask you something I've never asked anyone else in all these years. Could I get a picture with you?"

He said, "You mean can *I* get a picture with *you?*"

It's a beautiful picture, one of my proudest possessions. Edward G. Robinson was a fine man. Some years later, when I was living in Los Angeles, I gave a party and I called his house to invite him. The man who answered the phone asked who I was and then said, "He happens to be in Rome, where you oughta be." Edward got back in town a couple days after the party and called to say he was sorry he couldn't come, then he said, "Will you do me a favor?" "What is that?" I replied, and he said, "Will you ask us again?" Imagine Edward G. Robinson saying please ask us again!

Edward G. Robinson played the role of the "heavy" in a lot of movies, but he remained sweet and unassuming. Broderick Crawford was another story. He came into my place one night with a couple other men, but I didn't pay much attention until one of my waiters came over and said, "Madame, those men threw whiskey on the floor."

I went over to the men. "Is there something I can do for you?"

Broderick said, "Yeah, that whiskey of yours is gasoline. Send us some more drinks."

I said, "Well, even if it was gasoline, you wouldn't throw it on a lady's floor—and this *is* a lady's floor."

"Bring some more drinks," he said. And I said, "No, you can't get anything more to drink in here. In fact, get outta here."

He said, "I'll get out when I get ready," and I said, "No, you'll get out when *I'm* ready, and I'm ready now."

We went on a bit and I finally put him out. I heard that the next day a friend asked Broderick why he had given Bricktop such a hard time. He answered, "Bricktop? She wasn't even there." The friend said, "I've got news for you. Brick's the gal who threw you out."

Broderick Crawford had already been barred from just about every club in Hollywood. He was a "bad boy." I guess he'd played so many louts he'd become one himself. I didn't have much sympathy. Bricktop's didn't need his kind. I was running a club, not a sanitarium.

Frank Sinatra came to Bricktop's in Rome during the time Ava Gardner was filming *The Barefoot Contessa*. She was in the place all the time, but without him. At the time, Frank and Ava were separated and he was going down, but fast. He came to Italy and had no success there, either. Ava came to me one night and said, "Bricky, I'm going to bring my husband on New Year's Eve," and, sure enough, they came. She came right in, but he just stood there in the doorway with his hands in his pockets. I said, "Mr. Sinatra, come in. I don't have any photographers in here."

He came in and they sat down. She was sitting half on his lap, and it seemed to me that she was really trying to get him to enjoy himself. He looked so sad, and I found myself going over to them every little while and trying to make him feel at home. On one of those times he said, "You know, Bricktop, it's strange. Everybody in the world knows you but me." That's when I reminded him about the fight on 52nd Street and he turned to Ava and said, "I've been looking for this woman for

269

years." He came back again the next year. He was with that whole bunch they called the "Rat Pack"—Peter Lawford and all of them. I met him again after I got back to the United States. I'm very fond of him.

Another famous movie couple was associated with the Rome Bricktop's—Richard Burton and Elizabeth Taylor—but I don't claim any responsibility for that. The story that Bricktop's cradled their romance was a big, fat lie, and the idea that I had anything to do with it was an even bigger lie.

In 1961, Earl Blackwell organized a celebrity world cruise to launch a new Italian ship. Princess Soraya was on it, and the Considines, and a lot of other people. Earl invited me, and I decided to join the cruise in Naples and stay with it until it reached New York. By the time we had reached New York, it was late December. Meanwhile, back in Rome, Richard Burton and Elizabeth Taylor were filming *Cleopatra*, and Burton and his wife, Sybil, arranged to give a New Year's Eve party at Bricktop's. Elizabeth Taylor and Eddie Fisher were supposed to go to Paris for New Year's, but something happened and they wound up at the Burtons' party at Bricktop's. Not long afterward the story of the Burton-Taylor romance broke, and Bricktop's was in the headlines as the place where they'd made their first appearance together in public. I was in New York at the time, resting up after the cruise. Reporters kept calling me up. I told them I didn't know anything about it. Besides, when I'd heard about the party, it didn't sound to me like any notable event—Burton was with his wife and Elizabeth Taylor was with her husband, so it wasn't as if they had been out together. The combination of Bricktop's and the names Taylor and Burton was just too good for the columnists to resist, however.

Dorothy Kilgallen really played up that angle. She wrote in her column that I'd been a party to the romance since it had started, that I'd often closed the place so Liz and Richard could have it to themselves, and that I had sent them baskets of choice foods and vintage wines. There wasn't a word of truth to any of it. I didn't even know they were seeing each other.

I started getting anonymous letters accusing me of breaking up marriages. One said, "This is a pretty sad commentary on the state of the human race—your aiding and abetting these people. If you are so in-

terested in religious causes, I wonder why you don't protect marriage."
Finally, I wrote to Dorothy and asked her please to retract the story, but
of course she didn't.

Shirley MacLaine came to the Rome Bricktop's. I think she was in
town for a movie. Very late one night, when she was feeling no pain,
she sashayed over to the piano and started asking for numbers, and before long she was singing. There weren't more than a handful of people
in the place, and no one seemed to mind. Then a Hollywood newspaperman, a Bricktop's regular, came in, and he wasn't feeling any pain either.
He brushed past Shirley and, I think, deliberately lurched against her
derrière as he made his way to a table. "Nobody, but nobody, sings in
this place when Bricktop is here," he announced to no one in particular.
Shirley didn't pay any attention to him, just went right on singing.

Sensing trouble, I went over to him. He had a cutting tongue even
when he was sober, but he usually got away with it because he had a
great personality and usually knew what he was talking about; he was a
walking encyclopedia of show business. Still, I liked Shirley and didn't
want to have her insulted in Bricktop's. "Cool it, honey," I said to him.
"She's a big star and, besides, she's a terribly nice person."

"I don't come here and spend my money to hear that," he said. "She
can't sing. She's sharp."

I really hadn't been listening to her very closely. Now I did. He was
right. Not only was she pretty drunk, she was also pretty sharp. Luckily,
she soon got tired of singing and left. Some years later she made a
musical film, and the critics really panned her voice. My reporter friend
sent me all the reviews with a note that said, "That lady would be feeling
a lot better today if she'd listened to me years ago."

Although it didn't happen as constantly in Rome as it had in the Paris
days, musicians and professional singers still came to Bricktop's for
pleasure and wound up performing free of charge. Ella Fitzgerald would
relax in Rome after her European TV specials. She'd come to Bricktop's
and give impromptu concerts that delighted everyone who happened to
be lucky enough to be in the club at the time. And I'll never forget the
year Louis Armstrong came to the annual music festival at Spoleto.

Spoleto is a little mountain town about sixty kilometers from Rome.
While Louis and his band were preparing for the concert, Louis came

271

down with pneumonia, and his condition worsened so quickly that he was brought to Rome so he'd be nearer to good hospitals. The way the newspapers reported it, he was close to death, so you can imagine my surprise when a few days later I got a call from Angelo saying Louis had reserved a table for himself and his wife and a party of friends that night. I'd read in the papers that Louis and Louise were staying at the Grand Hotel, and I put in a call right away. When Louise said hello, I demanded, "Is Louis crazy? What's going on?"

She answered, "Nothing, Brick. You know Louis. He wants to give a party and tonight's the night."

I said, "But a few days ago he was dying."

"That was a few days ago," she laughed.

Well, when Louis Armstrong showed up on the Via Veneto that night, he attracted a crowd big enough to fill the Coliseum. I had a hard time getting into my own place. Once I did, we had a wonderful evening. Louis sang, and we talked about the days when Peter had played in his band.

Then there was the time Sophie Tucker came to Rome. It was 1960, I think. In her usual way, she took over the place. She insisted that I sing, and then she insisted that I have a spotlight on me. I had never worked with a spot, but I did that night, for her. When I got back to her table, she bawled me out about the clothes I was wearing. It was no use explaining to her that since my clients didn't dress anymore, I didn't either.

I missed a chance for a reunion with another old friend because of my chronic lateness, and I will always regret it. Cole Porter also came to Rome around 1960. He was staying at the Grand Hotel and sent word that he would be coming to Bricktop's on such-and-such a night. I wrote him a note saying I would be at the club at ten-thirty on the night he wanted to come. As usual, I was a bad timekeeper. Although I knew very well that when you told Cole ten-thirty you had better mean ten-thirty, I still managed to be five minutes late. As I got out of the cab, I saw a car drive away. Angelo told me that a woman had come downstairs looking for me, and I just knew I'd missed Cole. I wrote him a note saying how sorry I was. He wrote back, "The sign reads Bricktop's, but I didn't see any Brick."

I never saw Cole again. Racked with pain in his legs, he rarely went out or received visitors—even most of his old friends. I got to New York every once in a while during the Rome years. Business was slow in the late winter and spring, and so I'd take a vacation. Usually, I'd go to Madrid for the bullfights or to Chicago to visit my sister, stopping off in New York on my way back. Every time I got to New York, I'd call Cole at the Waldorf Towers. He would never see me, but each time I appeared on television with Mike Wallace or Arlene Francis, I'd get a call from his secretary saying that Cole had watched and enjoyed the show. A friend whose husband helped Cole with his business affairs told me that there were many nights when Cole would talk about nothing but Paris and Bricktop's. When I happened to be in New York, someone would say, "Brick is in town. Let's send for her," and he'd agree. By the time anyone got to the phone to call me, however, he'd changed his mind.

During a visit to New York in 1961, at the end of that Earl Blackwell celebrity cruise, I was sent for by Elsa Maxwell, who wanted me to attend a party at the Portuguese mission to the U.N. At the party she asked, "Have you seen Cole?" I told her I hadn't and she said, "He won't see me either." That made me feel better. I realized he had some sort of reluctance to see many of the people who'd belonged to the Paris part of his life. Maybe he didn't want us to see him so changed and in so much pain.

Two other old friends I did see at the Portuguese ambassador's party were the Duke and Duchess of Windsor. In fact, the Duke was the reason I had been invited. The ambassador's wife, Phyllis, gave the party, and she was afraid the Duke might get bored. She asked Elsa Maxwell what to do, and Elsa said, "Better get Bricktop," so Phyllis called and invited me.

I said, "I'll come, but not for dinner."

Phyllis laughed. "Same old Bricktop."

I brought a young pianist with me, a white boy, and he said, "I knew if I hung around you long enough, I'd eventually get to meet the Duke and Duchess of Windsor." We arrived just as everyone was coming out of the dining room. The Duchess and Elsa came out, and as soon as she saw me, the Duchess came right over.

"Bricky, you are a disgrace," she said. "It's been I don't know how many years since Lady Mendl and I sent you home, and yet you haven't a line, not even a wrinkle! What do you do?"

"Nuthin,' " I said. "That's just it—I don't do nuthin.' "

Just then the Duke emerged from the dining room. "Boy!" she hollered. "Look who's here."

He wanted to know what I was doing there. I told him I'd come to sing his favorite songs. "What are my favorite songs?" he asked. I named them, and pretty soon I was singing them. He started singing along with me, and we prompted each other when one of us forgot a word. The Duke was in great form that night. He wanted me to teach him the Twist.

The Duchess pretended horror. "Not that awful dance. I don't want you doing that thing."

He laughed. "But I used to know all the new dances, and Brick can tell you how many different girls I danced them with."

I said, "Yes, there was a different girl every night. But they all disappeared when you came into his life."

Around three or four a.m. we were just standing and talking, and I said, "Now will you do something for me?" I explained that I was trying to organize a concert at Carnegie Hall for the benefit of the Asthmatic Children's Hospital in Denver. Ralph Bunche had agreed to be a sponsor. Would they be sponsors, too?

The Duchess always did the answering for both of them. "You know we will, Brick."

Their names were added to the list of sponsors, and posters were printed up and distributed. People asked, "How did she ever get the Duke and Duchess of Windsor?" In fact, a lot of people didn't believe that I really did have them. Some of the organizers wanted a commitment in writing.

Somebody called the Duchess and she was highly insulted that anyone would question my word. "If Bricktop said it, it's right. Bricktop has *never* used any of us for publicity." The people out in Denver still wanted something in writing, however, and the whole benefit fell through because of that. I was so hot-headed I sent a cablegram out to Denver and canceled the whole thing—a sold-out concert at Carnegie Hall!

I returned to Rome. Hardly had I finished unpacking when I got a phone call from a committee sponsoring a Salute to Cole Porter at the Metropolitan Opera House to raise money for charity. "We can't do it without you," they said. I couldn't believe the bad timing.

"I just got back from New York," I said. "I can't afford another trip."

Hugh Shannon was in my apartment at the time. He shouted, "What can't you afford?" I told him and he said simply, "You can't afford not to."

So I flew back over and attended the concert, which Cole himself did not attend, much to my disappointment. I sat in a box with Cobina Wright and members of the committee while the stars came out on that big stage—Lisa Kirk, Celeste Holm, Julie Wilson, William Gaxton, Richard Rodgers, and the emcee, Milton Rosenstock. When the show was over, we all went upstairs to the second-floor bar and had ourselves another show. As Douglas Watt reported in the New York *Daily News*:

> Very late, when the formal show had ended downstairs in the vast auditorium and a cabaret entertainment was in progress in the second-floor bar, performer and writer seemed to achieve an identity that had been lacking throughout the rest of the gaudy evening.
>
> The dusky Bricktop, her hair now black, stood in front of a tiny piano while somebody maneuvering a baby spot tried unsuccessfully to focus it on her. Finally, it hit her from behind, leaving her features in darkness. Very simply, she explained how Cole Porter had been responsible for her rise to fame in Paris thirty years earlier. Then, movingly, she sang, "What Is This Thing Called Love?" and a random piece he'd written for her titled "Miss Otis Regrets."
>
> Missing was Ethel Merman, who reportedly had said she'd do "anything for Cole" but only if he showed up. But the little man who wasn't there found his truest interpreter in Bricktop.

Back in Rome again, I found that Bricktop's hadn't closed without me. I had some awfully good people working for me, and I didn't worry. There were those who came and went, drifted in and out depending on what other opportunities came along. They'd play a few weeks or a few months, then they'd get a better job. I never stepped in the way of artists when they got a chance to work in movies or television—even if it came at the height of the season. It was no big thing. When they came back, they knew they'd be welcome. I always said Hugh Shannon could have the key to the place any time he wanted to pick it up.

There were others who just seemed to belong with me and who stayed on and on. In the last years in Rome, people started calling them "Brick-top's Stock Company."

Elsie Byron was a Puerto Rican gal born in the States. I must have known her since she was fifteen or sixteen and singing in Paris. In Spain, Elsie was considered a top artist. She came to Italy with a band and was playing in Naples when things began to go sour. The company broke up and Elsie came to Rome, and I put her to work. She went over great, and one of her big fans was Archie Savage.

Archie came out of the Katherine Dunham troupe of the 1940s to become one of our best Negro dancers. He got caught up in the problems of a touring company, too. I told him to relax, that he could work at my place. I don't recall how many days he fumbled around the club, not knowing exactly what to do, but suddenly it was New Year's Eve and the place was packed, and even I was going around in circles. I said, "Archie, go out there and do a song."

Archie is probably the only person in the world who doesn't call me Brick or Bricky. "Madame, you know I'm not a singer," he said. "I'm a dancer. There's no place out there for me to dance."

I shooed him out on the floor before he had time to do any more protesting. A few seconds later I saw him trying to maneuver around with a glass in his hand. I called out, "Archie, take that glass out of your hand."

He looked as though he had lost his last friend. "But, Madame, I don't know any words."

I laughed. "This is New Year's Eve. Everyone is having a good time. Do the best you can."

He did, and he has turned out to be a fine entertainer. He has command of the floor and the audience. He likes to say he owes it to me, but that's nonsense. I didn't teach him how to be an entertainer. He had what it takes, he just didn't know it. It wasn't a question of voice but how to sell a song. When Archie went on with his long legs working into a dance, it was really something to see. All my entertainers had to double as checkers and assistants to the cashier. Archie was the best of them all. He carried himself well and never caused me a second's worry.

One of my favorite musicians was Angelino, an Italian who played guitar in the great combo I had. Several years later he got a chance to study with Andrés Segovia. The great artist of the guitar was impressed by Angelino's audition and wanted to know where he'd gotten his training. Angelino said he'd gotten it at Bricktop's. Segovia was puzzled. "Bricktop's? Isn't that a nightclub? Don't I know Bricktop from Paris?" Angelino explained that there was no better training in the world than being at Bricktop's night after night, watching great musicians like Louis Armstrong, Dizzy Gillespie, and André Previn perform.

Gimi Beni, a baritone, came to Rome on a Fulbright scholarship. After someone brought him to the club one night, Gimi started coming back on his own. He was at the bar when an old client told me, "That fellow has a beautiful voice; I just heard him humming." I sneaked over and had a listen, and he was good. I asked if he'd like to go out on the floor. Of course, he'd just been dying for an invitation. He went over great—that big voice just boomed through the room. Afterward we talked. Gimi told me about his studies and I asked if he'd like to sing at the club on the nights before his free days. "Those scholarships don't pay much," I said. "This would help you out." He had been coming in for a few weeks when the Fulbright people called him on the carpet about working at Bricktop's. They were willing to renew his scholarship for the next year, but questioned his working at the club. They renewed the scholarship after he explained, "I'm learning a lot at Bricktop's." Singing with Gimi was a joy. We worked out a lot of numbers together. He was a marvelous comedian. Today he is a popular opera singer, famous for his buffo roles.

Bricktop's also had its key people among the serving staff. There were the usual rows, but we stuck together through the long haul. Angelo, the headwaiter, grew stout through years of fine eating and a busy romantic life. Freddy was my bartender, an old-timer and one of the best in Europe. Yolanda was the cashier, and when she sat at that desk, you couldn't budge her with an earthquake. I never saw a human being with such concentration; once some money was missing and it turned up under her shoes. Poor Yolanda, she was so embarrassed, but Angelo roared—he thought it was the neatest trick of the week. I told Yolanda, "If I lose confidence in you, I'll lose confidence in myself." She was at her best at those times when even the best-run club goes haywire, like

New Year's Eve. She always got a bonus for her performance on those nights.

I was lucky with help in Rome, but the way I see it, I'd paid a fortune learning how to be lucky. There's no way for a nightclub owner to stop employees from cheating her unless she's learned every trick in the book, and invented a few of her own. Still, my Rome people were a rare group. They were so loyal, so careful to do things my way. In fact, they began unconsciously to imitate me, which may have been okay for the cashier, but not for the entertainers. Elsie Byron suddenly decided she wanted to stand at the bar and sing, as I did. People called out, "Come on, Elsie, get out on the floor. You're not Brick."

"You're not Brick." Those words told the story of the last two years of Bricktop's. As a club, it had been in business on and off, in widely separated parts of the world, for almost forty years, with all the ups and downs, triumphs and disasters, that are the special property of the nightclub world. Club operators learn to live with it all and probably wouldn't be happy if, for every good night, there wasn't a bad one to complain about. When there's no one to blame for the bad nights but yourself, however, it's a little bit different than cussin' out the waiters. I used to tell my entertainers that when they didn't feel well, they should stay home. "People don't come in here to hear your tales of woe. They have their own troubles and go to nightclubs to forget them." Around 1962 I decided it was time to follow my own advice. If Bricktop's was forty years old, its owner was over sixty-five—and feeling every year of it.

It began with arthritis. I never knew when it would come or when it would go away. Just as in Paris when I went through that nervous breakdown, I started to stay away from the place. Then I discovered that I had a heart condition. When you first find out about something like that, you pamper yourself. I found myself dressing and getting ready to go to work and then getting undressed and going back to bed. Other times I didn't even bother to get dressed. I found all sorts of excuses for not going to work. I realize now it wasn't all because of my health, that running Bricktop's just wasn't the same as it had been. Over the years the clientele had changed so much. Many nights I walked into the place and didn't know a soul. My staying away brought even more changes. A high-class place needs attention. It can't just roll along on its own, especially a place so intimately connected with its owner as Bricktop's.

Things got to the point where clients called first to ask if I was there. Usually, the waiters said, "Not yet, but she's expected." If I didn't show up, there were complaints. I finally called everybody together. "Don't bring people here under false impressions. I always call when I'm coming in, so let's start telling people the truth." It wasn't easy convincing them that that was the way to do it, because, like me, they knew I was destroying my own business.

I had never really thought about how Bricktop's would end. The club, wherever it was, had become part of me, and I couldn't imagine life without it. I should have had some sort of plan for a gala farewell party, or a quiet goodbye party with just a few friends, but I'd never been good at making decisions, and I hadn't improved with age. After months of thinking and worrying, I finally realized I'd exhausted any capacities I possessed to make up my mind. I turned the whole matter over to God, which is what I should have done to begin with. The feeling of relief came instantly, along with the excitement of wondering just which twist of fate would lead me away from my problems.

An old nightclub hand like me should have known: the landlord became the instrument of my fate. He didn't want more rent, but he had seen Bricktop's prosper for ten years and, like thousands of other owners of cabaret properties all over the world, he had decided he could make more money out of the property by running it himself. Gimi, Elsie, Angelo, Freddy, and I arrived one night to find that the locks had been changed. We walked back upstairs, went to a bar, took a table, ordered drinks, and sat there glumly. Someone said, "What do we do now?" I probably answered, "We'll find another place," but that was habit talking. Furious as I was, I was sort of relieved.

When influential Italians learned what had happened, they got behind me in pressing a suit against the landlord. I lost, not because I was an American but because, like thousands of Italians who lose court cases, I had poor legal representation. My attitude was that there was no use crying about it.

The New York *Daily News* of March 6, 1964, carried this headline: BRICKTOP, QUEEN OF NIGHT CLUBS, ABDICATES. The Reynolds Packard story said, "Singing, dancing, cigar-smoking Bricktop, who has reigned as American night club queen in Europe for 40 years, announced her abdication today. 'I'm tired, honey. Tired of staying up until dawn every day,' the 69-year-old, freckle-faced entertainer told me this afternoon. . . . Well known for her charities among Italian orphans, Bricktop never allowed bad language in her club. One of her favorite possessions is a book autographed to 'My child in Christ, Bricktop, who proves every walk of life can be spiritualized' from Bishop Sheen."

OLD WARHORSE

I STAYED ON IN Rome, mostly because I hated to leave. I love the city, a place where history walks beside you, whether you're wandering down a side alley, crossing a big boulevard, or crossing over the Tiber. I'm glad I did stay on for a while, because I got a chance to meet Martin Luther King, Jr., at one of the proudest times of his life—when he came to Europe to accept the Nobel Prize for Peace in the fall of 1964. He stopped off in Rome for an audience with the Holy Father. He was with Ralph Abernathy, and they were staying at the Hilton.

Abernathy called me from there. He said, "Bricktop, I am Ralph Abernathy, here with Dr. King. He'd like to know if you'll come out and have dinner with us." I said I was terribly sorry, but I was having a party for myself the next night. I always celebrate my birthday for two or three months; it's a good excuse to get drunk. "Why don't you come to *my* party?" I said.

Abernathy conferred with Dr. King, then came back to the phone. "Okay," he said, "but we'll have to leave by nine o'clock."

I said, "If you do, you won't get anything to eat. In Europe we don't eat before nine o'clock."

So they came. I sent Charlie Beale, the Negro piano player, in a car to get them. When Martin walked through the door, I said to myself, "Yeah, that's for me." He was one of the most calm, collected, together persons I have ever met in my life. I was in my house shoes and apron, cooking up blackeye peas. Nine o'clock came and went, and finally I put him and Abernathy out, along with everyone else, at about eleven forty-five. He hadn't expected me to be so down-to-earth. He later described me as "about the most fascinating person I have ever met." Not long after Dr. King's visit I returned to the United States. I'm glad I stayed around in Rome long enough to be able to show that great man some "down-home hospitality."

Early in 1965 Blonzetta became ill, and I flew to the States to be with her. I didn't know how long I'd be away, but I knew I'd be with her as long as she needed me. I moved in with Blonzetta and her husband. He was sick, too, so I nursed them both. I didn't do any entertainment work. The people who ran Maxim's Restaurant, the most elegant in Chicago, approached me with the idea of opening up an annex. It was the beginning of the discotheque era, and when I found out they wanted their annex to be a discotheque, I said, "Not me." That loud, screeching music wasn't my style of things.

I had plenty to keep me busy, though. I had so many invitations I could have gone out to lunch and dinner every day. All the high-society Negroes wanted me at their dinners and other affairs. I'd always tell them, "If I come, you gotta cook me some chitlins." That would set them back a bit. Several ladies told me, "I've never had a chitlin in my house in my life," but they realized they'd better have them if they wanted Bricktop. I did a lot for chitlins those two years in Chicago.

It was a sort of gag that I enjoyed putting on. Before I went to Europe, when I was working at Barron Wilkins's, none of those colored people in New York City, such as Madame Alelia Walker, wanted anything to do with me. I was invited to Carl Van Vechten's parties, but never to Jimmy Daniels's, or Clinton Moores's, or any of those big Negro society affairs. When I returned after fifteen years in Paris, however, every Negro doctor's wife in New York called me up—"Will you come here?" "Will you come there?" I wouldn't go anywhere. I felt the same way about the colored society folks in Chicago. They wouldn't have invited me if I hadn't been Bricktop, so if they wanted me, they were going to have to serve chitlins.

Blonzetta's husband died in 1966, and she died the next year. Before she died, she had me straighten out all her affairs, and it's a good thing she did. I wouldn't have been able to make head or tail of them after she'd gone. She had accounts in I don't know how many banks. She left me quite a bit of money. After she died, there was no reason for me to stay in Chicago.

For some time before Blonzetta's death, people had been talking to me about doing an autobiography and a movie about my life. Bob Wise, the big producer, and Jim Bacon, the columnist, were good friends, and they and others suggested that I move to Los Angeles. It was the center of the movie industry, and it would be the best place for me to be while they got the ball rolling on the picture.

When I first arrived in Los Angeles, I stayed at the Hilton Hotel. Then I moved to 1155 North La Cienega Boulevard and had a couple of different apartments there. I met Sidney Poitier in that building. He was staying with Joanna Shimkus, whom he later married. When I saw him in the flesh, I said for one of the few times in my life, "Yeah! Black *is* beautiful! If I was thirty years younger . . ." and Joanna said, "You're dangerous as it is."

I liked Los Angeles very much—the bigness of it, the fact that nobody sat on top of your head even if they lived right next door to you. It was a good time for me. Thanks to Blonzetta, I had money. I could pick up and travel any time I wanted to, and I still loved to travel, even with my arthritis and my heart condition.

I took a trip to New York. Earl Blackwell invited me to a party he was giving for the Duke and Duchess of Windsor, and of course I wasn't going to miss that. Came the night of the party, the Duke or the Duchess— I forget which one—was sick and they couldn't get there, and the Duke called Earl up and told him to get a recorder and record all the songs I used to sing for him. I also went down to Mexico a couple of times, to

Cuernavaca and Mexico City. I was just visiting—I couldn't have taken living in Mexico because of my heart.

Back in Los Angeles, I gave a lot of parties, and invited clients from the Rome days. I also gave a party for Shirley MacLaine. She called me up one day to say she was giving a big party for her husband—he spent most of his time in Japan and he was coming in for a visit. She said, "Bricky, come out here and show me how to give a party."

I said, "Me show *you* how to give a Hollywood party?"

She said, "Yeah, I mean one of those chic, elegant parties like you always gave in Rome." I said, "Well, then, you have to have chic, elegant people."

It was a tremendous party. Everybody was there. I sang all my songs. Jim Bacon wrote in the Los Angeles *Times* that when I left the floor, everybody just sighed. Danny Kaye was supposed to entertain after I did, but he said, "I'm not going to follow that." It was a great, great party, and I was glad to help out one of my favorite clients from the Rome days. Shirley had a heart of gold, even if she didn't have much of a singing voice.

I only stayed in Los Angeles a few months. Things weren't moving on the movie project, and in those days I still wanted things to move. When I wanted something done, I was used to seeing it done. However, time was taking care of everything and things were changing, and I had to learn to change with them.

I did quite a bit of moving around during that part of my life. People ask me now, "What were you looking for?" I was looking for Bricktop's. I found a couple of places in Los Angeles that would have been suitable. I even started to buy one place, but on good advice I didn't. I've usually been given good advice, and if I'd listened to people more, I wouldn't have made a few of the mistakes I made. I've always been pretty opinionated and hard-headed.

After Los Angeles, I returned to Rome, and arrived there in June 1968. Just as soon as I could, I took a walk along the Via Veneto, and didn't I feel like a queen that night! Old friends, taxi drivers, the papparazzi, even the police swarmed around me, and I felt as if I had come home. I got an unfurnished apartment, filled it with beautiful things, and continued my search for Bricktop's with more hope of finding it than I'd felt in a long time. But it wasn't to be. Although I used every contact I had to open up another place, Rome was getting to be like Paris after the war—tough on foreigners who wanted to start businesses. I didn't get the cooperation from the government that I should have had, and it was frustrating. Then I got sick. After about two years in Rome, I decided to leave. I didn't want to just live there. If I was going to just live and not run a business anywhere, I figured I might as well return to the United States.

Late one night, just before I left Rome, I took a kind of farewell walk along the Via Veneto. There on the sidewalk was one of my former waiters, working as a barker drumming up trade for the strip or topless show down in the cellar that had been Bricktop's. "I heard you were back, madame," he said. "I hoped you wouldn't see me. I feel so ashamed when I think of all the wonderful people who went down these stairs to Bricktop's. It doesn't make sense."

I gave him a sad smile. "I couldn't go on forever."

"No, you couldn't," he said. "But as long as there's a little intimate club on the Via Veneto, they'll remember Madame Bricktop."

On the way back to the United States, I stopped off in London for a month and spent Christmas there. I arrived back in the United States on December 29, 1970. In New York I stayed in hotels for a while, but that was pretty expensive, so I started looking around for an apartment. Back in Rome, Gimi Beni, the singer who had worked for me, had given me the name of his manager, and I'd gotten in touch with him. The manager's sister had moved to Germany, but she still kept an apartment on 68th Street and Broadway, so I moved into it and stayed in it several months, until I got my own apartment in the same building. I've lived in the same building ever since 1972.

As soon as I arrived back in New York, people started calling me— Hugh Shannon, Cy Coleman, Mabel Mercer, and all sorts of other people—inviting me to this and that. Cy Coleman and I recorded "So Long, Baby" around that time. It's the only recording I've ever done. A couple of times I was supposed to record all my songs, but for one reason or another the deal always fell through, and, frankly, that never bothered me much, since I do not consider myself a singer. One day I got a call from Huntington Hartford. He had a restaurant on 56th Street, and he

wanted me to run it for him. I went down to his apartment to talk business, and we had several meetings. He called in his business manager,
who started trying to talk terms as he would with any other entertainer,
but Huntington cut in. "Wait a minute," he said, "you can't talk that
way to Bricktop." Later, as he was seeing me to the door, he said,
"Bricky, anything they say, you go along with it, and then you and I will
have a private arrangement."

The night before I opened at Huntington Hartford's club, there was a
party there. Over three hundred people came; Josephine Baker came all
the way from Paris just to attend that party.

I haven't said anything about Josephine for a long time—not since I
was talking about the pre-war Paris days. That's because we didn't have
all that much contact. Our lives had taken very different paths, although
they did cross once in a while and we kind of followed each other's lives
through mutual friends and reading the newspapers. An awful lot was
written about Josephine, and still is being written—and a great deal of
that isn't true. She had a lot of men, sure, but she was never involved in
any *ménages-à-trois* that I know of, and she was never anybody's kept
woman. And that story about how when men got into Paris cabs and
asked to go to Josephine's, the cabbies would ask, "Do you mean the
club or her house?" . . . well, I just can't conceive of that. Josephine was
not a woman who had to sleep with a lot of men. She was a woman who
needed one man to love her and take care of her, to stand up to her but
not to use her. She never found him. I don't think she ever had a man in
her life who really loved her for herself—not Pepito, not Jean Lion, not
Jo Bouillon.

I think it was because she was always looking for love that she adopted
all those children, but she went overboard in that, just as she went overboard in everything else. She had to work so hard to support them that
she didn't have time to be a mother to them. Josephine couldn't adopt
just one or two children—no, she had to adopt eleven of them! She
never looked to the future, never sat down and considered in a rational
way what might be the consequences of her actions. When she was an
overnight success in Paris and had beautiful clothes for the first time in
her life, she just threw them around on the floor, with no idea that maybe
someday she might wish she'd taken care of them. It was the same with

everything else. She couldn't just buy a villa, she had to buy a whole village. Jack Jordan, who produced her comeback concert at Carnegie Hall, told me about riding through Paris with her once. She kept saying, "I used to own this building, I used to own that building." She'd lost them all by then.

In the end she lost just about everything—but she never lost her spirit. In June 1973, when she walked out on that stage at Carnegie Hall, she was as glamorous and exciting as she'd ever been. It was hard to believe that she was in her mid-sixties, had lost most of her hair, had seen her beloved Les Milandes sold right out from under her, and was so deeply in debt that she could never hope to get out. I introduced her that opening night. I said, "She was a simple little girl—she's still a simple little girl," and it was true. I don't think I've ever known anyone with a less complicated view of life, or whose life was more complicated than Josephine's.

Opening night at Huntington Hartford's club was even more well attended than the pre-opening night. There were four hundred people, which was too many. They spilled over into the area where I was supposed to do my entertaining, and it was impossible for me to sing. The place was just too big, and after about three or four nights I decided it wasn't for me. Grace Kelly and Prince Rainier came to town and wanted to come see me, but I wouldn't go back to the place even for them. Huntington was in the Bahamas at the time, and he came right back. We talked about opening up a smaller room, but I just didn't like the terms his associates were offering—they wanted more control than I was willing to give up.

A couple years later, in 1974, Hugh Shannon came to me and said, "Bricky, I've got a lovely spot, just great for you and me, called Soerabaja, on East 74th Street. We can have the room upstairs and run it like you want to." We opened up in November, and it was a huge success. Every night the place was jammed—*everybody* came. One night a waiter came to me and said there was a man named George Badonsky who wanted to talk to me. He was from Chicago and owned a restaurant called the Tango, where he'd never offered any entertainment. He wanted me to go out to Chicago and provide entertainment at his club.

I was happy where I was, so I put him off, told him to call me when he got back to Chicago, and thought I was rid of him.

He called. He was still interested and wanted to know how much money I wanted. I named an outrageous sum, thinking to put him off that way. He laughed and said, "You can't scare me. I'll pay it—with pleasure." Well, I couldn't turn down that kind of money. I went to Chicago.

I've described other nights and gigs as sensational successes, I know, but I think for me, personally, that one was the most sensational. Never before in my life had I enjoyed that kind of success as a *singer*-entertainer, and at a place that wasn't even called Bricktop's. All of Chicago came out to see me, and I was in Kup's—Irv Kupcinet's—column *eighteen days straight*. The other columnists did write-ups about me, too, and they were overly kind about both my singing, if you want to call it that, and my personality—the way I walked around and greeted people and all that. I was there six or eight weeks, and I went back again the same year, 1975, for another several weeks.

Unfortunately, during that second time I got sick, and I mean *really* sick. I had a heart attack. For a few days I didn't know where or who I was. I started losing weight; in nine days I lost almost twenty pounds. The doctor told me I'd better keep at it, because so much of my weight was water and my heart was just drowning. I was never on a special diet or anything, but my anemia and my arthritis and all, combined with the fact that I kept on working, caused my weight just to drop off. When I started losing, I weighed 210. Within a couple of years I was back to 130 pounds, what I had weighed when I'd first gone to Paris. I've never put any of that weight back on.

Even after the heart attack I wasn't off my feet long. I kept on working. I went back to Chicago in 1976 and 1977. I didn't go back in 1978 because I went to London instead to entertain at the Playboy Club. I was a great success there, too, and the only thing that disturbed me was the Arabs. You couldn't keep them quiet. They'd come in from the gambling rooms to the restaurant/cabaret room, and they wouldn't stop talking for a minute.

I went back to Chicago in 1979 because my boss had opened up a new place and it wasn't going. It was called the Bastille, and I went out for about ten days just to get it off the ground. The same year, in New York, I worked with Hugh Shannon at "21," where we had a Bricktop Hour.

I haven't worked much since 1979. My arthritis bothers me too much. I turn down most invitations to go places now. I don't like to have too many visitors either, but I keep in touch by telephone with all my friends. I have a lot of friends. They call me up and say, "Bricky, can I do anything for you? Can I bring you something?" I'm in touch with Mabel Mercer and Alberta Hunter and Earl Blackwell, and was with Hugh Shannon until his recent death—too early at the age of sixty-one. I get calls and letters from young people who say, "My mother or father used to go to Bricktop's. They always talked about you." I like to hear from young people. I'm pretty much a loner now, however, just as I always have been. I've got a lot of memories to keep me company, and I'm at peace with myself. Not many people can look back on their lives, as I can, and say that if they had it to do over, they'd do it just about the same.

The one thing that really bothers me about being old is that I'm one of the last living persons who knew all those great people. Since they're dead, everybody thinks he or she is going to get some dirt about them out of me, but that's not my style. I wouldn't ever betray the memory of a friend or someone who was nice to me. It's not my business—it's not anyone's business—and I'm not telling it, and that's that. One of the reasons I am at peace with myself is that I've tried very hard to live my life without hurting anyone, and I have no intention of changing at my age.

It's a good philosophy. *Ciao*, babies.

INDEX

Abatino, Giuseppe ("Count" Pepito), 109–110, 186, 286
Abbey, Leon, 132
Abernathy, Reverend Ralph David, 281–282
"Ace in the Hole" (song), 266
Achard, Marcel, 244
Addams, Jane, 17
Adler, Polly, 251–252
Aga Khan, the, 102–103
Alamo Café, Harlem, 75
Alderson, W. Va., 4–7, 50, 64, 73, 81, 136, 140–141, 245
Al Field's Minstrels, 20
"All Alone" (song), 258
"All Night Long" (Brooks), 47
Al Turney's, Chicago, 57–58
American hospital, Paris, 139–140
Amin (secretary to King Farouk), 254, 256
Anderson, Marian, 208
Angelina (violinist), 124
Angelino (guitarist), 277
Angelo (headwaiter), 251, 272, 277, 279
Applegate family, 7, 9
Arlen, Harold, 266
Armour, Lolita, 9
Armour, Philip and Malvina, 9–10
Armstrong, Louis, 60, 132, 182, 271–272, 277
Around the World in 80 Days (film), 232
Astaire, Fred and Adele, 93, 144
Atlantic City, N.J., 74

"Babylon Revisited" (Fitzgerald), 98
Bacon, Jim, 283–284
Badonsky, George, 287–288
Bagnole, Duchessa du, 254
Baker, Edith, 175
Baker, Josephine, *xi–xiv*, 107–110, 180, 184, 186–187, 210, 285–286
Baker, Stanley, 267
Ball, Mabel, 76–77, 153
Ballentine, Danny, 260
"Ballin' the Jack" (song), 236
Bamville Club, Harlem, 75
Band Box, Paris, 165, 225
Bankhead, Eugenia, 113–115
Bankhead, Tallulah, *xiv*, 113–115
Banks, Adah, 47–49
Barefoot Contessa, The (film), 216, 269
Barnes, Cliff, 217
Barnes, Mae, 217, 221
Baron, the (Paris gangster), 166–170, 242
Barron's Exclusive Club, New York City, 34, 75–78, 80, 82, 166, 170
Barrymore, John, 20, 77
Basie, Count, 200
Bastille, Chicago, 288
Beale, Charlie, 282
Belasco, David, 77
"Begin the Beguine" (Porter), 123, 178–179
Being Geniuses Together (McAlmon and Boyle), 17, 126
Belfant, Etta Smith (Blonzetta), 4–20 *pas-*

Belfant, Etta Smith (Blonzetta) (*cont.*)
sim, 36–37, 73–74, 137, 139–140, 182,
196, 201, 282–283
Belfant, Peter, 74, 283
Bells, The (show), 47
Beni, Gimi, 277, 279, 285
Berlin, Germany, 133–135
Berlin, Irving, 125, 211
Biarritz, France, 72, 94, 133, 139, 156, 172,
175–176, 178, 187–188, 191, 241, 246–247
Big Jim Colisimo's, Chicago, 56
Big Mouth Florence (prostitute), 31
Billingsley, Sherman, 212–213
Blackbirds (show), 133
Black Bottom (dance), 116
Black Mag (madam), 39
Blackwell, Earl, 270, 273, 283, 289
Blake, Eubie, 79
Bloomingdale, Donald, 239–240, 242
"Blue Room" (song), 175, 266
"Blue Skies" (song), 266
Blumenthal, A.C., 223–225
Bogart, Humphrey, 267
Bonnocini, Frank, 213
Booth, Shirley, 267
Bordoni, Irene, 164
Boswell Sisters, 55
Bougival, France, villa in, 145–147, 152,
163, 171, 180, 184, 193
Bouillon, Jo, 286
Bowman, Billy, 71–72
Boyer, Lucienne, 121
Boyle, Kay, 17, 126
Boys' Town, Italy, 261–263
Branch, Miss (teacher), 15
Bricktop (Ada Smith Ducongé): appear-
ance, *xiii*, 4–5, 19, 22–23, 26, 28, 33, 36,
88, 130, 158, 165, 174, 208, 288; boardinghouse operator, 218–219; Bougival
villa, 145–147, 152, 158, 163, 171, 180,
184, 193; celibacy vow, 227; character
and personality, *xii–xv*, 3, 5, 10, 13, 33,
43, 54, 63, 68, 72, 82, 85, 88, 92, 98–99,
101, 106–107, 111–112, 130–131, 138,
143, 167, 169, 185, 193–194, 198, 204,
212, 227, 230, 239, 279, 284, 289; charity
work, 110–111, 229, 261–262, 264, 274–
275; dancer/dance teacher, 16, 26, 77,
101–103, 106, 110–113, 116–117, 174, 247,
274; deportment, *xiii*, 6, 11, 30, 98, 130,
175; early life, 3–23; friends, 30–32, 34,
40–42, 50, 58, 71, 97, 106–107, 111–112,
129–130, 172, 200, 205, 208, 211, 215,
217–218, 221, 230, 235–236, 239, 258,
289; gambling and pool playing, 68, 72,

Bricktop (Ada Smith Ducongé) (*cont.*)
145, 188; hostess, *xii*, 98, 104, 106, 121–
122, 125, 130–131, 141, 143, 156–158, 161,
180, 186, 189, 194, 213–214, 217–218, 247,
288; illnesses, *xii*, 5, 12–13, 72, 84–85,
88, 140–141, 143–144, 206, 231, 237, 278,
285, 288–289; lateness, 46, 166, 263,
272; legend/symbol of Paris "golden
years," *xiii–xiv*, 102, 119, 121–122, 127,
141, 143, 146, 191, 209, 227, 239–240,
246, 265, 267; Los Angeles apartments,
65, 283; marriage, 145; myths about,
xii, 107, 199, 235, 256, 258, 270; name
and nicknames, *xii*, 32, 34, 61–62, 75,
167, 199, 261; New York apartments,
xii, 216–217, 234–235, 285; Paris apartments, 90, 93, 136–137, 158, 174, 177,
193–194, 200; party entertainer, 104,
106, 174–175, 190–191, 203, 230, 245,
247, 257, 273–274; personal habits, 5,
26, 28, 33, 46, 84, 137, 157–158, 190, 208,
256, 272; association with pimps and
prostitutes, 29, 31–32, 34, 37, 39–41, 61–
63, 65, 218–219; racial heritage and
pride, *xv*, 4, 6, 78, 112, 129, 132, 185;
and racial prejudice, 58, 71, 134–135,
188, 208–211; religion and Catholicism,
xii, 6, 182, 219–220, 224, 227–228, 237,
254, 262, 279; Rome apartments, 245,
284; salary and finances, 24, 26, 28, 41,
66–67, 75, 87, 93–95, 119, 144, 158, 188–
189, 193, 195–196, 198, 200, 211, 216,
220–221, 240, 242, 258, 263–264, 283;
saloonkeeper/nightclub operator, 3, 50,
55, 94, 98, 102, 106, 111, 117, 119–121,
126–127, 130, 149–151, 157, 160, 168, 179,
225–226, 248, 251–252, 265; singer, *xiii*,
39–43, 45, 47, 49–50, 53, 55, 59–60, 67–
68, 71, 74–76, 80–81, 89–92, 117, 121,
177–179, 201, 213–215, 244, 247, 258,
260, 266–267, 274, 285, 288; singing recorded, 285; in vaudeville, 24–35, 37–
38, 61, 137; World War II, 201–206
Bricktop's, Biarritz, 172, 176, 187, 246.
See also Merry Sol
Bricktop's, Mexico City, 227. *See also*
Chavez's; Reforma Hotel
Bricktop's, Paris, *xiv*, 77, 98, 119–126, 143,
145, 149, 151, 155, 158, 161, 165 176–
177, 179, 184, 194, 198, 214, 243–247,
289. *See also* Band Box; Le Grand Duc;
Music Box
Bricktop's, Rome, 10, 216, 251–254, 258–
259, 265–272, 275, 278–279, 285. *See also*
Ambassador Hotel

Briggs, Arthur, 145, 203, 237
Briggs, Georgina, 237
Broadway theater, New York City, 57, 66, 76, 79, 93, 120, 141–142, 164
Broadway Jones's Supper Club, Harlem, 75
Bromfield, Louis, 98
Brooks, Shelton, 42, 47, 56
Broomfield, Jack, 50
Brother Rat (play), 254
Brown, Elvira, 30
Brown, Rose, 38–40
Bruce, Carol, 213
Buchwald, Art, 238–239, 244
Budapest, Hungary, 133
Bullard, Gene, 82, 84–88, 118–119, 145, 167, 203
Bunche, Ralph, *xi*, 132, 274
Burns, Ralph, 259–260
Burton, Richard, *xiv*, 270
Burton, Sybil, 270
Byron, Elsie, 276, 278–279

Cabaret de Champion. *See* Café Champ
Cabarets. *See* Nightclubs/saloons
Café Champ, Chicago, 44–49, 53, 66
Cameron, Lucille, 47–48
Cannes, France, 142, 172, 199–201
Cantinflas (Mario Moreno), *xiv*, 232–233
Cantor, Eddie, 144
Capri, 133, 237, 254, 257, 260, 263, 266
Carnegie Hall, New York City, 274, 287
Carol, King of Rumania, 257
Carpenter, Thelma, 222
Carpentier, Georges, 183
Carstair, Jo, 200
Cartier, Paris, 136
Casanova, Paris, 86, 120
Cascais, Portugal, 257
Casino de la Forêt, La Touquet, France, 142
Casino de Paris, 186
Castle, Vernon and Irene, 89, 100–101
CBS. *See* Columbia Broadcasting System
Cerutti, Frank, 217
Cerutti's, New York City 217, 220
Chamberlain, Neville, 201
Champs-Elysée Theatre, Paris, 186
Chappie (boyfriend), 36–37, 132
Charleston (dance), 101–103, 105, 110–111, 113, 116
Charleston, Yellow, 82
Chationne, Henri, 230–231
Chavez (nightclub owner), 226, 231–232
Chavez's, Mexico City, 227, 229–232

Chevalier, Maurice, 145, 183–184
Chez Florence, Paris, 77, 115, 117, 124, 166
Chez Joséphine, 109
Chicago, Ill., *xiii*, 6–15, 18, 20, 23, 26, 29, 32, 34, 36, 43, 53, 63, 73, 288; Negro society in, 283; saloons in, 11, 14–15, 18–19, 25, 38–40, 44, 49, 53, 56–60; segregation in, 11
Chippy Mama (prostitute), 31
Chorea (St. Vitus's Dance), 12–13
Clair, René, 157
Clam House, Harlem, 75
Cleopatra (film), 370
Cochran, Charles B., 128–129
Cocteau, Jean, 157
Cole, Kid, 89–90
Cole, Louis, 141–142, 146
Coleman, Cy, 285
Colisimo, Big Jim. *See* Big Jim Colisimo's
Colony Club, New York City, 210
Columbia Broadcasting System, 159
Connie's Inn, New York City, 80–81, 85, 210
Considine, Bob, 260, 270
Cooper, Opal, 81, 86, 203
Cooper and Robinson, 55
Copacabana, New York City, 209
Coq Rouge, New York City, 213
Cotton Club, New York City, *xii*, 75, 78, 208, 218
Coward, Noel, *xiv*, 122, 164, 267
Crane, Jeff, 144, 150, 196–197
Crawford, Broderick, 268–269
Crawford, Joan, 75, 208
Cromwell, Jimmy, 221
Crosby, Oma, 27–28, 30, 32–34. *See also* Oma Crosby Trio
Crutchfield, Billy, 50–51
Cunard Line, 204–205
Cy (piano player), 214

Dago (prostitute), 72
Dali, Salvador, 244
Dancer, Earl, 66–67
Daniels, Jimmy, 282
"Darktown Strutter's Ball" (song), 68, 267
Darrieux, Danielle, 246
David, Twinkle, 59
Davis, Benny, 57, 59
Davis, Bette, 267–268
Dean, Jack, 91–94
Deauville, France, 94, 150, 156, 197
De Forrest, Maude, 107
Delaney, Walter, 62, 69, 132, 228

Del Rio, Dolores, 225
Deluxe, the, Chicago, 60
Depression, the Great: in Europe, 142, 182–183, 187, 194–197, 200, 216, 250; in the United States, 57, 144, 158, 161, 178, 196
Desmond, Jody, 258–259
Devan, André, 107
De Wolfe, Elsie. *See* Mendl, Lady Elsie
Diamond, Alice (Mrs. Jack), 76–77, 170
Diamond, Jack "Legs," *xiii*, 76–77, 166, 170
Dixon, Mrs. George, 104
Dodge, Betty, 247
Dodge, Horace, 155–156
Dodge, Lois (Mrs. Horace), 155–156
Dolly Sisters, 141–142
Dôme, Paris, 95
Donahue, Jimmy, 176–177
Dreamland, Chicago, 60
Ducongé, Ada Smith. *See* Bricktop
Ducongé, Peter, 132–133, 136–137, 139, 144–147, 152, 159, 163, 169, 172, 180–183, 193, 195–196, 240, 261, 272
Duke, Doris, 221–222
Dunham, Katherine, 276
Du Pont, Ethel, 188

"East Side, West Side" (song), 163
Ebony, xi
Edward VII, King of England, 172
Edward VIII, King of England. *See* Windsor, Duke of
Eiffel Tower, 138
El Garon, Paris, 148–149
Eliot, T. S., *xiv*, 136
Ellen, Miss (Hattie Smith's partner), 4
Ellington, Duke, *xiii*, 78, 120, 138, 186–188
Elmer Snowden's Washingtonians, 77–78, 81
El Morocco, New York City, 210
"Embraceable You" (Gershwin), 266
Estoril, Portugal, 257
Europe: Americans in, 83, 111, 153, 257; racial prejudice in, 103, 128–129, 134–135. *See also* Depression; *individual countries*
Everleigh sisters, 39
"Everybody Loves My Baby" (Williams), 117

Fallon, Father Thomas, 224
Farmer, Michael, 123–125, 145, 149, 152, 161–162, 172
Farouk, King of Egypt, 254–256

Fay, Frank, 75
Fears, Peggy, 223
Fellowes, Daisy (Mrs. Reginald), 104, 203
Field, Al. *See* Al Field's Minstrels
Fields, Benny, 57–59
Fields, Dorothy, 165
Fields, Herbert, 165, 225
Fifty Million Frenchmen (show), 164–165
Finkelhoffe, Freddie, 254–255
Fisher, Eddie, 270
Fisher, Snow, 124
Fiske, Dwight, 123
Fitzgerald, Ella, 271
Fitzgerald, F. Scott, *xii–xiv*, 95–98, 108, 119, 126, 152, 236
Fitzgerald, Scottie, 95, 97–98
Fitzgerald, Zelda, 95–97
Flanner, Janet, 243
Four Cohans, 20
Foy, Charley, 57
France, Americans in, 202–204; anti-Americanism in, 182, 241; popularity of Negro entertainers in, 160; post-war bureaucracy in, 182, 237. *See also individual cities*
Francine, Anne, 213
Franciosa, Anthony, 252
Francis, Arlene, 273
Freiburg's, Chicago, 56
Fricka, Monsieur and Madame, 199–201
Frisco, Joe, 56–57
Front Page, The (film), 277
Furness, Lady Thelma, 172, 191

Gable, Clark, 103
Gabor sisters, 142
Gaither, Ed, 29
Gangsters: American, 76, 146, 167, 170, 229, 231; French, 86, 166–167, 170
Gardner, Ava, *xiv*, 216, 252, 269
Gaxton, William, 275
George, Duke of Kent, 174–175, 193, 198
George and Gus's saloon, St. Paul, 49
George, Yvonne, 175
Gerald's Bar, Paris, 115
Germany, 134–135. *See also* Berlin
Gertie Jordan's theatrical boardinghouse, Chicago, 36–37, 50, 54
Gibson Theatre, New York City, 33
Gilbert, Morris, 213
Gillespie, Dizzy, 277
Gilmore, Buddy, 100–101
Gilpin, Charles, 20
Gino (headwaiter), 247–248, 258
"Go Down, Moses" (song), 255

Goetz, Ray, 107, 164–165, 225
Grace, Princess of Monaco, 287
Grady, Lottie, 20
Grand Casino, Biarritz, 172–173, 188
Grand Theatre, Chicago, 61
Grappelly, Stéphane, 200
Great White Hope, The (play), 185
Green, Cora, 54–56, 59–61, 80
Greenwich Village Follies (show), 142
Greer, Sonny, 77
Gordon, Sidney, 254–255
Grock (clown), 183
Guggenheim, Peggy, 95
Gunzburg, Nicolas, Baron de, 150, 154, 197
Gut Bucket (cornetist), 81

Hall, Gerald, 113–114
Hanna, Leonard, 125, 211
Hardwick, Otto, 78
Harlem, *xiii*, 75, 79, 182, 208; nightclubs
  in, 75, 80, 82; Renaissance, 75, 94, 107,
  120
Harper, Leonard, 80
Harris, Sam, 227, 229, 233–234
Harry's New York Bar, Paris, 123, 146, 262
Hart, Guy, 61–62
Hartford, Huntington, 285–287
Harvey, Laurence, 267
Hay, Mary, 93
Hayes, Helen, 7
Haymarket Theatre, Chicago, 16
Haywood, Billy, 217
Hazel (Peter Ducongé's mistress), 180–
  181
Hecht, Ben, 77
Heifetz, Jascha, 124
"Hello, Central, Give Me No Man's Land"
  (song), 68
Hemingway, Ernest, *xiv*, 98, 236
Henderson, Bertha (Mrs. George), 63–64
Henderson, Fletcher, 138
Henderson, George, 62–63
Henley, Bill, 146
Henri, Marquis de la Falaise de la Coud-
  raye, 161
Herman, Woody, 259
"Hesitation Blues" (song), 68
Hight, Mattie, 54
Hildegarde, 121
Hill, Virginia, 229–231
Hitler, Adolf, *xiv*, 201
Hollywood, Ca., 98, 124, 141–142, 152, 253,
  267, 269, 271
Hollywood Reporter, 267
Holm, Celeste, 275

Hoskins, Hugh. *See* Hugh Hoskins's saloon
Hotsy Totsy Club, New York City, 76
"How Deep Is the Ocean?" (Berlin), 266
Hoyningen-Huené, George, 158
Hughes, Franklin, 237
Hughes, Howard, 151–152
Hughes, Langston, *xiv*, 86, 211–212
Hugh Hoskins's saloon, Chicago, 60
Hunter, Alberta, 60, 289
Hutchinson, Leslie, 110, 114–117, 129
Hutton, Barbara, 176–177

"If I Knew You Were Comin', I'd Have
  Baked a Cake" (song), 245
"I'll See You Again" (Coward), 267
"I'm a Little Blackbird" (song), 267
"I'm a Little Old Lido Lady" (song), 111
"I'm in Love Again" (Porter), 101
Immerman, Connie, 80–82, 210
Immerman, George, 80
International Herald Tribune, 154, 247
Inter-Ocean, 7
"It's All Right With Me" (Porter), 266
"It's the Wrong Time" (song), 259

Jack the Bear (prisoner), 17–18
Jackson Brothers, 90, 92
Jacobi (nightclub manager), 157, 200
Jamerson, Mr. and Mrs. George, 86–87, 89,
  93, 116–118
James Sisters (Ethel and Riva), 39
Jannings, Emil, 183
Jeffries, Jim, 43
Jessel, George, 144
Jet, xi
Jews, 14, 165–166, 211
Jiki Club, Rome, 247–248
Johnson, Etta Duryea (Mrs. Jack), 46, 48
Johnson, Irene Pineau (Mrs. Jack), 184
Johnson, Jack, *xiii*, 42–49, 58, 66, 75, 183–
  185
Jolson, Al, 54, 75
Jones, Bobby, 87, 132
Jones, Florence, 81–82, 87, 89, 91–92, 115,
  120
Jones, James Earl, 185
Jones, Palmer, 81–82, 87, 89, 115
Jones, Roy, 39–41. *See also* Roy Jones's
  saloon
Jones, Walter, 42
Joplin, Scott, 19
Jordan, Charlie, 10
Jordan, Gertie. *See* Gertie Jordan's theatri-
  cal boardinghouse
Jordan, Jack, *xii–xiii*, 287

Joseph, Charles, 226
Joyce, Peggy Hopkins, 153–155

Kaye, Danny, 284
Kefauver, Senator Estes, 231
Keith School, Chicago, 15
Keith vaudeville circuit, 55, 58, 78, 141
Kelly, Grace. *See* Grace, Princess of Monaco
Kentucky Club, New York City, 78
Kilgallen, Dorothy, 210, 259, 270–271
King, Dr. Martin Luther, Jr., *xiv*, 281–282
Kinky-Doo Trio, 37–38
Kirk, Lisa, 275
Kirkland, Jerry, 217
Kirkpatrick, Sidney, 39
Knickerbocker, Cholly (Maury Paul), 207
Kollmar, Dick, 210
Kovacs, Kalman, 133
Kupcinet, Irv, 288

Ladd, Alan, 166
La Revue Négre (show), 107
Latin Quarter, New York City, 209
Lawford, Peter, 271
Lawrence, Amos, 116
Leary, Beth, 172
Le Boeuf sur le Toit, Paris, 157, 200, 214
Leeds, Billy Dee, 107, 168
Left Bank, New York City, 210
Le Grand Duc, Paris, 82, 84–96 *passim*, 108–109, 113–119, 126, 166, 212, 250
"Les Six," 157
Lester Mapp's saloon, San Francisco, 58, 66–68, 70–71
Levine, Isadore, 53–54, 56, 59, 77
Lewis, Charlie "Dixie," 87, 203, 247, 253
Lillie, Beatrice, 144
Lion, Jean, 286
Little Caesar (film), 167
"Little Gray Home in the West" (song), 54
Logan, Ella, 254–255
London, England, 113–114, 128–129, 165, 167, 285; racial prejudice in, 128–129
Loos, Anita, 153
Lopez, Arturo, 103, 107, 239–240, 242–243
Los Angeles, Ca., 62, 66, 268, 283–284
Los Angeles Times, 284
Louis, Joe, 208
"Love for Sale" (Porter), 127, 178–179
Lulu Belle (show), 77
Lupescu, Magda, 257–258
Lyles, Aubrey, 24, 79
Lyman, Tommy, 51–52

McAlmon, Robert, 95, 126
MacArthur, Charles, 77
MacCabe's Georgia Troubadours, 25–26
McCormack, John, 106
McCormic, Mary, 124
McDermott, Loretta, 56
McDowall, Roddy, 267
McKenney, Justine, 74
MacLaine, Shirley, *xiv*, 271, 284
Macoco (South American millionaire), 149
Magnani, Anna, *xiv*, 252–253
Mainbocher, 93
"Manhattan" (song), 121
"Man I Love, The" (song), 266
Man Ray, 99, 126
Man Who Came to Dinner, The (film), 163
Mapp, Lester, 67. *See also* Lester Mapp's
Margaret, Princess of England, 252
Marina, Princess of Greece, 175, 198
Marlborough, Duke of, 104
Mars Club, Paris, 259
Martin, Dewey, 258–259
Martin, Neil (interior decorator), 158
Martin, Neil (pimp), 62–63
Matthews, Eddie, 229–230
Maxim's, Paris, 86
Maxwell, Elsa, 91–92, 101–105, 111, 122, 125, 130, 146, 164, 198, 204, 273
Mdivani, Prince Alexis, 176–177
"Mean to Me" (song), 213
"Melancholy Baby" (song), 51–52, 163, 266
Mendl, Lady Elsie, *xiv*, 104–107, 133, 154, 193–194, 201, 203–205, 207, 211, 274
Mendl, Sir Charles, 105, 193
Mercer, Johnny, 266–267
Mercer, Mabel, 159–161, 173–175, 177, 179, 187–189, 198–201, 211, 214, 219, 244, 289
Merman, Ethel, 275
Merry Sol, Biarritz, 172, 187–188
Metropolitan Opera House, New York City, 275
Mexico City, Mexico, *xiv*, 220–223, 227, 234, 284; bureaucracy in, 232–233, 236; foreign colony in, 221, 223, 232; nightclubs in, 221, 224–225
Milhaud, Darius, 157
Miller and Lyles, 23–25, 79
Miller, Flournoy, 24, 79
Miller, Henry, 131
Miller, Marilyn, 123–124, 152
Mills, Florence, *xiii*, 26, 54–56, 59–61, 78–80, 135

Minstrel shows, 25–26, 140
Minuit, Mexico City, 223–225, 227, 233
"Miss Otis Regrets She's Unable to Lunch Today" (Porter), *xiv*, 178–179, 213, 266, 275
Mistinguett, 145, 184
Mitchell, Lizzie, 30
Mitchell, Louis, 89, 94, 115, 117–118
Mitchell, Tony (Mrs. Louis), 91–92
Mitchell's, Paris, 89
Molyneux, Eddie, 130, 158, 205, 216, 231
Monte Carlo, Monaco, 72, 133, 166, 170
Montmartre, Paris, 97, 134, 137, 241, 244; appearance, 85, 143, 237; nightclubs in, 86–87, 105, 146, 167–169, 171, 202, 237–238; people of, 91, 106, 143–144, 169, 195–196
Montparnasse crowd, Paris, 94–95, 98–99
"Moon River" (song), 266
Moore, Grace, 124, 193
Moores, Clinton, 282
Moreno, Mario. *See* Cantinflas
Morgan, Helen, 123
Mornet, Count Gosta, 155
Morton, Jelly Roll, 64
Motts, Bob, 20–21
Mountbatten, Lady Caroline, 153–154
Movie stars, American, in Europe, 77, 123, 153–154, 161, 251, 260, 267
Moyses, Louis, 157
Munn, Luisa Wanamaker, 208, 211
Murphy, Gerald, 164
Murray's, Los Angeles, 64–65
Music Box, Paris, 116–117, 119
Music Is My Mistress (Ellington), 73
Mussolini, Benito, 201
Mussolini, Jimmy, 169, 187, 199, 243
"My Belle" (song), 177
"My Hair is Curly" (song), 124
"My Hero" (song), 48

Negri, Pola, 176
New Whirl, Atlantic City, 74
New York City, N.Y., 33–34, 75–76, 78, 98, 126, 207–209, 211, 220, 222; nightclubs in, 209–210, 212–215, 217; segregation in, 208–211, 214
New York Daily News, 251, 275, 279–280
New York Herald Tribune, 238, 244
New York Journal, 207
New York World-Telegram, 213
New Yorker, The, 243
"Night and Day" (Porter), 178–179
Nightclubs/saloons: entertaining in, 74–76, 88, 93–94; integrated, 74–75; opera-

Nightclubs/saloons (*cont.*)
tion, 94, 117, 126, 149–151, 166, 191, 250, 260, 278; segregated, 75. *See also* Bricktop: hostess; saloonkeeper/nightclub operator; Saloons
Nijinsky, 103
Novarro, Ramon, 219
Nurse, Miss (teacher), 15

O'Brien, Dolly, 103, 124
Oliver, King, 60
"One for My Baby" (Mercer and Arlen), 266–267
On Your Toes (show), 164
Oriental Gardens, Washington, D.C., 78
O'Toole, Peter, 266–267

Packard, Reynolds, 251, 279
Palace Theater, New York City, 32–33, 165, 183
Panama Club, Chicago, 53–57, 59–60
Panama Trio, 55, 59–62
Pantages vaudeville circuit, 35
Paradise Club, Atlantic City, 74
Paramount Pictures Corp., 164
Paris, France, *xiii–xiv*, 76–77, 85–86, 93–95, 165, 171, 217, 237; Americans in, 86, 94–95, 127, 164, 203–205, 238; anti-Semitism in, 165–166; August in, 90, 171, 217; fashion in, 86, 89–90, 93, 108; gangsters in, 86, 166–167, 170; "golden era" in, 94–95, 148, 236, 245, 251; jazz in, 86, 120, 127, 138, 186; Negro entertainers in, 81–83, 86–88, 90, 107, 109, 127, 132, 159; nightclubs in, 86, 100, 116–117, 148; post-war anti-American feeling in, 238–239, 248–249; post-war bureaucracy in, 240–242; society parties in, 103–106, 190
Paris Opera, 103, 107
Parker, Lawrence, 219–220
Patou, Jean, 130, 184, 231
Pecci Blunt, Contessa, 248
Pekin Theatre, Chicago, 19–23, 37
Piaf, Edith, 239
Picasso, Pablo, 98–99
Pittsburgh Courier, *xi*
Place du Trocadéro, Paris, 138
Playboy Club, London, 288
Poiret, Paul, 107–108
Poitier, Sidney, 283
Polignac, Marquise de, 103, 116, 174
"Poor Papa" (song), 267
Porter, Cole, *xiv*, 98, 101–103, 105, 107, 110–112, 117–123, 127–131, 140, 142, 146,

Porter, Cole (*cont.*)
153–154, 161, 164–165, 178–180, 184, 191, 198–199, 203–204, 208–209, 211, 257, 272–273, 275
Porter, Linda (Mrs. Cole), 102, 107, 110, 112, 146
Previn, André, 277
Primrose and West, 20
Prohibition, *xiii*, 70, 74–75, 80

Quinn, Anthony, 267
Quo Vadis (film), 248

Rainey, Ma, 30
Rainier, Prince of Monaco, 287
Ramsey, Mr. (nightclub manager), 74
Raymond, Nigger Nate, 215
Reardon, Billy, 124, 146
Rédé, Alexis, Baron de, 177, 244
Reforma Hotel, Mexico City, 223, 226, 232
Reinhardt, Django, 199–200
Reyes, Reva, 226–227, 229–231
Rheims, France, 174
Richardson, Sammy, 81–82, 120
Ricks, Bertha, 74
Ritz, Paris, 104–106
Riviera, the, 142, 170, 237. *See also* individual cities
Robeson, Essie (Mrs. Paul), 128–130, 197
Robeson, Paul, 128–129, 197–198
Robilant, Count Andrea, 111
Robinson, Bill "Bojangles," *xiii*, 30, 55, 208
Robinson, Edward G., 167, 268
Rodgers, Richard, 275
Rome, *xiv*, 133, 237, 247–248, 252, 258, 266–267, 272, 275, 278, 281, 284–285; American colony in, 248; bureaucracy in, 285; as film center, 267, 269, 271, nightclubs in, 247–248, 263–266
Rome American, 253
Roosevelt, Franklin D., Jr., 187–188, 210
Rose, Lillian, 71
Rosenstock, Milton, 275
Rothschild family, 104, 154
Rothstein, Arnold, 215
Roy Jones's saloon, Chicago, 38–41, 43–44, 53
Rubirosa, Porfirio, 245–246
Running Wild (show), 80
Russell (partner in Oma Crosby Trio), 27

Sablon, Jean, 244
St. Jean-de-Luz, France, 191, 193
"St. Louis Woman" (song), 267

St. Martin de Porres, *xiv*
Salador, Suzi, 121
Saloons, 28–29, 44; decor, 18–19, 28–29, entertaining in, 39–42, 45–49, 67–68, 74–76; integrated, 59; segregated, 51, 58
Sanders of the River (film), 198
San Faustino, Jane, Princess di (Jane Campbell), 111
San Sebastian, Spain, 172
Sans Souci, Paris, 239
Saratoga, N.Y., 32, 218–220
Sarre, Count of. *See* Umberto, King of Italy
Satie, Erik, 157
Saunders, Gertrude, 79
Savage, Archie, 276
Savini, Jimmy. *See* Savini's
Savini's, New York City, 212–213
Schiaparelli, Elsa, 130, 152, 239–240, 242–245, 249
Schultz, Dutch, 146
Scott, Mrs. (neighbor), 14–15
Seeley, Blossom, 58–59
Segovia, Andrés, 277
Sélect, Paris, 95
"September in the Rain" (song), 267
"September Song" (song), 266
Shannon, Betty (Mrs. Hugh), 246
Shannon, Hugh, 98, 236–237, 244–246, 259, 275–276, 285, 287, 289
Shaw, Vic, 39
Shea, Thomas, 47–48
Sheen, Bishop Fulton J., 220, 263, 280
Shields, Frank, 163
Shimkus, Joanna (Mrs. Sidney Poitier), 283
Short, Bobby, 157, 191
Show Boat (show), 128
Shubert, Jake, 120
Shuffle Along (show), 79, 124
Shuffle Inn, New York City, 80
Siegel, Bugsy, 229
"Silver Rose" (song), 267
Simon, Simone, 244
Simpson, Wallis, 191–193. *See also* Windsor, Duchess of
Sinatra, Frank, *xiv*, 215–216, 266, 269
Sissle, Harriet (Mrs. Noble), 79
Sissle, Noble, 79
Smith, Ada. *See* Bricktop
Smith, Bessie, 30
Smith, Ethel, 4, 7, 10, 12–14, 19–22, 26, 36–37, 73
Smith, Etta (Blonzetta). *See* Belfant, Etta Smith

Smith, Hattie E. Thompson, 3–29 *passim*, 32, 34–39, 42, 49–50, 61–62, 64–65, 72–74, 81–84, 90, 130–131, 136, 157, 201; visits Bricktop in Europe, 137–140, 146–147, 152, 173, 184, 188–196 *passim*
Smith, Robert, 4, 7, 20, 22, 26, 36–37, 49, 73
Smith, Thomas, 4–7, 219
Snowden, Elmer, 77. *See also* Elmer Snowden's Washingtonians
Soerabaja, New York City, 287
"So Long, Baby" (song), 285
Soraya, Princess, 270
Spain, 90, 187, 252, 276
Speakeasies, 67, 70–71
Spoleto, Italy, 271
Steinbeck, John, 266
Steinman, Sam, 267
Stock market crash, 144
Stork Club, New York City, 210
Strassburger, Ralph Beaver, 150
Streeter, Ted, 266
Stuart, Daddy and Florence, 50
Swanson, Gloria, 161–162, 172
Sweatman, Wilbur, 30. *See also* Wilbur Sweatman's Rhythm Kings

Tango, the, Chicago, 287
Tanguay, Eva, 20, 55
Taylor, Elizabeth, *xiv*, 252, 270
Ten Georgia Campers, 35
Tender is the Night (Fitzgerald), *xii*
Tennessee Ten, 78
Teresa Hotel, New York City, 208, 216
"Thanks for the Memory" (with special lyrics), 243
Theatre Owners Booking Agency (TOBA) vaudeville circuit, 27, 30, 37, 45, 54, 66
Thomas, Louis, 81
Thompson, Kid, 78–79
Three Deuces, New York City, 214–215
Three Eddys, 104
Times (London), 162
TOBA. *See* Theatre Owners Booking Agency
Todd, Mike, 225, 232
Tony's, New York City, 214
Tropic of Cancer (Miller), 131
Troubetzkoy, Princess. *See* Hutton, Barbara
Tubercular Children of Italy, benefit for, 110–111
Tucker, Sophie, 20, 23, 165–166, 272
Turney, Al. *See* Al Turney's
"21" Club, New York City, 210, 289

Twin Cities Stag Club, Minneapolis, 49
Two Weeks in Another Town (film), 268

Ulric, Lenore, 77
Umberto, King of Italy, 257, 267
Uncle Tom's Cabin (play), 16
United States: gangsters in, 76, 146, 167, 170, 229; Negro racial consciousness in, 25, 72; race relations in, 5, 10–11, 48, 51, 59, 178, 185, 208–209. *See also* Depression
U.S.S. *America*, 84
U.S.S. *Washington*, 206–207

Van Allen, Louise, 176
Vancouver, British Columbia, 71–72, 215
Vanderbilt, Consuelo (Duchess of Marlborough), 104
Van Gogh, Vincent, 116
Van Vechten, Carl, 86, 282
Vaudeville, 58, 141–142, 159; Negro, 24–28, 30–38 *passim*, 54, 61; "Pot Circuit" of, 30
Venice, Italy, 94, 110–113, 257, 262
Verdura, Duke of, 244
Victor's, Rome, 248
Vodery, Will, 218
Vogue, 93, 197, 243

Wacker, Mr. and Mrs. Charles, 172
Wake Up and Dream (show), 128
Walker, Ada Overton, 23
Walker, Madame Alelia, 282
Walker, Earl, 44
Walker, George, 23
Walker, Mayor Jimmy, 93, 162–163
"Walkin' the Dog" (Brooks), 56
Wallace, Mike, 273
Waller, Fats, 80
Ward, Fannie, 91–95
Washington, D.C., 77, 81, 140
Washingtonians, The, 77–78, 81
Waters, Ethel, 30, 66, 183
Watt, Douglas, 275
Watts Country Club, 62, 64
Waugh, Evelyn, 236
Webb, Clifton, 93, 144
Welles, Orson, 267
"What Is This Thing Called Love?" (song), 275
"When the Red, Red Robin Comes Bob-Bob-Bobbing Along" (song), 245
Whetsol, Arthur, 77–78
White, Harvey, 87, 160
White, Sammy, 86

Whiteman, Paul, 200
Whitman Sisters, 45
Wicks, Lola, 37
Wilbur Sweatman's Rhythm Kings, 80
Wilkins, Barron, 34, 75, 77–82, 282. *See also* Barron's Exclusive Club
Williams, Bert, 20, 23, 75
Williams, Carolyn, 61–63
Williams, Esther, 267
Williams, Spencer, 109, 117, 186
Williams, "Tack" Annie, 31–32
Wilson, Garland, 221
Wilson, Julie, 275
Wiman, Dwight, 95, 164
Wiman, Steve (Mrs. Dwight), 95
Windsor, Duchess of, *xiv*, 193–194, 204–205, 211, 245, 273–274, 283. *See also* Simpson, Wallis
Windsor, Duke of, *xiv*, 116–117, 125, 172–

Windsor, Duke of (*cont.*) 175, 179, 191–194, 244–245, 267, 273–274, 283
Winston, Harry, 156
Wise, Bob, 283
Women's Wear Daily, 131, 197
Wooley, Monty, 163–164
World War I, 53, 61, 70, 84, 94
World War II, *xiv*, 94, 162, 200–205, 215, 235, 238, 248
Wright, Cobina, 275
Wright, Needham, 34

Young, Billy, 25

Zelli's, Paris, 108–109, 179
Ziegfeld Follies, 23, 56, 141, 153–154, 218, 223
Zito (caricaturist), 108–109

BRICKTOP makes her home in New York City. Her coauthor, JAMES HASKINS, has written more than fifty nonfiction adult and children's books, including *Black Theater in America*, *The Cotton Club*, *Katherine Dunham*, *Always Movin' On: The Life of Langston Hughes*, and *I'm Gonna Make You Love Me: The Story of Diana Ross*. He is a professor of English at the University of Florida, and divides his time between New York City and Gainesville, Florida.